LUNA MUNRO

Ticino Travel Guide 2025

Discover the Heart of Swiss-Italian Charm: Lakes, Mountains, and Hidden Gems

Copyright © 2024 by Luna Munro

All rights reserved. No part of this publication may be reproduced, stored or transmitted in any form or by any means, electronic, mechanical, photocopying, recording, scanning, or otherwise without written permission from the publisher. It is illegal to copy this book, post it to a website, or distribute it by any other means without permission.

Luna Munro asserts the moral right to be identified as the author of this work.

First edition

This book was professionally typeset on Reedsy.
Find out more at reedsy.com

Contents

Reader's Experience	ix
Disclaimer	xi
Discovering Ticino	xii
Quick Facts	xviii
Why Visit	xxv
1. New Developments and Attractions in 2025	xxv
2. Exciting Festivals in 2025	xxvi
3. Perfect for First-Time Visitors	xxvii
4. A Treat for Returning Tourists	xxviii
Planning Your Trip	1
When to Visit	1
Spring in Ticino (March to May)	1
Summer in Ticino (June to August)	2
Fall in Ticino (September to November)	4
Winter in Ticino (December to February)	5
Entry Requirements and Travel Documents	7
1. Visa Requirements for Schengen Area Countries	7
2. Visa Requirements for Non-Schengen Countries	8
3. Visa Requirements for Visa-Required Countries	9
4. Entry Requirements for British Citizens	11
5. Health-Related Entry Requirements (Including COVID-19 Regulations)	11
6. What Travel Documents Are Necessary for Entry?	13
Packing Tips for Ticino's Climate	14
1. General Packing Tips for Ticino	14
2. Packing for Spring (March to May)	15

3. Packing for Summer (June to August)	16
4. Packing for Fall (September to November)	17
5. Packing for Winter (December to February)	19
Budgeting for Your Trip to Ticino: Costs and Saving Tips	20
Language and Cultural Etiquette in Ticino	25
Health and Safety: Staying Safe in Ticino	27
Traveling with Kids: Family-Friendly Tips	29
Sustainable Travel in Ticino	31
Getting to Ticino	34
Flying to Ticino: Nearest Airports	34
Train Travel: Scenic Swiss Rail Journeys	37
Car Rentals and Road Trips: Driving to and Around Ticino	40
Cross-Border Travel from Italy and Beyond	44
Getting Around Ticino	48
Public Transportation: Buses, Trains, and Boats	48
Renting a Car: What You Need to Know	52
Cycling in Ticino: Bike Rentals and Scenic Routes	54
Walking Tours: Exploring Ticino on Foot	58
Family-Friendly Transportation Options in Ticino	61
Where to Stay in Ticino	67
Luxury Hotels and Resorts for a Lavish Stay	67
Mid-Range and Boutique Hotels: Where Comfort Meets Charm	69
Unique Stays: Special Themes and Historical Significance	72
Budget-Friendly Stays and Hostels for the Savvy Traveler	74
Family-Friendly Accommodations: Hotels with Pools, Kids Clubs, and Babysitting Services	76
Unique Stays: From Agriturismos to Chalets and Bed & Breakfasts	79
Camping and Glamping: Outdoorsy Stays in Ticino	83
Itineraries for Every Traveler	86
3 Days in Ticino: A Perfect Introduction	86

Day 1: Exploring Lugano	86
Day 2: Lake Maggiore and Ascona	87
Day 3: Bellinzona and the Castles	89
5-Day Family-Friendly Itinerary	90
Day 1: Arrival in Lugano	90
Day 2: Fun at Monte Tamaro	91
Day 3: Bellinzona and the Castles	91
Day 4: Day Trip to Locarno	92
Day 5: Lugano's Lido and Funicular to Monte Brè	93
Adventure Seeker's 7-Day Itinerary	93
Day 1: Arrival in Lugano and Introduction to the Outdoors	93
Day 2: Explore Valle Verzasca	94
Day 3: Rock Climbing in Ponte Brolla	95
Day 4: Canyoning in the Maggia Valley	96
Day 5: Monte Tamaro and Adventure Park	96
Day 6: Paragliding and Mountain Biking	97
Day 7: Kayaking on Lake Maggiore and Farewell Dinner	98
Luxury 4-Day Escape	99
Day 1: Arrival and Spa Day	99
Day 2: Private Yacht Tour and Wine Tasting	100
Day 3: Shopping and Helicopter Tour	101
Day 4: Day Trip to Ascona and Farewell Dinner	101
Top Attractions in Ticino	103
Lake Lugano: A Perfect Spot for Water Sports and Relaxation	103
Lake Maggiore: A Blend of Adventure and Tranquility	106
Bellinzona's Castles - UNESCO World Heritage Sites	110
Castelgrande: The Largest and Oldest Fortress	110
Montebello Castle: A Picture-Perfect Medieval Fortress	112
Sasso Corbaro Castle: The Highest and Most Secluded Castle	113
How to Visit All Three Castles in One Day	114
Ascona: A Lakeside Gem with a Mediterranean Vibe	115
Locarno: A Blend of History and Culture	117

Visiting During Festival Season	120
Natural Beauty of Valle Verzasca	121
Outdoor Activities in Valle Verzasca	121
The Sacred Monte Madonna del Sasso	124
Religious and Historical Significance	124
Religious and Historical Significance of Madonna del Sasso	126
What Visitors Can See and Experience at the Sanctuary	127
How to Reach Madonna del Sasso	128
When to Visit Madonna del Sasso for the Best Experience	129
Nearby Attractions to Combine with Your Visit	130
Exploring the Brissago Islands: A Botanical Paradise	131
Swissminiatur: A Family Favorite in Ticino	134
Outdoor Adventures and Activities	**137**
Best Hiking Trails for All Levels	137
Water Sports: Kayaking, Paddleboarding, and Boating in Ticino	141
Mountain Biking in Ticino's Stunning Landscapes	144
Paragliding and Zip-lining: Ticino for Thrill Seekers	147
Rock Climbing in Ticino's Valleys	150
Scenic Drives Through Ticino's Alpine Roads	153
Parco Ciani: Lugano's Favorite Family Park	156
Al Maglio Zoo: A Fun Day with Animals	157
Swissminiatur: A Family Favorite in Melide	158
Monte Tamaro Adventure Park: A Full Day of Family Fun	159
Special Events and Seasonal Activities	160
Beaches and Lakeside Fun	**162**
Best Beaches on Lake Maggiore and Lake Lugano	162
Family-Friendly Beach Spots with Shallow Waters	164
Special Events and Seasonal Activities at the Beaches	166
Water Sports: Swimming, Boating, and More	167
Lakeside Dining: Cafés and Restaurants with a View	171
Dining in Ticino	**174**

Ticino's Culinary Scene: What to Expect	174
Must-Try Local Dishes: Risotto, Polenta, and More	175
Dining Traditions and Outdoor Dining	179
Best Fine Dining Restaurants in Ticino	180
Family-Friendly Restaurants and Cafés	183
Street Food and Market Eats: Where the Locals Go	185
Wine Tasting in Ticino's Vineyards	188
Vegetarian, Vegan, and Dietary Options	189
Designer Boutiques and Local Fashion Finds	191
Artisan Crafts and Souvenirs to Bring Home	194
Markets: What to Buy and Where	197
Malls and Shopping Centers: A Guide for Families	199
Tax-Free Shopping for Tourists	201
Nightlife and Entertainment	204
Bars and Nightclubs: Where to Go in Lugano	204
Music Festivals and Outdoor Concerts in Ticino	207
Cultural Events: Theater, Opera, and More	209
Family-Friendly Evening Activities	213
Cultural Experiences in Ticino	216
Art Galleries and Museums to Explore	216
Ticino's Traditional Festivals	220
Architectural Wonders of Ticino	223
Churches, Chapels, and Sacred Sites to Visit	226
Day Trips from Ticino	230
A Day in Milan: Italian Culture and Shopping	230
Lake Como: An Enchanting Escape	233
The Swiss Alps: Adventure Beyond Ticino	236
Hidden Gems for Day Trips and Excursions	238
Ticino for Families	241
Family-Friendly Attractions and Activities	241
Best Playgrounds and Parks for Kids	245
Educational Spots: Kid-Friendly Museums in Ticino	247

Traveling with Babies and Toddlers: What You Need to Know	251
Practical Information	254
Emergency Numbers and Healthcare in Ticino	254
Embassies and Consulates in Ticino	258
Accessibility: Tips for Seniors and Travelers with Disabilities	261
Staying Connected: Wi-Fi, SIM Cards, and Internet Access	264
Using Swiss Francs in Ticino	266
Using Credit Cards in Ticino	268
Tipping Culture in Ticino	270
Final Tips for a Memorable Ticino Trip	271
How to Avoid Tourist Traps in Ticino	271
Money-Saving Hacks for Budget Travelers	272
Making the Most of Your Ticino Adventure	276
Must-Know Tips for First-Time Visitors	278
Conclusion	282

Reader's Experience

When it comes to travel guidebooks, Luna Munro knows how to make every trip unforgettable. Her Sanibel guide were spot-on, helping me find the perfect hidden beaches and dining spots. This guide was like having a local by my side, leading me to the best places I would have missed on my own." **-Rebecca Sinclair, New York City**

"I've always relied on her guidebooks, and the Doha edition was no exception. The level of detail and the clear directions in this guide saved us so much time and hassle. It's not just about where to go, but also how to make the most of every place. This is now a must-have on all our trips!" - **Brian Lawson, London**

"As someone who loves off-the-beaten-path destinations, the Zaragoza guide gave me all the tips I needed to experience the local culture. The author's knowledge and love for these places shine through every page. This guide made my trip unforgettable, from finding the best food spots to discovering lesser-known attractions." - **Emily Martinez, Barcelona**

"We used the Sanibel travel guide for our family vacation, and it was perfect! The recommendations were exactly what we needed, especially with kids. Every tip was spot on, from beach activities to where to grab quick meals. This guide made our trip stress-free, and I can't wait to use the next one for our next destination!" - **Tina Johnson, Chicago**

"Having used the Doha guide last year, I can confidently say these travel guides are top-notch. The thorough research and practical advice made our trip so much easier and more enjoyable. Every detail from transportation tips to finding hidden

*gems was on point."- **Mark Reynolds, Sydney**

Disclaimer

This book serves as a reliable companion for your journey, offering detailed insights and practical tips to enhance your travel experience. Although every effort has been made to ensure the accuracy of the information at the time of writing, please be aware that travel conditions and local details may change.

This guide does not include images or maps. Instead, it focuses on providing valuable content to help you prepare for a memorable trip.

Use this guide as your starting point, and let your adventures complete the story.

Discovering Ticino

Ticino is Switzerland's Italian-speaking region, often referred to as the country's Italian gem. This part of Switzerland offers a unique combination of Swiss efficiency and Italian charm that you won't find anywhere else in the country. While the rest of Switzerland may be more known for its German or French influences, Ticino stands out with its Mediterranean atmosphere, laid-back lifestyle, and sunny climate. You feel like you've crossed into Italy, but you're still benefiting from Switzerland's world-renowned infrastructure, safety, and cleanliness.

The Perfect Blend of Two Cultures

In Ticino, you can experience the warmth and spontaneity of Italian culture while enjoying the precision and order that Switzerland is famous for. This blend is what makes Ticino such an attractive destination. When you walk through the streets of Ticino's towns and cities, you'll hear Italian spoken, see Italian-style architecture, and taste Italian food, but everything runs on time, and the streets are impeccably clean. It's a blend of two very different cultures, but in Ticino, they work together seamlessly.

Ticino is famous for its relaxed, Mediterranean vibe, especially when compared to the busier, more rigid regions in other parts of Switzerland. Here, life moves a little slower. The locals enjoy long lunches, leisurely strolls along the lake, and plenty of time outdoors. It's not uncommon to see people sitting in cafés for hours, chatting with friends or reading the newspaper. This leisurely pace is part of the Italian influence, but the Swiss side of things ensures that public transport is reliable, shops are well-stocked, and services are top-notch.

The Italian charm is apparent in the everyday interactions as well. Ticinese people are warm and welcoming, always ready with a smile or a friendly conversation. This is quite different from other parts of Switzerland, where people might be more reserved. In Ticino, don't be surprised if a local strikes up a conversation with you at a café or offers you directions without being asked. This friendliness and openness are a big part of why visitors feel so comfortable here.

Language and Culture

Italian is the official language of Ticino, but you'll find that many people also speak French, German, and English, especially in tourist areas. In the cities like Lugano, Locarno, and Bellinzona, it's easy to get by with English, but learning a few basic Italian phrases will go a long way and be appreciated by locals. Phrases like "Buongiorno" (Good morning), "Grazie" (Thank you), and "Arrivederci" (Goodbye) are simple but can make your interactions more pleasant.

The culture here is a mix of Italian passion and Swiss practicality. On one hand, you have the Italian love for food, art, and socializing. On the other hand, you have Swiss efficiency, punctuality, and organization. This means you can expect high-quality services and excellent infrastructure, but also lively markets, open-air festivals, and spontaneous gatherings. Ticino is known for its love of food, with local markets selling fresh, seasonal produce and restaurants serving up traditional dishes like risotto, polenta, and locally-cured meats.

Ticino is also a region where festivals play a big role. The locals celebrate everything from food to music to local traditions, often with vibrant public events. The Locarno Film Festival, for example, is one of Europe's most prestigious film festivals, attracting filmmakers and movie lovers from all over the world. There are also smaller festivals that celebrate local food, like the chestnut festivals in the fall, where you can sample roasted chestnuts, chestnut-flavored ice cream, and other delicacies made from this local ingredient.

Geographic Highlights and Landscape

Ticino's geography is one of its most striking features. The region is nestled between the southern Alps and the Italian border, which gives it a diverse landscape that's perfect for outdoor enthusiasts. On one side, you have towering mountains and deep valleys, and on the other, you have serene lakes with Mediterranean flair. This makes Ticino ideal for both hikers looking to explore the Alpine trails and travelers seeking a relaxing getaway by the water.

The most famous geographic features in Ticino are its two lakes: **Lake Lugano** and **Lake Maggiore**. Both lakes offer stunning views, crystal-clear water, and plenty of activities for visitors. You can take boat trips across the lakes, swim in designated areas, or just relax on the shores, enjoying the Mediterranean climate. Lake Lugano is especially popular because of the city of Lugano, which is the largest city in the region. Lugano combines the beauty of the lake with all the conveniences of a modern city, making it the perfect base for exploring Ticino.

If you're more interested in mountains and hiking, Ticino has that covered too. The Verzasca Valley is one of the most beautiful spots in the region, known for its emerald-green river and dramatic landscapes. The valley is dotted with small villages where time seems to stand still, and the hiking trails offer spectacular views of the surrounding mountains. **Verzasca Dam**, made famous by the opening scene of the James Bond film *GoldenEye*, is also located here. Adventure seekers can even try bungee jumping off the dam for an adrenaline-filled experience.

Another notable geographic highlight is the **Bellinzona Castles**, which are recognized as a UNESCO World Heritage Site. These medieval fortresses are incredibly well-preserved and offer a glimpse into the region's history. The castles are perched on a hillside, offering panoramic views of the surrounding area. The main castle, **Castelgrande**, is the oldest and largest of the three, and it's open to the public for tours. Exploring the castles and the charming town of Bellinzona is like stepping back in time.

Towns and Cities of Ticino

Lugano is the largest and most cosmopolitan city in Ticino, offering a mix of cultural attractions, shopping, and dining. The city is set against the backdrop of Lake Lugano, with mountains rising up on all sides, making it one of the most picturesque cities in Switzerland. Lugano is often compared to cities like Monte Carlo or the Italian Lakes for its upscale atmosphere, but it still retains a relaxed, down-to-earth vibe that makes it approachable for all kinds of travelers.

Some of the key highlights of Lugano include:

- **Piazza della Riforma**: This central square is the heart of the city, where you'll find cafés, restaurants, and shops. It's a great place to sit and people-watch or enjoy a coffee while soaking up the atmosphere.
- **Parco Ciani**: This lakeside park is perfect for a leisurely stroll or picnic. It's filled with beautiful flower gardens, sculptures, and shady trees, making it a favorite spot for both locals and tourists.
- **Monte Brè**: For panoramic views of Lugano and the surrounding mountains, you can take a funicular ride up to Monte Brè. Once at the top, you can enjoy hiking trails or relax with a meal at the restaurant overlooking the lake.

The city of Locarno, located on the shores of Lake Maggiore, has a distinctly Mediterranean feel with its palm trees, warm climate, and colorful houses. Locarno is famous for its international film festival, which takes place every summer in the **Piazza Grande**, one of the largest open-air squares in Europe. The city is also home to several historic churches, including the **Madonna del Sasso**, a pilgrimage site that offers stunning views over the lake and mountains.

Bellinzona, the capital of Ticino, is a smaller city but is rich in history. Its three castles—**Castelgrande**, **Montebello**, and **Sasso Corbaro**—are the main attractions, but the city itself is also worth exploring. Bellinzona has a charming old town with narrow streets, colorful buildings, and weekly markets where you can buy local produce and crafts. The castles are open to the public, and you can easily spend a day wandering through their halls, climbing the towers, and enjoying the views from the top.

Practical Travel Information for Ticino

Ticino is well-connected to the rest of Switzerland and Italy, making it easy to reach by train, car, or plane. **Lugano Airport** offers flights to major European cities, but many visitors arrive by train from other parts of Switzerland or Italy. The **Gotthard Base Tunnel**, the world's longest and deepest railway tunnel, has made travel to Ticino faster and more convenient than ever. Trains from Zurich to Lugano, for example, take just under two hours, making it easy to visit Ticino as part of a broader Swiss itinerary.

If you're coming from Italy, you can take a train from **Milan** to Lugano, which takes about an hour. This makes Ticino a popular day trip destination for those staying in northern Italy. However, to really experience all that Ticino has to offer, it's best to stay for at least a few days. There are plenty of hotels, guesthouses, and rental apartments to suit all budgets, from luxurious lakeside resorts to more affordable family-run establishments.

Public transportation in Ticino is excellent, with buses, trains, and boats connecting the major towns and attractions. The **Ticino Ticket**, which is provided free to hotel guests, gives you unlimited access to public transportation in the region, making it easy to explore without needing a car. If you do decide to drive, be aware that parking in the cities can be limited, especially during peak tourist season. However, driving is a good option if you plan to explore the more remote valleys and mountains.

For those who enjoy outdoor activities, Ticino is a paradise. Hiking, cycling, and water sports are popular, and the region's natural beauty makes it a great destination for nature lovers. The warm climate also makes it possible to enjoy these activities for much of the year, with mild winters and hot, sunny summers. Whether you're looking to relax by the lake, explore historic towns, or embark on an outdoor adventure, Ticino has something for everyone.

Quick Facts

Ticino is a distinct region in Switzerland with its own character, language, and lifestyle. Located in the southern part of the country, it is the only Swiss canton where Italian is the official language. It offers a warm, Mediterranean climate, beautiful lakes, and a blend of Swiss efficiency with Italian charm.

Population and Area

Ticino has a population of approximately 350,000 people. The population density is around 130 people per square kilometer, making it a sparsely populated region compared to Switzerland's more urbanized areas like Zurich or Geneva. The total area of Ticino is 2,812 square kilometers, which gives it a variety of landscapes, from bustling cities to remote valleys and mountain ranges.

Key Cities

Lugano

Lugano is the largest city in Ticino, with a population of about 63,000 people. It is the economic and cultural hub of the region and lies along the shores of Lake Lugano. This city offers a cosmopolitan atmosphere with numerous restaurants, high-end shops, and cultural institutions like museums and theaters. It's known for its stunning lake views and Mediterranean feel, making it a favorite destination for both tourists and locals alike.

- **Address**: Piazza della Riforma, 6900 Lugano, Switzerland
- **How to Get There**: From Zurich, you can take a direct train to Lugano,

which takes about two hours. Alternatively, from Milan, it's just a one-hour train ride.
- **Cost**: Free to explore the city, though attractions like museums may have entry fees (around CHF 10-15).

Bellinzona

Bellinzona, the capital of Ticino, is known for its medieval castles, which are a UNESCO World Heritage Site. With a population of around 19,000, Bellinzona is a quieter city compared to Lugano but offers rich historical significance. The city's three castles—**Castelgrande**, **Montebello**, and **Sasso Corbaro**—are its main attractions. Bellinzona is also the administrative center of Ticino, housing the cantonal government.

- **Address**: Via Orico, 6500 Bellinzona, Switzerland (Castelgrande)
- **How to Get There**: Direct trains from Lugano take about 30 minutes, and it's easily accessible from other parts of Switzerland via the Gotthard Base Tunnel.
- **Entry Cost**: CHF 5 for Castelgrande; combo tickets for all three castles are around CHF 15.

Locarno

Locarno, on the northern shore of Lake Maggiore, is famous for its annual **Locarno Film Festival**. With a population of about 15,000, this city attracts artists, filmmakers, and tourists from around the world. It has a charming old town, beautiful lakefront promenades, and plenty of outdoor activities like hiking and swimming. Locarno enjoys more than 2,300 hours of sunshine a year, making it one of the sunniest places in Switzerland.

- **Address**: Piazza Grande, 6600 Locarno, Switzerland (for the main town square)
- **How to Get There**: Trains from Bellinzona take about 20 minutes; from Lugano, it's about 50 minutes by train.
- **Costs**: Exploring the town and lake is free, but film festival tickets or

museum entries vary (CHF 10-20).

Ascona

Located just a few kilometers from Locarno, Ascona is a small town on the shores of Lake Maggiore. With a population of only around 5,000 people, Ascona is known for its elegant lakefront promenade, art galleries, and boutique shops. The town is quieter than Locarno but offers luxurious hotels and a more relaxed atmosphere. It's also home to the **Monte Verità**, an arts and cultural center that was once a retreat for artists and philosophers in the early 20th century.

- **Address**: Lungolago Motta, 6612 Ascona, Switzerland
- **How to Get There**: Easily reachable by bus or a 10-minute drive from Locarno. It's also connected by boat services across Lake Maggiore.
- **Costs**: Free to explore the lakefront. Entry to Monte Verità costs about CHF 10.

Official Language and Local Dialects

Ticino's official language is Italian, but it's slightly different from the Italian spoken in Italy. Locals speak a version of Lombard, a dialect of Italian, but standard Italian is universally understood and spoken. In tourist-heavy areas like Lugano and Locarno, you'll also find that many people speak English, French, and German, especially in hotels, restaurants, and public services.

In smaller towns and rural areas, however, Italian is predominant, and knowing a few phrases can go a long way. Basic greetings like **"Buongiorno"** (Good morning), **"Grazie"** (Thank you), and **"Arrivederci"** (Goodbye) will help you connect with locals. While it's not necessary to be fluent, showing an effort to use Italian will be appreciated.

Currency and Costs

Like the rest of Switzerland, Ticino uses the **Swiss franc (CHF)**. It's worth noting that many places near the Italian border, such as Mendrisio or the markets in Locarno, will accept euros, but you may not get a favorable exchange rate. For the most accurate transactions, it's best to use Swiss francs.

Ticino is a bit more affordable compared to major Swiss cities like Zurich or Geneva, but it's still Switzerland, so prices for accommodations, dining, and activities can be on the higher side. Below is a breakdown of typical costs you might encounter:

Accommodation:

- Luxury hotels: CHF 250-500 per night
- Mid-range hotels: CHF 150-250 per night
- Budget hotels or guesthouses: CHF 80-150 per night
- Hostels: CHF 40-80 per night

Meals:

- Fine dining: CHF 60-120 per person
- Casual dining: CHF 20-40 per person
- Takeaway food (sandwiches, snacks): CHF 10-15 per person

Attractions:

- Museum entry: CHF 10-20
- Castle entry (Bellinzona): CHF 5-15
- Boat rides on Lake Lugano or Lake Maggiore: CHF 15-30

Transportation:

- Public transport ticket (1-day pass): CHF 10-20 depending on the area
- Train from Zurich to Lugano: CHF 40-60 one way

- Car rental: CHF 70-100 per day

ATMs are widely available in all towns and cities, and credit cards are accepted almost everywhere, especially in tourist-friendly areas. Cash is still used in local markets or smaller businesses, so it's helpful to carry some Swiss francs with you.

Climate and Best Time to Visit

Ticino's Mediterranean climate makes it one of the warmest parts of Switzerland. Summers are hot, with temperatures often reaching 30°C (86°F), especially around the lakes, while winters are mild, with temperatures rarely dropping below 5°C (41°F). The region receives plenty of sunshine, particularly in Locarno and Ascona, where you can expect over 2,300 hours of sunshine annually.

The best time to visit Ticino depends on what you want to do. If you're looking to enjoy outdoor activities like hiking, swimming, or boating, late spring to early autumn (May to September) is ideal. The lakes are warm enough for swimming by June, and the hiking trails are open from May through October. Autumn is a great time to visit for food festivals and wine tastings, especially in September and October when the grape harvest is in full swing.

Winter is quieter in Ticino, but it still offers plenty to do, especially if you enjoy skiing or snowshoeing in the nearby mountains. While it's not as popular for winter sports as other Swiss regions like the Valais or Graubünden, Ticino does have some ski resorts in the northern areas near **Airolo** and the **Lepontine Alps**.

Natural Landscape and Outdoor Activities

Ticino's diverse geography means that there's something for everyone, whether you enjoy lakeside relaxation or high-altitude hiking. The region is home to two major lakes, **Lake Lugano** and **Lake Maggiore**, both of which offer a wide range of activities like swimming, boating, and paddleboarding.

You can take boat cruises on both lakes, which offer spectacular views of the surrounding mountains and charming lakeside towns.

For hiking enthusiasts, Ticino has some of the best trails in Switzerland. The **Sentiero Verzasca** trail, for example, takes you through the stunning Verzasca Valley, with its crystal-clear river, ancient stone bridges, and picturesque villages like **Lavertezzo**. The **Monte Brè** hike offers panoramic views of Lake Lugano and the surrounding Alps. Another must-visit spot is the **Monte Tamaro**, which is accessible by cable car and offers both hiking and mountain biking trails, as well as a thrilling zip line.

In addition to the lakes and mountains, Ticino has several beautiful parks and gardens. **Parco Ciani** in Lugano is a lakeside park with well-maintained walking paths, flower gardens, and sculptures, making it a great place to relax or go for a walk. For something more unique, the **Brissago Islands** on Lake Maggiore are home to a botanical garden that features exotic plants from all over the world, thanks to the region's mild climate.

- **Address (Parco Ciani)**: Viale Carlo Cattaneo, 6900 Lugano, Switzerland
- **Address (Brissago Islands)**: Accessible by boat from Ascona or Locarno
- **Costs**: Entry to Parco Ciani is free. Entry to the Brissago Islands botanical garden is CHF 8, with additional costs for boat transport (CHF 15-25 depending on the route).

Festivals and Local Events

Ticino has a packed calendar of events, from local food festivals to international film premieres. The **Locarno Film Festival**, held every August, is one of Europe's top film festivals, attracting filmmakers, celebrities, and movie enthusiasts from around the world. The films are screened in the **Piazza Grande**, a massive outdoor square that can seat up to 8,000 people, creating a unique cinema experience under the stars.

- **Address (Piazza Grande)**: Piazza Grande, 6600 Locarno, Switzerland
- **Costs**: Tickets for festival screenings range from CHF 15-30.

In autumn, many towns in Ticino celebrate the grape harvest with wine festivals, where you can sample local wines, enjoy live music, and join in the celebrations. The **Sagra dell'Uva** in Mendrisio is one of the largest, featuring traditional costumes, folk music, and plenty of food and wine.

- **Address (Mendrisio)**: Centro Storico, 6850 Mendrisio, Switzerland
- **Costs**: Entry is free, though food and wine are sold separately (expect to pay CHF 5-10 per glass of wine).

There are also smaller festivals celebrating local foods like chestnuts and risotto, particularly in rural areas. These festivals are a great way to experience the local culture, meet the friendly people of Ticino, and try some authentic Ticinese cuisine.

Why Visit

1. New Developments and Attractions in 2025

In 2025, Ticino is introducing several new projects that will attract visitors. One of the most anticipated is the **Lugano Art & Cultural Center**, set to open in the spring of 2025. This modern cultural hub will be home to rotating art exhibits, performances, and interactive spaces for families. It's expected to bring in contemporary artists from across Europe and showcase local Ticinese talent. The center is located near **Parco Ciani** in Lugano, making it easy for visitors to stop by while exploring the city.

- **Address**: Viale Carlo Cattaneo, 6900 Lugano, Switzerland
- **How to Get There**: Take a train to **Lugano Station** and walk 15 minutes toward the lake.
- **Entry Cost**: CHF 15 for adults, CHF 8 for children under 12.

Another new addition for 2025 is the **Green Pathway Network**, a series of eco-friendly walking and biking trails that connect Ticino's towns and rural areas. The initiative focuses on promoting sustainable tourism, allowing visitors to travel between popular destinations like Lugano, Locarno, and Bellinzona without needing a car. This is a great opportunity for outdoor enthusiasts and those looking to reduce their environmental footprint.

- **Cost**: Free
- **Trail Access Points**: Trails start at various points in Lugano, Locarno, and Bellinzona. Most are marked and easy to navigate. You can rent

bikes from local shops in these cities for around CHF 25 per day.

2. Exciting Festivals in 2025

Ticino is known for its lively festivals, and 2025 will see a full calendar of events for all interests. Whether you're a film buff, food lover, or music fan, there's something happening throughout the year.

Locarno Film Festival (August 2025)

The **Locarno Film Festival**, one of Europe's most prestigious film festivals, is a must-visit event in 2025. Held every August in Locarno's **Piazza Grande**, the festival screens international films under the stars. In 2025, the festival will celebrate its 78th edition and promises to showcase the best in world cinema. What's unique this year is a special focus on sustainability, with films exploring environmental issues and eco-friendly festival practices like banning single-use plastics.

- **Address**: Piazza Grande, 6600 Locarno, Switzerland
- **How to Get There**: Trains from Lugano to Locarno take around 50 minutes. From Locarno train station, it's a 10-minute walk to Piazza Grande.
- **Ticket Price**: CHF 20-40 per screening.

Bellinzona Medieval Festival (September 2025)

For those interested in history and culture, the **Bellinzona Medieval Festival** is a highlight in September 2025. Held within the walls of Bellinzona's UNESCO-listed castles, this festival transports you back to medieval times with re-enactments, knights' tournaments, and markets selling handmade crafts. You can explore all three castles—**Castelgrande**, **Montebello**, and **Sasso Corbaro**—while enjoying live performances and sampling local food. This festival is particularly family-friendly, with activities for children like archery lessons and interactive history exhibits.

- **Address**: Via Orico, 6500 Bellinzona, Switzerland
- **How to Get There**: Take a 30-minute train from Lugano to Bellinzona. The festival is held in the castles, which are within walking distance from the train station.
- **Entry Cost**: CHF 10 for adults, CHF 5 for children under 12. Combo tickets for all three castles and the festival are CHF 25.

Festa della Vendemmia (October 2025)

In October 2025, don't miss the **Festa della Vendemmia**, or Grape Harvest Festival, in Mendrisio. This festival celebrates Ticino's rich winemaking tradition, with local vineyards showcasing their best wines. You can take part in wine tastings, vineyard tours, and enjoy live music and local food. There are also grape-stomping contests, where visitors can experience traditional winemaking methods firsthand. It's a great way to connect with the local culture and sample some of Ticino's best **Merlot**, which the region is famous for.

- **Address**: Piazza del Ponte, 6850 Mendrisio, Switzerland
- **How to Get There**: From Lugano, Mendrisio is a 20-minute train ride. The festival is held in the town center, a short walk from the train station.
- **Cost**: Entry is free, but wine tastings typically cost around CHF 5 per glass.

3. Perfect for First-Time Visitors

Ticino is ideal for first-time visitors to Switzerland because it offers a different experience compared to the more well-known German- and French-speaking regions. In Ticino, you get the charm and warmth of Italy, but with the orderliness and reliability that Switzerland is known for. It's an accessible region where everything runs smoothly—trains are punctual, streets are clean, and services are efficient. For first-time visitors, this means you can relax and focus on enjoying the beauty of the region without the usual travel hassles.

Ticino's compact size makes it easy to explore multiple destinations within a few days. For example, you can stay in Lugano and take day trips to **Locarno**, **Bellinzona**, and **Ascona**. Public transportation, including trains, buses, and ferries, is extensive and easy to use. A **Ticino Ticket**, which you receive when staying at participating hotels, gives you unlimited access to the region's public transport, making it simple to get around without a car.

- **Cost**: The Ticino Ticket is free for hotel guests, and you can use it on buses, trains, and boats across the region.
- **Availability**: Offered at most hotels and guesthouses across Ticino in 2025.

For first-time visitors, the cultural experience in Ticino is also unique. The region's Italian influence is reflected in its food, language, and daily life. Expect to enjoy long, leisurely lunches, interact with friendly locals, and take part in lively festivals that celebrate the best of Italian and Swiss traditions. Whether you're strolling along Lake Lugano, visiting the Bellinzona Castles, or enjoying a meal at a local **grotto** (rustic restaurant), you'll find that Ticino has an approachable, welcoming vibe.

4. A Treat for Returning Tourists

For those returning to Ticino in 2025, there's always something new to discover. While the region's key attractions like Lake Lugano and the Verzasca Valley are timeless, there are plenty of lesser-known gems and new experiences to explore.

New Hiking Trails and Outdoor Adventures
One of the big draws for returning tourists in 2025 is the expansion of hiking trails in Ticino's rural areas. The **Verzasca Valley**, known for its emerald-green river and dramatic rock formations, is opening new trails

that offer more challenging routes for experienced hikers. These trails take you deeper into the valley's less-traveled areas, providing stunning views and a sense of solitude.

For thrill-seekers, the famous **Verzasca Dam**, where you can try bungee jumping, continues to be a popular spot. In 2025, they're introducing night jumps during the summer months, allowing visitors to experience the adrenaline rush under the stars.

- **Address (Verzasca Dam)**: Via Valle Verzasca, 6633 Lavertezzo, Switzerland
- **How to Get There**: Take a bus from Locarno to **Lavertezzo**; the dam is a short walk from the bus stop.
- **Cost**: Bungee jumps cost CHF 195 per person. Night jumps start at CHF 230.

New Culinary Experiences

Ticino's food scene is always evolving, and 2025 brings new culinary experiences for returning visitors. One highlight is the rise of **farm-to-table** dining. Several new **agriturismos** (farm stays) around the **Maggia Valley** are offering visitors the chance to dine on meals made entirely from locally sourced ingredients. You can enjoy traditional Ticinese dishes like **polenta**, **risotto**, and **freshwater fish**, all prepared with seasonal ingredients grown on-site. These agriturismos also offer cooking classes, where you can learn to make regional dishes with guidance from local chefs.

- **Address (Agriturismo La Piana)**: Via alla Piana, 6673 Maggia, Switzerland
- **How to Get There**: Drive 20 minutes from Locarno or take a bus to Maggia.
- **Cost**: Meals range from CHF 40-70 per person. Cooking classes cost around CHF 120 for a half-day experience.

Wellness and Relaxation

Ticino is also growing as a wellness destination, with new spas and wellness retreats opening in 2025. For returning visitors looking for a relaxing getaway, the new **Alpine Spa & Wellness Resort** near **Monte Tamaro** offers luxury treatments with stunning views of the surrounding mountains. This retreat focuses on holistic wellness, combining traditional spa therapies with outdoor activities like yoga, meditation, and forest bathing.

- **Address**: Monte Tamaro, 6802 Rivera, Switzerland
- **How to Get There**: Take a funicular from Rivera to Monte Tamaro.
- **Cost**: Spa day passes start at CHF 150. Full retreat packages range from CHF 600-1,200.

Planning Your Trip

When to Visit

Ticino's climate is one of the key reasons why this region is so popular with both Swiss and international visitors. It enjoys a mild, Mediterranean-like climate that makes it a year-round destination, but each season offers something different depending on what you're looking to do.

Spring in Ticino (March to May)

Spring is one of the best times to visit Ticino, especially if you enjoy outdoor activities like hiking or visiting the region's beautiful gardens. From March through May, the weather begins to warm up, with daytime temperatures averaging around 15°C (59°F) in March and rising to 20°C (68°F) by May. Spring also brings the blooming of flowers, especially in places like **Parco Ciani** in Lugano and the **Brissago Islands** on Lake Maggiore, where you can see exotic plants and flowers in full bloom.

Spring is also a fantastic time for hiking because the temperatures are comfortable, and the trails are less crowded than in the summer. The **Verzasca Valley** is particularly beautiful in spring, with its clear waters and lush green surroundings. Popular trails include the **Sentiero Verzasca**, which starts in the village of **Sonogno** and takes you through scenic villages and along the river. Another great hiking area is **Monte Brè**, which overlooks Lake Lugano and offers stunning views of both the lake and surrounding mountains.

- **How to Get There (Verzasca Valley)**: From Lugano, take a train to Locarno, then a bus to **Lavertezzo** or **Sonogno** to start your hike.
- **Costs**: Public transport from Lugano to the Verzasca Valley costs about CHF 10-15 each way. Access to hiking trails is free.

Spring is also when Ticino's festival season kicks off. One notable event is **Pasqua in Città** (Easter in the City), a festival held in **Lugano** to celebrate Easter. The event includes traditional food stalls, Easter egg hunts for children, and outdoor performances. Another event is the **Camelie Locarno** (Camellia Festival), which takes place in late March. This festival celebrates the beautiful camellia flower with exhibitions, flower arrangements, and guided tours of Locarno's **Camellia Park**.

- **How to Get There (Camelie Locarno)**: The festival is held at **Parco delle Camelie** in Locarno, accessible by train from Lugano (50 minutes).
- **Costs**: Festival entry is CHF 10 per person.

Why Visit in Spring: Spring is ideal for those who enjoy outdoor activities like hiking and prefer mild temperatures. It's also perfect for travelers looking to experience local festivals without the larger crowds of summer. The blooming flowers and gardens make for particularly scenic landscapes during this season.

Summer in Ticino (June to August)

Summer is peak season in Ticino, and for good reason. The weather is hot, with temperatures ranging from 25°C (77°F) to 30°C (86°F), making it perfect for lake activities, outdoor dining, and festivals. The summer months are ideal for travelers who want to enjoy Ticino's lakes—**Lake**

Lugano and **Lake Maggiore**—which are warm enough for swimming and water sports by June.

Lake Lugano is a popular spot for boating, paddleboarding, and swimming. The lakeside parks, like **Parco Ciani**, are full of locals and tourists enjoying picnics, sunbathing, or taking a dip in the lake. Boat tours are available throughout the summer, offering scenic trips between towns like Lugano, **Morcote**, and **Gandria**.

- **Boat Tours (Lake Lugano)**: Departures from **Lugano Pier**, with stops at Gandria and Morcote.
- **Costs**: Boat tour prices range from CHF 15-35 depending on the route.

Summer is also the season for some of Ticino's biggest festivals. The **Locarno Film Festival** is the highlight of the year, attracting filmmakers, celebrities, and cinema lovers from around the world. Held every August, the screenings take place in **Piazza Grande**, one of the largest open-air squares in Europe, creating a unique movie-watching experience under the stars.

Another major summer event is the **Estival Jazz Festival** in Lugano, which is a free open-air jazz concert series held in **Piazza della Riforma**. Visitors can enjoy performances by internationally renowned jazz musicians while soaking up the summer atmosphere in the heart of the city.

- **How to Get There (Estival Jazz)**: The festival is held in **Piazza della Riforma**, a short walk from Lugano's main train station.
- **Costs**: Free entry.

If you're interested in outdoor adventures, summer is also a good time for more challenging hikes, such as **Monte Tamaro** or the **Maggia Valley**. **Monte Tamaro** is accessible by funicular and offers hiking, mountain biking, and a zip line. It's a favorite spot for families due to its adventure park at the top of the mountain.

- **How to Get There (Monte Tamaro)**: Take the funicular from Rivera, which is a 15-minute train ride from Lugano.
- **Costs**: CHF 25 for a round-trip funicular ticket. Adventure park activities have additional fees (zip line costs CHF 20).

Why Visit in Summer: Summer is perfect for travelers who want to enjoy the lakes, festivals, and outdoor events. It's also the best time for water sports and hiking in the higher elevations. However, because it's peak season, be prepared for larger crowds and higher accommodation prices. Booking early is recommended if you're visiting in July or August.

Fall in Ticino (September to November)

Fall is another excellent time to visit Ticino, especially for food lovers and those looking to experience the region's rich agricultural traditions. September and October are the harvest months, when Ticino's vineyards are busy producing some of the country's best wines, particularly **Merlot**. Fall temperatures are cooler than summer, with averages around 15-20°C (59-68°F), making it ideal for exploring both the towns and the countryside.

One of the highlights of fall is the **Festa dell'Uva** (Grape Harvest Festival) in **Mendrisio**, where you can sample local wines, enjoy traditional foods, and watch parades featuring locals in traditional dress. Many vineyards in the **Maggia Valley** and **Mendrisio** offer tours and tastings during the harvest season, and it's a great opportunity to see the winemaking process firsthand.

- **How to Get There (Mendrisio)**: Take a 20-minute train from Lugano to Mendrisio. The festival is held in the town's historic center.
- **Costs**: Entry to the festival is free, but wine tastings cost around CHF 5 per glass.

Fall is also a great time for hiking, as the summer crowds have thinned, and the weather is still pleasant. The forests take on beautiful autumn colors, particularly in areas like the **Maggia Valley** and **Vallemaggia**, where the trails are lined with chestnut trees. The **Chestnut Festival** in **Ascona** is a unique fall event where you can taste chestnut-based dishes and learn about the region's history of chestnut farming.

- **How to Get There (Ascona)**: Ascona is a 15-minute bus ride from Locarno or 50 minutes by train and bus from Lugano.
- **Costs**: Free entry to the Chestnut Festival; food costs CHF 5-15 per dish.

Fall is also a time when you can explore Ticino's towns and cities at a more relaxed pace. The major attractions like the **Bellinzona Castles** or **Monte Brè** are less crowded, and you can enjoy the cooler temperatures while sightseeing. If you prefer cultural activities, many of Ticino's museums, such as the **Museo d'Arte della Svizzera Italiana** in Lugano, host special fall exhibitions.

- **Costs (Museo d'Arte della Svizzera Italiana)**: Entry is CHF 15 for adults, CHF 8 for children under 12.

Why Visit in Fall: Fall is ideal for travelers interested in food, wine, and outdoor activities without the crowds of summer. The cooler weather makes it comfortable for hiking and exploring, while the harvest season offers unique opportunities to experience local food and wine festivals.

Winter in Ticino (December to February)

Ticino is not typically associated with winter sports like other parts of Switzerland, but it's still a great destination in the winter months, especially if you're looking for a milder winter experience. Temperatures range from 5°C (41°F) to 10°C (50°F) in the towns, making it a pleasant place to visit for sightseeing and cultural activities. While snow is rare in the cities, the nearby mountains receive enough snow for skiing, snowshoeing, and winter hiking.

The **Airolo-Pesciüm** ski resort is one of the main winter sports areas in Ticino. Located in the northern part of the region, near the **Gotthard Pass**, it offers a range of ski slopes for all levels, as well as snowshoe trails and cross-country skiing. It's a quieter alternative to the more famous Swiss ski resorts, making it perfect for families or beginners who want to avoid the crowds.

- **How to Get There (Airolo-Pesciüm)**: Take a 90-minute train ride from Lugano to Airolo. From there, a short bus or shuttle ride will take you to the ski lifts.
- **Costs**: A full-day ski pass costs CHF 50-65, depending on the season. Equipment rentals are available on-site for around CHF 40 per day.

If you're visiting Ticino during the winter but aren't interested in skiing, there are still plenty of things to do. The region's Christmas markets are a big draw, especially in **Lugano** and **Locarno**. The **Lugano Christmas Market** fills **Piazza della Riforma** with stalls selling handmade crafts, local foods, and holiday decorations. There's also an ice-skating rink set up in the square, making it a fun winter activity for families.

- **How to Get There (Lugano Christmas Market)**: The market is held in **Piazza della Riforma**, a short walk from the main train station.
- **Costs**: Free to explore the market. Ice-skating costs CHF 10-15 for skate rentals.

Winter is also a great time to visit Ticino's spas and wellness centers. The cooler weather makes it the perfect season to enjoy a thermal bath or spa treatment, and Ticino has several options. The **Termali Salini & Spa** in **Locarno** is one of the most popular, offering outdoor thermal baths with views of Lake Maggiore and the surrounding mountains. You can relax in the warm waters while taking in the snowy scenery.

- **Address**: Via G. Respini 7, 6600 Locarno, Switzerland
- **How to Get There**: The spa is a 10-minute walk from the Locarno train station.
- **Costs**: Day passes start at CHF 50, with additional costs for spa treatments.

Why Visit in Winter: Winter is ideal for travelers looking for a quieter, more relaxed visit. While the cities remain mild, the nearby mountains offer winter sports, and the holiday season brings festive markets and activities. It's also the best time for spa and wellness experiences, with fewer crowds and cooler temperatures.

Choosing the Best Time for Your Trip

The best time to visit Ticino depends on what you're looking to do. If you're interested in outdoor activities like hiking and lake visits, spring and summer are the best seasons. For those who prefer food and wine, fall is ideal with its harvest festivals and vineyard tours. Winter is perfect for a quieter getaway, especially if you want to enjoy the region's spas, Christmas markets, or skiing in the nearby mountains.

Entry Requirements and Travel Documents

1. Visa Requirements for Schengen Area Countries

If you are from a **Schengen Zone** country, you do not need a visa to enter Switzerland, including Ticino. The Schengen Area is made up of 27 European countries that have abolished border controls between them. Citizens from Schengen countries can move freely between member states without needing to show a passport or visa. All you need to carry with you is a valid national ID card or passport.

Countries included in the Schengen Area:

- Austria
- Belgium
- Germany
- France
- Italy
- Spain
- Portugal
- Sweden
- Finland
- Greece
- Netherlands
- And others

For example, if you're traveling to Ticino from Italy or France, you won't need to go through immigration control at the Swiss border. However, it's always recommended to carry your passport or ID card with you while traveling, as some local authorities may request it.

2. Visa Requirements for Non-Schengen Countries

If you're traveling from outside the Schengen Zone, such as from the **United States**, **Canada**, **Australia**, or **Japan**, you can enter Switzerland **visa-free** for short stays (up to 90 days) as a tourist. This applies to stays for tourism, business, or family visits, as long as you don't exceed the 90-day limit within a 180-day period. However, you must have a valid passport, and the passport must be valid for at least three months beyond the date you plan to leave Switzerland.

Key Requirements:

- **Passport**: Must be valid for at least three months beyond your planned departure date.
- **Visa**: No visa required for short stays (up to 90 days) for citizens of the United States, Canada, Australia, Japan, and most other visa-exempt countries.
- **Proof of Sufficient Funds**: You may be asked to show proof that you have sufficient financial means to support yourself during your stay.
- **Return or Onward Ticket**: Some travelers may be asked to show proof of their return or onward travel ticket when entering Switzerland.

For stays longer than 90 days or for other purposes such as studying or working, you will need to apply for a long-stay visa (national visa) at the Swiss embassy or consulate in your home country.

Swiss Consulate (United States): Swiss Consulate General in New York

- **Address**: 633 Third Avenue, 30th floor, New York, NY 10017
- **How to Contact**: Tel: +1 212 599 5700
- **Website**: Swiss Consulate General in New York

Swiss Consulate (Canada): Swiss Consulate General in Montreal

- **Address**: Place du Canada, 1010 Sherbrooke St. West, Montreal, QC H3A 2R7
- **How to Contact**: Tel: +1 514 932 7181
- **Website**: Swiss Consulate General in Montreal

3. Visa Requirements for Visa-Required Countries

If you're a citizen of a country that requires a visa to enter Switzerland, such as **India**, **China**, or **South Africa**, you will need to apply for a **Schengen visa** before traveling. The Schengen visa allows you to visit Switzerland and other Schengen countries for up to 90 days within a 180-day period.

The process for obtaining a Schengen visa involves submitting an application at the Swiss consulate or embassy in your home country, along with supporting documents such as:

- A valid passport (with at least two blank pages and valid for at least three months beyond the planned departure date).
- A completed and signed visa application form.
- Passport-sized photos.
- Proof of travel insurance with coverage of at least €30,000.
- Proof of accommodation (hotel reservations, invitation letter if staying with family).
- Proof of sufficient funds for the trip (bank statements, sponsorship letters).
- Return or onward flight tickets.

Processing Time: It's recommended to apply for your visa at least 15 days before your planned trip, but ideally, you should apply 30-45 days in advance in case of delays.

Swiss Embassy (India): Swiss Embassy in New Delhi

- **Address**: Nyaya Marg, Chanakyapuri, New Delhi 110021
- **How to Contact**: Tel: +91 11 4995 9500
- **Website**: Swiss Embassy in New Delhi

Swiss Embassy (China): Swiss Embassy in Beijing

- **Address**: Sanlitun Dongwujie 3, Chaoyang District, Beijing 100600
- **How to Contact**: Tel: +86 10 8532 8888
- **Website**: Swiss Embassy in Beijing

Cost of Schengen Visa: The standard cost for a Schengen visa is **€80 (CHF 85)** for adults and **€40 (CHF 45)** for children aged 6 to 12. Children under six years old are exempt from visa fees.

4. Entry Requirements for British Citizens

Since **Brexit**, British citizens no longer have the same freedom of movement within the Schengen Zone. However, for short stays (up to 90 days), UK passport holders do not need a visa to enter Switzerland. British tourists can stay in Ticino and other parts of Switzerland for up to 90 days within a 180-day period without a visa, similar to travelers from the U.S. or Canada.

- **Passport Validity**: Your passport must be valid for at least six months beyond your planned departure date from Switzerland.

It's important to note that stays beyond 90 days or for purposes such as work or study will require a visa.

- **Swiss Embassy (UK)**: Swiss Embassy in London
- **Address**: 16–18 Montagu Place, London W1H 2BQ
- **How to Contact**: Tel: +44 20 7616 6000
- **Website**: Swiss Embassy in London

5. Health-Related Entry Requirements (Including COVID-19 Regulations)

As of 2025, Switzerland has lifted most COVID-19-related entry restrictions, but it's always wise to check for the latest updates before traveling, as regulations may change based on global health conditions.

Current Health Regulations (as of 2025):

- **Vaccination**: Switzerland does not currently require travelers to provide proof of COVID-19 vaccination for entry.
- **Testing**: There are no mandatory COVID-19 testing requirements for

entry, whether you're vaccinated or not.
- **Quarantine**: No quarantine is required upon entry for travelers from most countries, but it's advisable to check closer to your travel dates to ensure that no new regulations have been introduced.

It's still important to travel with comprehensive travel insurance that covers health emergencies, including COVID-19. Most travelers are not asked to show proof of insurance at the border, but it's better to have it in case you need medical assistance during your trip.

Switzerland has an excellent healthcare system, and Ticino is no exception. If you need medical attention during your stay, the major hospitals in Ticino include:

Ospedale Regionale di Lugano (Lugano Regional Hospital)

- **Address**: Via Tesserete 46, 6900 Lugano, Switzerland
- **How to Contact**: Tel: +41 91 811 60 00
- **Website**: Lugano Regional Hospital

Ospedale San Giovanni Bellinzona (Bellinzona Regional Hospital)

- **Address**: Via Ospedale 12, 6500 Bellinzona, Switzerland
- **How to Contact**: Tel: +41 91 811 80 00
- **Website**: Bellinzona Hospital

Travel Insurance:

You are strongly recommended to have travel insurance that covers medical treatment up to a value of **€30,000**. Many insurers now offer COVID-19 coverage as part of their standard travel insurance packages, so check with your provider before traveling. While travel insurance is not required for entry, it's essential for peace of mind during your trip.

6. What Travel Documents Are Necessary for Entry?

To summarize, here's a quick checklist of the travel documents you'll need for your trip to Ticino, depending on your country of origin:

Citizens of Schengen Zone Countries:

- Valid national ID card or passport.

Citizens of Visa-Exempt Countries (U.S., Canada, Australia, etc.):

- Valid passport (must be valid for at least three months beyond your departure date).
- Proof of sufficient funds (optional, but may be requested at the border).
- Return or onward travel ticket (may be requested).

Citizens of Visa-Required Countries:

- Valid passport (must be valid for at least three months beyond your departure date).
- Schengen visa.
- Proof of travel insurance with coverage of at least €30,000.
- Return or onward travel ticket.
- Proof of sufficient funds.

Health Regulations (for all travelers):

- Travel insurance with COVID-19 coverage (recommended but not required).
- No current vaccination, testing, or quarantine requirements for entry, but check closer to your travel date for updates.

Packing Tips for Ticino's Climate

1. General Packing Tips for Ticino

Ticino enjoys a Mediterranean-like climate, but the weather can vary depending on where you are and the time of year. If you're in the valleys or by the lakes, the temperatures tend to be warmer, but if you're heading into the mountains, you'll need to be prepared for cooler conditions. Regardless of the season, there are a few basic items that you'll want to pack no matter when you visit.

- **Comfortable Walking Shoes**: Ticino is best explored on foot, whether you're walking around cities like Lugano or hiking in the Verzasca Valley. Bring comfortable, sturdy shoes that are suitable for walking on both paved streets and more rugged terrain. If you're planning to hike, make sure you pack proper hiking boots or shoes with good traction.
- **Layers**: Even in summer, the temperature can vary greatly between the valleys and the mountains, so packing layers is key. Lightweight sweaters, jackets, and long-sleeved shirts will help you adjust to changing weather conditions.
- **Waterproof Jacket**: Ticino can get rainy, particularly in spring and fall. A lightweight, waterproof jacket or raincoat is a must, especially if you plan to spend time outdoors. Many hiking trails don't have much shelter, so being prepared for unexpected showers is a good idea.
- **Sunscreen and Hat**: The sun can be strong in Ticino, especially in summer. Even if you're hiking in the mountains or spending the day by the lake, you'll need protection from the sun. A good sunscreen and a wide-brimmed hat will keep you safe from sunburn.
- **Travel Adapter**: Switzerland uses Type J electrical outlets, so if you're coming from outside the country, you'll need a travel adapter. Make sure you bring one to charge your phone, camera, or other electronics.

2. Packing for Spring (March to May)

Spring in Ticino is mild and pleasant, but temperatures can still be unpredictable, especially in the mountains. The days start to warm up in March, but evenings can be chilly, particularly if you're near Lake Lugano or in higher elevations like Monte Brè.

Clothing:

- **Lightweight Jacket or Sweater**: A light jacket is essential for spring mornings and evenings, especially in March and April when temperatures can dip to around 10°C (50°F). A fleece jacket or a thin down coat will work well for cooler days.
- **Long-Sleeved Shirts and T-Shirts**: Bring a mix of short- and long-sleeved shirts so you can adjust to the changing temperatures. Temperatures can range from 12°C (54°F) in early spring to 20°C (68°F) by May.
- **Comfortable Pants or Jeans**: For walking around the cities or visiting parks like **Parco Ciani** in Lugano, comfortable pants or jeans are a good choice. You might also want to pack a pair of lighter, breathable pants for warmer days.
- **Rain Gear**: Spring is known for its showers, so pack a compact umbrella or a lightweight rain jacket. Waterproof shoes or boots are a good idea if you plan to do a lot of walking or hiking, especially on muddy trails in the valleys.

Footwear:

- **Waterproof Hiking Boots**: If you're planning to hike in the Verzasca Valley or around Monte Brè, waterproof hiking boots with good ankle support are a must. Trails can be wet and muddy in spring, and proper footwear will make your hikes much more enjoyable.

Activities and Extras:

- **Binoculars**: Spring is a great time for birdwatching, especially in Ticino's nature reserves like the **Bolle di Magadino**, near the mouth of the Ticino River. If you're interested in wildlife, pack binoculars to spot local bird species.
- **Reusable Water Bottle**: Whether you're walking around towns or hiking, bring a reusable water bottle. You'll find public fountains with fresh drinking water in most towns and villages, so it's easy to refill throughout the day.

3. Packing for Summer (June to August)

Summer is the busiest time to visit Ticino, with warm temperatures and plenty of sunshine. Whether you're planning to spend your days by the lake or hiking in the mountains, you'll want to pack for both hot days and cooler nights, especially if you're heading to higher elevations.

Clothing:

- **Lightweight, Breathable Fabrics**: Ticino's summer temperatures can reach 30°C (86°F), especially in the valleys and around the lakes. Pack lightweight clothing like cotton or linen shirts, shorts, and skirts to stay cool during the day.
- **Swimsuit**: If you're planning to swim in Lake Lugano or Lake Maggiore, don't forget your swimsuit. Many lakeside parks and public beaches, like **Lido di Lugano**, offer swimming areas and are popular spots to cool off in the summer heat.
- **Sunglasses and Hat**: The sun can be strong, especially around the lakes. Sunglasses and a wide-brimmed hat will protect you from the sun whether you're lounging by the water or exploring the towns.

Footwear:

- **Sandals**: Pack a comfortable pair of sandals for walking around cities like **Locarno** or **Ascona**, where you'll be strolling along lakefront promenades or sitting at outdoor cafés. Sandals are also great for the lakeside beaches.
- **Hiking Shoes**: If you're hiking in the mountains, pack lightweight hiking shoes with good grip. Summer is the perfect time to explore the trails around **Monte Tamaro** or **Cardada-Cimetta**. While the temperatures are warm in the valleys, it can get cooler at higher altitudes, so be prepared with a light jacket or sweater.

Activities and Extras:

- **Quick-Dry Towel**: Many visitors spend time at the lake or hiking to remote spots with water access. A quick-dry towel is easy to pack and perfect for lake swims or picnics by the water.
- **Waterproof Bag**: If you're planning any boat trips on Lake Lugano or exploring the Verzasca River, consider bringing a waterproof bag to protect your electronics and valuables.
- **Sunscreen and After-Sun Lotion**: The summer sun in Ticino is strong, so pack plenty of sunscreen, ideally with a high SPF. After-sun lotion or aloe vera gel can help soothe sunburns if you spend too much time in the sun.

4. Packing for Fall (September to November)

Fall in Ticino brings cooler temperatures and a mix of sunny and rainy days. It's also the harvest season, making it a fantastic time to visit for food lovers. If you're attending fall festivals like the **Festa dell'Uva** in Mendrisio or the **Chestnut Festival** in Ascona, you'll want to dress comfortably for both outdoor and indoor activities.

Clothing:

- **Light Sweaters and Jackets**: Early fall still has warm days, but temperatures drop significantly in the evenings. Pack a mix of lightweight sweaters and jackets that you can layer as needed. By November, temperatures in the valleys can drop to around 10°C (50°F) during the day.
- **Long Pants**: As the weather cools, long pants or jeans will be more comfortable for walking around. If you're planning to visit vineyards or take a food tour, casual but comfortable clothing is best.
- **Rain Jacket**: Fall tends to be rainy in Ticino, so don't forget a waterproof rain jacket or coat. It's also a good idea to pack a small umbrella for city tours or walking between festival venues.

Footwear:

- **Waterproof Shoes or Boots**: Waterproof shoes or boots are a good idea in the fall, as rain is common, and some streets or trails can get slippery. If you're attending outdoor festivals, comfortable waterproof shoes will make sure your feet stay dry while you enjoy the events.

Activities and Extras:

- **Scarf and Gloves**: By late fall, particularly in November, it can get quite chilly, especially in the evenings. Pack a scarf and gloves to stay warm if you're visiting mountain areas or walking around the cities in the evening.
- **Small Backpack**: If you're attending festivals or visiting markets, a small backpack is useful for carrying purchases, festival souvenirs, or an extra layer of clothing.

5. Packing for Winter (December to February)

Winter in Ticino is much milder than other parts of Switzerland, especially in the cities and around the lakes. However, if you're heading into the mountains, you'll need to prepare for colder temperatures and snow. While snow is rare in Lugano and Locarno, you'll find plenty of winter activities in areas like **Airolo** and **Cardada-Cimetta**.

Clothing:

- **Warm Coat**: A warm, insulated coat is essential if you're visiting in winter, especially if you plan to spend time in the mountains. Temperatures in the cities like Lugano can hover around 5°C (41°F), but it will be much colder in higher elevations, particularly if you're skiing or snowshoeing.
- **Thermal Layers**: For those planning to ski or enjoy other winter sports, thermal layers are a must. Even if you're just walking around towns like Bellinzona or Locarno, thermal tops and leggings will keep you comfortable on cold days.
- **Hat, Gloves, and Scarf**: These are essential in winter, especially if you're heading to mountain resorts like **Airolo-Pesciüm** for skiing. Even in the cities, it can get quite cold in the evenings, so pack warm accessories to stay comfortable.

Footwear:

- **Insulated Boots**: If you're visiting in winter, insulated boots are necessary, particularly if you're visiting higher-altitude areas. Even if there's no snow in the cities, it's best to wear warm, waterproof boots, especially if you're exploring the region's castles or outdoor Christmas markets.

Activities and Extras:

- **Ski Gear**: If you plan to ski in **Airolo-Pesciüm** or **Cardada-Cimetta**, you can rent skis, poles, and helmets on-site, but it's always a good idea to bring your own ski jacket and pants for comfort and fit. Ski passes at Airolo-Pesciüm cost around CHF 50-65 for a day pass.
- **Warm Socks**: Pack plenty of warm, wool socks for winter hiking or skiing. Even if you're not doing winter sports, having warm socks will keep your feet comfortable in colder conditions.
- **Hot Water Bottle**: If you're staying in mountain cabins or older buildings, it can get chilly at night. A travel-sized hot water bottle can help keep you warm while sleeping.

Budgeting for Your Trip to Ticino: Costs and Saving Tips

Accommodation Costs

Accommodation in Ticino varies depending on the type of lodging you choose and the time of year. In high season (summer and early fall), prices tend to be higher, especially around popular tourist spots like **Lugano** and **Locarno**. Here's an overview of what to expect:

Luxury Hotels: If you're looking for top-end luxury, expect to pay anywhere between **CHF 250-500 per night** for a 5-star hotel. Some of the best options include the **Grand Hotel Villa Castagnola** in Lugano, which offers lakeside views and high-end amenities.

- **Address**: Viale Castagnola 31, 6900 Lugano, Switzerland
- **Cost**: CHF 300-450 per night (depending on the season).

Mid-Range Hotels: For mid-range accommodations, plan on spending **CHF 150-250 per night**. These hotels offer comfortable rooms with a good range of amenities. In Locarno, the **Hotel Belvedere** is a solid option for travelers looking for comfort without splurging.

- **Address**: Via ai Monti 44, 6600 Locarno, Switzerland
- **Cost**: CHF 180-220 per night.

Budget Hotels and Hostels: For those on a tighter budget, budget hotels and hostels offer more affordable options, typically ranging from **CHF 80-150 per night**. The **Hotel Besso** in Lugano is a great option for budget-conscious travelers.

- **Address**: Via Besso 24, 6900 Lugano, Switzerland
- **Cost**: CHF 80-130 per night.

Hostels: A bed in a hostel dormitory will cost around **CHF 40-70 per night**. Hostels like the **Youth Hostel Lugano Savosa** offer clean, basic accommodations for travelers who don't mind sharing spaces.

- **Address**: Via Cantonale 13, 6942 Savosa, Switzerland
- **Cost**: CHF 40-60 per night for dorms; private rooms are available for around CHF 80-100.

Money-Saving Tip for Accommodation:
If you're visiting during the high season, it's best to book your accommodation well in advance to lock in better prices. Another tip is to look for guesthouses or **Agriturismos** (farm stays) in the countryside, which often offer lower rates than hotels in the city centers. Websites like **Airbnb** also have options for renting private apartments or rooms at more affordable prices.

Dining and Meal Costs
Eating out in Ticino can be expensive, especially if you're dining at restaurants around the main tourist areas. However, there are ways to enjoy the local cuisine without breaking the bank.

Fine Dining: If you want to treat yourself, fine dining at high-end restaurants in Lugano or Locarno can cost between **CHF 60-120 per person**. At places like **Grotto Ticinese**, you can enjoy gourmet Ticinese cuisine with local wines.

- **Cost**: CHF 70-100 for a full meal with wine.

Mid-Range Dining: Expect to pay around **CHF 30-50 per person** at mid-range restaurants. Many local **grottoes** (traditional restaurants) serve classic Ticinese dishes like risotto, polenta, and fresh fish at reasonable prices. **Grotto Morchino** is a great option for traditional fare at a reasonable price.

- **Address**: Via al Grotto 32, 6912 Pazzallo, Switzerland
- **Cost**: CHF 35-50 per person.

Casual Dining and Street Food: For casual dining, Ticino offers plenty of cafés and takeaway spots where you can get a sandwich or pizza for around **CHF 10-20**. Bakeries and cafés are also good for quick breakfasts or snacks.

- **Cost**: CHF 10-15 for a sandwich or slice of pizza.

Money-Saving Tip for Dining:
Take advantage of **lunch specials** (called "**menu del giorno**" or "plat du jour"), which offer a full meal (main dish, salad, and drink) at a discounted price, usually around **CHF 20-25** at mid-range restaurants. Additionally, shopping for groceries and making your own meals is an effective way to save money. Larger supermarkets like **Coop** and **Migros** in Lugano and Locarno offer a wide selection of fresh, local products.

Transportation Costs
Public transportation in Ticino is excellent and well-organized, with buses, trains, and boats connecting major towns and tourist spots. While

transportation can be pricey, there are ways to keep costs down.

- **Ticino Ticket**: If you're staying at a hotel, guesthouse, or campsite in Ticino, you'll receive a **Ticino Ticket**. This pass gives you **free unlimited access** to public transportation (buses, trains, and boats) throughout the region, as well as discounts on some cable cars and attractions.
- **Cost**: Free for hotel guests (ask your accommodation about the ticket).
- **Train Tickets**: Train travel is efficient but can be expensive if you're buying single tickets. For example, a train ride from **Zurich** to Lugano costs around **CHF 40-60** one way. If you plan to use the trains often, consider buying a **Swiss Travel Pass**, which offers unlimited train, bus, and boat travel across Switzerland for a fixed price.
- **Swiss Travel Pass Cost**: CHF 232 for 3 days, CHF 363 for 8 days.
- **Local Buses**: If you don't have the Ticino Ticket, expect to pay around **CHF 2.50-4.50** for a local bus ride, depending on the distance.

Money-Saving Tip for Transportation:

To save on transportation, try to take advantage of the **Ticino Ticket**, which is available to most visitors staying in hotels. For longer journeys or multiple day trips, the **Swiss Travel Pass** is also worth considering, as it includes travel throughout the entire country and discounts on many mountain excursions.

Activities and Attractions

Ticino is full of outdoor activities and cultural attractions, many of which are free or low-cost. You can enjoy hiking, swimming in the lakes, and exploring towns like Lugano and Locarno without spending a lot of money.

Museums and Galleries: Most museums in Ticino charge an entry fee of **CHF 10-20**. One of the top museums in Lugano is the **Museo d'Arte della Svizzera Italiana**, which showcases Swiss-Italian art from the Renaissance to modern times.

- **Address**: Piazza Bernardino Luini 6, 6900 Lugano, Switzerland
- **Cost**: CHF 15 for adults, CHF 8 for children.

Boat Tours: A boat trip on Lake Lugano or Lake Maggiore is a must-do, and prices range from **CHF 15-35** depending on the length of the tour. For example, a round-trip boat tour from **Lugano to Gandria** costs about CHF 18.

- **Address (Lugano Pier)**: Riva Vincenzo Vela, 6900 Lugano, Switzerland.

Castles of Bellinzona: A visit to the UNESCO-listed castles of **Bellinzona** is another budget-friendly activity. You can explore the **Castelgrande**, **Montebello**, and **Sasso Corbaro** for **CHF 15** with a combined ticket.

- **Address**: Via Orico 13, 6500 Bellinzona, Switzerland
- **Cost**: CHF 5 for each castle, CHF 15 for a combined ticket.

Money-Saving Tip for Activities:

Many outdoor activities, like hiking in the **Verzasca Valley** or walking along the **Lugano lakefront**, are free. Ticino's parks, gardens, and public spaces are open to everyone, making it easy to explore without spending much.

Local Currency and Payment Tips

Switzerland uses the **Swiss Franc (CHF)**, and most places in Ticino accept credit cards, including Visa and MasterCard. However, smaller shops, cafés, and some local markets may only accept cash or have a minimum amount for card payments.

- **Currency Exchange**: If you need to exchange money, it's best to do so at a bank or official exchange office, as they typically offer the best rates. ATMs are widely available in all towns and cities, and you can

withdraw Swiss francs directly from your bank account using a debit or credit card.
- **Credit Cards vs. Cash**: Credit cards are accepted almost everywhere in Ticino, but it's always a good idea to carry some cash, especially when visiting smaller towns or paying for local transportation. If you're shopping at local markets or eating at small restaurants, you may find that some places prefer cash.

Money-Saving Tip for Currency:

To avoid high ATM fees, consider using a travel credit card that doesn't charge foreign transaction fees. When paying with a card, always choose to pay in Swiss francs rather than your home currency to avoid unfavorable exchange rates.

Language and Cultural Etiquette in Ticino

Ticino is the only Swiss canton where **Italian** is the official language. While many people, especially in tourist areas, speak English, it's always appreciated when visitors make an effort to speak a few words of Italian. Here are some key phrases that will help you get by:

- **Buongiorno** – Good morning/Good day
- **Buonasera** – Good evening
- **Grazie** – Thank you
- **Prego** – You're welcome
- **Per favore** – Please
- **Dov'è...?** – Where is...?
- **Quanto costa?** – How much does it cost?
- **Scusi** – Excuse me
- **Arrivederci** – Goodbye

Most locals will greet you with "**Buongiorno**" or "**Buonasera**," depending on the time of day. It's polite to greet shopkeepers and people you meet with these phrases. A simple **"Grazie"** (thank you) goes a long way in making your interactions pleasant.

Dining Etiquette in Ticino

When dining out in Ticino, meal times are usually similar to those in Italy. Lunch is typically served between 12:00 and 2:00 PM, and dinner starts around 7:00 PM. Ticinese people tend to eat later in the evening, so many restaurants may not open for dinner service until after 7:00 PM.

- **Tipping**: Tipping in Ticino is not mandatory, as service charges are usually included in the bill. However, it's customary to round up the bill or leave a small tip if the service was excellent. For example, if your bill is CHF 47, you could leave CHF 50. A 5-10% tip is generally appreciated for good service at restaurants or cafés.

Cultural Etiquette in Ticino

- **Respect for Personal Space**: While Ticino is influenced by Italian culture, it still follows many of the more reserved Swiss customs, particularly when it comes to personal space and greetings. Don't assume people will greet you with a hug or a kiss on the cheek unless you know them well. A simple handshake is the standard greeting when meeting new people.
- **Quiet Hours**: Like the rest of Switzerland, Ticino has quiet hours, especially in residential areas. It's considered impolite to make excessive noise between **10:00 PM and 7:00 AM**, so if you're staying in a guesthouse or apartment, be mindful of this.
- **Dress Code**: Ticino is generally relaxed when it comes to dress, but in upscale restaurants or cultural events, it's best to dress smartly. In churches and religious sites, it's polite to dress modestly, covering shoulders and knees.

Health and Safety: Staying Safe in Ticino

Emergency Numbers and Services

In Ticino, emergency services are efficient and widely available. Here are the key emergency numbers that you should keep handy during your trip:

- **Police**: 117
- **Ambulance**: 144
- **Fire Department**: 118
- **General Emergency (European Emergency Number)**: 112

If you need medical assistance, Ticino's hospitals and clinics provide high-quality care. Emergency rooms operate 24/7, and doctors usually speak Italian, German, and English, so language won't be an issue.

Key Healthcare Facilities in Ticino:
Ospedale Regionale di Lugano (Lugano Regional Hospital)

- **Address**: Via Tesserete 46, 6900 Lugano
- **Contact**: +41 91 811 60 00
- **How to Get There**: 10 minutes by taxi from Lugano city center, or take bus line 5 or 6 from Lugano train station.

Ospedale San Giovanni Bellinzona (Bellinzona Regional Hospital)

- **Address**: Via Ospedale 12, 6500 Bellinzona
- **Contact**: +41 91 811 80 00
- **How to Get There**: 15 minutes by taxi from Bellinzona train station, or take bus line 1 from the city center.

Clinica Luganese Moncucco

- **Address**: Via Moncucco 10, 6900 Lugano

- **Contact**: +41 91 960 81 11
- **How to Get There**: A 10-minute drive from Lugano city center.

Travel Insurance:

It's always a good idea to travel with comprehensive travel insurance that covers medical emergencies, accidents, and cancellations. Make sure your policy covers outdoor activities if you plan on hiking, skiing, or other adventure sports in Ticino. Most travel insurance policies will cover emergency medical expenses, including hospital stays, doctor visits, and medical evacuation if necessary.

Precautions for Outdoor Activities

Ticino is a paradise for outdoor lovers, with its mountains, lakes, and valleys offering everything from hiking and cycling to water sports. However, it's important to take a few safety precautions, especially if you're planning to spend a lot of time outdoors.

- **Hiking Safety**: Ticino's hiking trails are well-marked and maintained, but always carry a map, plenty of water, and snacks. Some trails, like those in the Verzasca Valley or Monte Tamaro, can be strenuous, so be sure to wear appropriate hiking shoes with good traction. Check the weather forecast before you go, as rain can make the trails slippery.
- **Swimming and Water Safety**: Swimming in **Lake Lugano** or **Lake Maggiore** is a favorite summer activity, but always stick to designated swimming areas, especially if you're not a strong swimmer. Some parts of the lakes can have strong currents or deep sections. The local **Lido di Lugano** and **Lido Locarno** offer supervised swimming areas with lifeguards, perfect for families.
- **Sun Protection**: The sun in Ticino can be strong, especially in summer. Whether you're hiking, lounging by the lake, or exploring the towns, always wear sunscreen with a high SPF and a hat to protect yourself from sunburn.

- **Altitude Sickness**: If you're planning to hike at high elevations, such as Monte Brè or Monte Tamaro, be aware of the signs of altitude sickness, especially if you're not used to mountain climbing. Drink plenty of water, take breaks, and descend if you start to feel dizzy or short of breath.

Traveling with Kids: Family-Friendly Tips

Ticino is a family-friendly destination with plenty of activities to keep kids entertained, from outdoor adventures to fun attractions designed for young visitors. Here are some practical tips to make traveling with kids in Ticino a breeze.

Kid-Friendly Attractions
Swissminiatur

- Located in **Melide**, just outside Lugano, Swissminiatur is an open-air museum where you can see Switzerland's most famous landmarks in miniature. It's a great place for kids to explore, and the gardens and miniature trains are always a hit with young visitors.
- **Address**: Via Cantonale, 6815 Melide
- **Cost**: CHF 19 for adults, CHF 12 for children (ages 6-15), free for children under 6
- **How to Get There**: A 10-minute train ride from Lugano to Melide, then a short walk from the station.

Falconeria Locarno

- The Falconeria in Locarno offers live bird of prey shows, where children can see eagles, falcons, and owls in action. It's both educational and fun, with interactive demonstrations.

- **Address**: Via delle Scuole 12, 6600 Locarno
- **Cost**: CHF 25 for adults, CHF 12 for children
- **How to Get There**: Take a train from Lugano to Locarno (50 minutes), then a short walk or taxi to the Falconeria.

Splash e Spa Tamaro

- A perfect option for a rainy day, Splash e Spa is a water park and wellness center in Rivera. It features water slides, wave pools, and play areas for children, as well as a spa section for adults.
- **Address**: Via Campagnole, 6802 Rivera
- **Cost**: CHF 35 for adults, CHF 25 for children
- **How to Get There**: A 20-minute train ride from Lugano to Rivera, followed by a short walk.

Dining with Kids

Most restaurants in Ticino are family-friendly, especially the local **grottoes**, which often have outdoor seating and large tables perfect for families. Kid-friendly meals usually include pasta, pizza, and risotto, which are always popular with young visitors.

Grotto Morchino in **Pazzallo** is a great option for families, with a relaxed outdoor atmosphere and traditional Ticinese dishes that even picky eaters will enjoy.

- **Address**: Via al Grotto 32, 6912 Pazzallo
- **Cost**: CHF 35 per person on average for a meal.

Pizza al Volo in Lugano serves quick, affordable pizza by the slice, perfect for a fast meal between sightseeing stops.

- **Address**: Via Nassa 62, 6900 Lugano

- **Cost**: CHF 10-15 for a pizza slice and drink.

Transportation with Kids

- **Ticino Ticket**: Families staying at hotels or campsites in Ticino will receive the **Ticino Ticket**, which allows free travel on buses, trains, and boats throughout the region. This makes it easy to explore with kids without worrying about extra transportation costs.
- **Trains and Buses**: Public transportation in Ticino is family-friendly, with most trains and buses offering space for strollers and luggage. If you're traveling with small children, the local **Ferrovia Monte Brè** funicular is an exciting way to reach the top of **Monte Brè**, and the view from the top will impress both adults and children.

Childcare and Family Discounts

Some hotels and resorts in Ticino offer childcare services and kids' clubs, particularly in the summer months. Resorts like **Parco San Marco Lifestyle Beach Resort** offer babysitting services and family rooms. Be sure to inquire about family discounts at attractions, as many museums, water parks, and even transportation services offer reduced prices for children.

Sustainable Travel in Ticino

If you're an eco-conscious traveler, Ticino is a great place to visit sustainably. The region offers plenty of ways to minimize your carbon footprint, from eco-friendly accommodations to green transportation options.

Eco-Friendly Accommodations

Several hotels and guesthouses in Ticino have adopted eco-friendly practices, from using renewable energy to sourcing local ingredients for their restaurants.

EcoHotel Locanda del Giglio

- This eco-friendly hotel near Monte Brè focuses on sustainability by using solar panels, recycling, and locally sourced food. It's perfect for travelers looking for a green getaway with breathtaking views.
- **Address**: Via al Bosco 39, 6945 Lugano-Castagnola
- **Cost**: CHF 150-200 per night
- **How to Get There**: Take a bus from Lugano to Castagnola, then a 10-minute taxi ride to the hotel.

Hotel & SPA Cacciatori in **Cademario** also follows sustainable practices, using energy-efficient systems and promoting local produce.

- **Address**: Via Cantonale 75, 6936 Cademario
- **Cost**: CHF 220-300 per night
- **How to Get There**: A 20-minute drive from Lugano city center.

Green Transportation Options

Using public transportation in Ticino is not only convenient, but it's also an eco-friendly way to get around. The **Ticino Ticket** gives you unlimited access to buses, trains, and boats, making it easy to explore the region without a car.

- **Biking**: Ticino is increasingly bike-friendly, with bike rental services available in cities like Lugano and Locarno. You can rent a bike from **Rent a Bike Lugano** for about **CHF 30 per day** and explore the local bike trails.
- **Address**: Stazione FFS, 6900 Lugano
- **Cost**: CHF 25-30 for a day rental.
- **E-Bikes**: For a greener option, consider renting an **e-bike** for the day. E-bike rentals are available at many train stations, and the bike trails around **Monte Tamaro** and along **Lake Lugano** are perfect for a leisurely ride with minimal environmental impact.

Sustainable Activities

- **Hiking**: One of the best ways to enjoy Ticino while minimizing your environmental footprint is by hiking. Trails like the **Sentiero Verzasca** or the routes around **Monte Tamaro** allow you to explore the region's natural beauty without leaving a negative impact.
- **Local Markets**: To support local communities and minimize your environmental impact, visit local markets like the **Mercato di Bellinzona**, where you can buy fresh, local produce, cheeses, and crafts directly from Ticinese farmers and artisans.
- **Address**: Piazza Nosetto, Bellinzona
- **Market Days**: Saturdays, 8:00 AM – 1:00 PM.

Getting to Ticino

Flying to Ticino: Nearest Airports

When planning your trip to Ticino, the region is well-connected to several airports, making it relatively easy to get there whether you're flying from within Europe or coming from overseas. While Ticino itself has a small regional airport, many travelers use larger nearby airports in Italy for international flights. Here's what you need to know about the nearest airports, airlines, and the best routes to get to Ticino.

Lugano Airport (LUG)

Lugano Airport is the closest airport to the heart of Ticino. It's a small regional airport located about 6 kilometers from Lugano's city center, in the suburb of Agno. While the airport doesn't handle long-haul international flights, it serves a few key routes within Europe, making it convenient for travelers coming from cities like Zurich or Geneva.

- **Address**: Via Aeroporto 15, 6982 Agno, Switzerland
- **How to Get There**: A 10-minute taxi ride from Lugano city center, or you can take bus line 60, which runs directly to the airport from Lugano's main train station.

Airlines Serving Lugano Airport:

- **Swiss International Air Lines**: Offers flights between Lugano and Zurich, with easy connections to other European and international destinations. From Zurich, you can catch direct flights to cities like New York, London, Paris, and more.
- **Helvetic Airways**: Operates seasonal flights to Lugano from various cities within Switzerland and Europe. It's a good option for short-haul flights to Lugano.

Flight Connections:

- From **Zurich Airport**: Zurich is the largest hub for flights connecting to Lugano. You can fly directly from Zurich to Lugano in about 45 minutes, and flights are available multiple times a day.
- From **Geneva Airport**: You can also fly from Geneva to Lugano, though these flights are less frequent. The journey takes just under an hour.

Tips for Flying to Lugano:
While Lugano Airport is convenient, the flights can be more expensive than flying into Milan or Zurich due to the limited number of routes. If you're coming from overseas, you'll likely need to connect through Zurich, Geneva, or another major European city.

Milan Malpensa Airport (MXP)
For most international travelers, **Milan Malpensa Airport** is the best airport to fly into when visiting Ticino. Located about 70 kilometers south of Lugano, Malpensa is Italy's second-busiest airport and offers flights from all over the world. It's a major hub for long-haul flights, including routes from the United States, Asia, and the Middle East.

- **Address**: 21010 Ferno VA, Italy
- **How to Get There**: The easiest way to get from Malpensa to Ticino is by taking the **Malpensa Express** train to **Mendrisio** or **Lugano**. The train journey takes about 1 hour and 30 minutes, with frequent

departures throughout the day. Alternatively, you can rent a car or take a shuttle service. If you're driving, the journey to Lugano takes about an hour via the **A9 highway**.

Airlines Serving Milan Malpensa:

- **Emirates, Qatar Airways, American Airlines**, and **Delta Air Lines**: These airlines offer long-haul flights from the United States, Middle East, and Asia.
- **easyJet, Ryanair**, and **Lufthansa**: For budget-friendly European flights, you can use airlines like easyJet and Ryanair, which connect to many cities across Europe.

Tips for Flying to Milan Malpensa:

- **Cost Efficiency**: Milan Malpensa often offers cheaper flights compared to Swiss airports, especially for budget carriers or long-haul routes. If you're looking to save on airfare, flying into Malpensa and then traveling to Ticino by train is a cost-effective option.
- **Shuttle Services**: Several shuttle services operate between Malpensa and Lugano. Prices start at around **CHF 25-30** for a one-way ticket, and shuttles run several times a day.

Other Airport Options:

- **Milan Linate Airport (LIN)**: Linate is another option for travelers flying into northern Italy. It's smaller than Malpensa but still offers a range of European flights, primarily for short-haul destinations. From Linate, you can either drive or take a combination of bus and train to reach Ticino in about 1 hour and 30 minutes.
- **Zurich Airport (ZRH)**: As Switzerland's largest airport, Zurich is a good alternative for travelers coming from North America or Asia. From Zurich, you can either catch a short flight to Lugano or take the

train directly to Ticino, which takes around 2 hours.

Train Travel: Scenic Swiss Rail Journeys

Traveling to Ticino by train is one of the most scenic ways to arrive, especially if you're coming from other parts of Switzerland or Italy. The region is well-connected to Switzerland's extensive rail network, and trains are clean, comfortable, and on time. If you're looking to soak in the views of the Swiss Alps, a train journey to Ticino is a memorable experience in itself.

The Gotthard Panorama Express

The **Gotthard Panorama Express** is one of Switzerland's most famous scenic train routes, and it's the perfect way to arrive in Ticino. The journey starts in **Lucerne**, with passengers boarding a boat for a cruise across Lake Lucerne, then transferring to a panoramic train that travels along the historic Gotthard route. The train winds through the stunning Reuss Valley, passes through spiral tunnels, and crosses the famous **Gotthard Pass** before descending into the sunny landscapes of Ticino.

- **Route**: Lucerne to Lugano, with stops along the way in Flüelen and Bellinzona.
- **Duration**: 5.5 hours (combined boat and train journey).
- **Cost**: Tickets for the Gotthard Panorama Express start at **CHF 89** for second class and **CHF 149** for first class, one way. Swiss Travel Pass holders travel for free but need to pay a small reservation fee of **CHF 16**.

How to Book: You can book tickets directly on the **SBB Swiss Railways** website or at any train station in Switzerland. If you're traveling during peak season (June to September), it's best to book in advance to secure a seat, especially in first class, which offers the best views.

First Class vs. Second Class:

- **First Class**: Offers larger seats, more legroom, and panoramic windows, ideal for enjoying the stunning scenery. It's more expensive, but for scenic journeys like the Gotthard Panorama Express, it's worth the upgrade.
- **Second Class**: More affordable and still very comfortable. The difference between first and second class is primarily the space and window size, but both classes are a great way to travel.

The Gotthard Base Tunnel

For travelers who prefer a faster journey into Ticino, the **Gotthard Base Tunnel** is the world's longest and deepest railway tunnel, cutting through the Swiss Alps to connect the northern and southern parts of Switzerland. The tunnel reduces travel time significantly and is ideal for those who want to get to Ticino quickly.

- **Route**: Zurich to Lugano via the Gotthard Base Tunnel.
- **Duration**: Around 2 hours from Zurich to Lugano.
- **Cost**: Standard tickets from Zurich to Lugano start at **CHF 40-60** for second class, one way.

While the Gotthard Base Tunnel route is not as scenic as the Gotthard Panorama Express, it's the fastest way to travel between Zurich and Ticino.

Other Scenic Rail Routes to Ticino

- **Bernina Express**: While not a direct route to Ticino, the **Bernina Express** is another scenic Swiss train journey worth mentioning. You can take this iconic route from **Chur** through the Engadine region and into Italy's **Tirano**, then transfer to a train heading north into Ticino

via **Milan**. It's a longer journey, but the views of glaciers, mountains, and valleys are breathtaking.
- **Cost**: From CHF 59 for second class. Reservations are required, and it's best to book tickets in advance, especially in summer.

Booking Train Tickets and Rail Passes

If you're planning to travel around Switzerland, especially for multiple days, buying a **Swiss Travel Pass** can save you money and simplify your travel experience. The Swiss Travel Pass allows unlimited travel on trains, buses, and boats throughout Switzerland for a set number of days.

- **Swiss Travel Pass Costs**:
- **3 days**: CHF 232 (second class), CHF 369 (first class)
- **8 days**: CHF 363 (second class), CHF 564 (first class)

Where to Buy: You can purchase the Swiss Travel Pass online via the Swiss Railways (SBB) website, or in person at any train station in Switzerland. The pass also gives you free or discounted entry to many museums and attractions throughout the country.

Money-Saving Tip: If you're only traveling within Ticino and not planning on extensive rail travel across Switzerland, it might be more economical to buy individual tickets or regional passes, such as the **Ticino Ticket**, which offers free travel on buses and trains within the region for hotel guests.

First Class vs. Second Class on Swiss Trains

- **First Class**: If you prefer a quieter, more spacious experience, first-class tickets offer larger seats, more legroom, and often fewer passengers. On scenic routes like the Gotthard Panorama Express, first-class panoramic carriages are ideal for enjoying the stunning views.
- **Second Class**: For budget-conscious travelers, second class is still very comfortable. Swiss trains are known for their cleanliness and efficiency,

so even in second class, you'll have a pleasant journey.

Baggage and Accessibility

Swiss trains offer plenty of space for luggage, with overhead racks and designated areas for larger bags. If you're traveling with heavy luggage or bicycles, most trains, including those to Ticino, have dedicated luggage compartments.

All major Swiss trains are accessible to travelers with reduced mobility. Trains have wide doors, ramps, and accessible toilets, and staff are available to assist if needed.

Car Rentals and Road Trips: Driving to and Around Ticino

Driving in Ticino is one of the best ways to explore the region at your own pace, especially if you want to visit remote villages, mountain passes, or enjoy scenic routes that are harder to reach by public transportation. Here's everything you need to know about renting a car, road conditions, and planning a memorable road trip through this stunning region.

Car Rental Options in Ticino

Car rentals in Ticino are straightforward and available in major towns like **Lugano**, **Bellinzona**, and **Locarno**. If you're flying into nearby airports like **Milan Malpensa** or **Zurich**, you can also rent a car directly from the airport and drive to Ticino. The most popular car rental companies include:

1. Europcar: Europcar has multiple locations in Ticino, including at Lugano Airport and in the city center. They offer a wide range of vehicles from compact cars to larger vans, perfect for families or groups.

- **Address (Lugano)**: Via Clemente Maraini 41, 6900 Lugano
- **Cost**: From CHF 70 per day for a compact car. Prices vary based on the season and vehicle type.

2. Hertz: Hertz is a reliable option with locations at airports and in central Lugano. Their fleet includes everything from economy cars to luxury vehicles.

- **Address (Lugano)**: Via San Gottardo 13, 6900 Lugano
- **Cost**: Starting at CHF 60 per day.

3. Avis: Avis is one of the most well-known car rental companies and is available at **Milan Malpensa Airport**, making it convenient for those arriving from Italy.

- **Address (Milan Malpensa)**: Terminal 1, 21010 Ferno VA, Italy
- **Cost**: From EUR 50 per day.

Tips for Renting a Car:

- **Book in Advance**: Especially in the summer months, car rentals can be in high demand, so it's best to book your car well in advance to secure the best rates.
- **Automatic vs. Manual**: Many rental cars in Europe are manual, so if you're more comfortable driving an automatic, make sure to specify this when booking.
- **Check for the Vignette**: All vehicles in Switzerland, including rental cars, must have a **vignette** (toll sticker) for highway use. Most rental cars will already have this, but double-check to avoid fines.

Road Conditions and Scenic Routes in Ticino

Ticino offers some of the most scenic drives in Switzerland, with well-maintained roads that wind through valleys, along lakes, and up into the mountains. Swiss roads are known for being in excellent condition, and driving here is a pleasure for those who enjoy taking in the views as they travel.

Top Scenic Routes:

1. **Lugano to Bellinzona via Lake Lugano**: This drive takes you along the shores of **Lake Lugano**, offering stunning lake views with the mountains in the background. Stop at the small town of **Gandria** to explore its charming narrow streets or take a short boat ride across the lake.

- **Distance**: 30 km
- **Time**: 30-40 minutes without stops

2. **Verzasca Valley**: If you're looking for a picturesque mountain drive, head to the **Verzasca Valley**. This narrow, winding road takes you past traditional stone houses, lush green forests, and the famous **Verzasca Dam**, where you can even try bungee jumping. The drive ends in **Sonogno**, a beautiful village where you can stop for a meal.

- **Distance**: 25 km from Locarno to Sonogno
- **Time**: 45 minutes

3. **Monte Ceneri Pass**: The **Monte Ceneri Pass** connects the northern and southern parts of Ticino. The road winds through forests and offers sweeping views of the Ticino valley. It's a great option for drivers who want to see a different side of Ticino away from the lakefront towns.

- **Distance**: 16 km from Lugano to Bellinzona via the pass
- **Time**: 20 minutes

4. **Lake Maggiore and Centovalli**: For a longer day trip, drive from Locarno along **Lake Maggiore** and into the **Centovalli Valley**. This route takes you through small villages nestled in the mountains, with plenty of opportunities to stop and hike or have a picnic.

- **Distance**: 40 km from Locarno to the Italian border
- **Time**: 1 hour

Road Conditions:

- **Highways and Local Roads**: Swiss highways (marked with a green sign) are in excellent condition and easy to navigate. Ticino's local roads, especially in the mountains, can be narrow and winding, so drive carefully and be mindful of cyclists and hikers.
- **Winter Driving**: If you're visiting Ticino in winter, roads are generally kept clear of snow, but mountain passes may require **snow chains** or winter tires. Check the weather forecast and road conditions before heading out.

Parking in Ticino:

- **Parking in Cities**: In cities like Lugano and Locarno, street parking is available but limited. Look for blue zones, where you can park for free for up to one hour with a parking disc, which can be picked up at most gas stations. There are also paid parking garages, which charge around **CHF 2-4 per hour**.
- **Parking in Smaller Towns**: In smaller towns and villages, parking is usually easier to find, and many attractions, like the **Verzasca Valley** or **Monte Brè**, have dedicated parking lots for visitors. These often charge a flat fee of around **CHF 5-10** for the day.

Fuel Costs and Tolls

Fuel prices in Switzerland are generally higher than in neighboring Italy or France, so it's worth factoring this into your budget if you plan on driving a lot.

- **Average Fuel Costs**: As of 2025, fuel prices in Ticino average around

CHF 1.90-2.10 per liter. Gas stations are easy to find in the cities and along major highways, but they may be more sparse in remote areas, so plan ahead if you're driving through the mountains.

Toll Roads:

- **Swiss Vignette**: To drive on Swiss highways, your car needs a **vignette**, which is a toll sticker that costs **CHF 40** for a year. Most rental cars will already have one, but if you're driving your own car into Switzerland, you can purchase the vignette at the border or at most gas stations.
- **Tunnels and Passes**: While the vignette covers most roads, certain tunnels and mountain passes, like the **Gotthard Tunnel**, may have additional fees.

Cross-Border Travel from Italy and Beyond

Ticino's location near the Italian border makes it a popular destination for travelers coming from Italy and other neighboring countries. Whether you're driving, taking the train, or traveling by bus, here's how to navigate cross-border travel into Ticino.

Driving from Italy to Ticino

Driving from Italy to Ticino is one of the most convenient ways to cross the border, especially if you're coming from **Milan** or other northern Italian cities. The drive is scenic and fairly straightforward, with well-marked roads and quick border crossings.

Key Border Crossings:

- **Chiasso**: This is the main border crossing if you're driving from **Milan** to Ticino. It's located on the **A9 highway**, which turns into the **A2**

highway once you cross into Switzerland. The drive from Milan to Lugano takes about 1 hour, depending on traffic.
- **Ponte Tresa**: This smaller border crossing is perfect if you're heading to **Lugano** from the northern Italian lakes, such as **Lake Como** or **Varese**. The crossing is less busy than Chiasso, but the roads are narrower, making it a scenic option for a leisurely drive.

Documents Needed:

- **Passport**: If you're an EU citizen, you can travel between Italy and Switzerland using your national ID card, though carrying a passport is always recommended. Non-EU citizens, such as Americans, Australians, or Canadians, will need a valid passport.
- **Driver's License**: If you're renting a car, your regular driver's license is sufficient. Non-EU travelers may also need an **International Driving Permit (IDP)**, so check with your rental company ahead of time.
- **Insurance**: Make sure your rental car has the proper insurance coverage for both Switzerland and Italy. Most rental companies include this as part of the package.

Tips for Cross-Border Driving:

- **Border Checks**: Border checks between Switzerland and Italy are generally quick and hassle-free. However, during busy times (like summer holidays), there can be short delays, so it's a good idea to avoid peak travel times.
- **Speed Limits**: Be aware that speed limits change when you cross into Switzerland. On highways, the limit is **120 km/h**, while in cities, it's **50 km/h**.

Taking the Train from Italy to Ticino

Traveling by train is one of the most convenient ways to cross the border from Italy into Ticino. The Swiss train system is fast and reliable, and there are direct train connections between major Italian cities and Ticino.

Trains from Milan:

The **EuroCity** trains run directly from **Milan Central Station** to **Lugano** and **Bellinzona**, with several departures throughout the day. The journey takes just under an hour to Lugano and a little longer to Bellinzona.

- **Cost**: Tickets start at around **EUR 20-30** for second class, depending on how far in advance you book. First-class tickets are also available for around **EUR 50-60**.
- **Booking**: You can book tickets online through the **Trenitalia** or **SBB Swiss Railways** websites, or purchase them at the station.

Trains from Other Italian Cities:

If you're coming from other cities like **Florence**, **Rome**, or **Venice**, you'll likely need to transfer in Milan. Trains from these cities to Milan run frequently, and connections to Ticino are quick and easy.

Border Formalities:

There are no formal border checks when traveling by train from Italy to Ticino, but make sure to carry your passport or ID card, as random checks can occur.

Bus and Shuttle Services from Italy

If you prefer not to drive or take the train, there are several bus and shuttle services that connect Italian cities with Ticino. These are particularly useful for travelers flying into **Milan Malpensa** or **Linate Airport**.

- **Malpensa Shuttle**: This shuttle runs regularly between **Milan Malpensa Airport** and **Lugano**, with tickets costing around **CHF 25-30** one way. The journey takes about 1 hour and 15 minutes.
- **Booking**: Tickets can be booked online or at the airport.
- **Eurolines**: For longer bus journeys, Eurolines offers connections

between major Italian cities and Ticino. This is a budget-friendly option, with tickets starting at **EUR 15-25**, depending on the route.

Getting Around Ticino

Public Transportation: Buses, Trains, and Boats

Ticino has a reliable and extensive public transportation system that makes it easy to travel between towns, villages, and scenic spots. Whether you're visiting lakeside towns or heading into the mountains, buses, trains, and boats can take you just about anywhere in the region. Here's a detailed guide to using Ticino's public transport system, including schedules, ticket prices, and passes to save you money.

Trains in Ticino

The train network in Ticino is one of the most efficient ways to travel between major towns like **Lugano**, **Bellinzona**, and **Locarno**. Trains are run by **Swiss Federal Railways (SBB)**, and the routes are well-connected to Switzerland's national railway system, making it easy to travel from Ticino to other parts of the country.

Train Routes:

- **Lugano to Bellinzona**: This is one of the most popular routes, and the journey takes just under 30 minutes. Trains depart regularly, typically every 30 minutes.
- **Bellinzona to Locarno**: This journey takes around 20 minutes, with scenic views of the **Magadino Plain** along the way.

- **Lugano to Zurich**: If you're traveling beyond Ticino, there are fast connections to Zurich via the **Gotthard Base Tunnel**, with the trip taking about 2 hours.

Ticket Prices:

Train ticket prices in Ticino vary depending on the distance and whether you travel in first or second class. For example:

- **Lugano to Bellinzona**: CHF 12-18 for a second-class ticket (one way). First-class tickets cost around CHF 25-30.
- **Locarno to Bellinzona**: CHF 9-12 for second class, CHF 20 for first class.

Rail Passes:

If you're staying in Ticino for a few days and plan to use public transport regularly, investing in a rail pass can save you money.

- **Swiss Travel Pass**: This pass allows unlimited travel on Switzerland's trains, buses, and boats for a set number of days. It also includes free entry to many museums and discounts on mountain cable cars.
- **Cost**: CHF 232 for 3 days, CHF 363 for 8 days (second class).
- **Ticino Ticket**: If you're staying at a hotel, campsite, or guesthouse in Ticino, you'll receive a **Ticino Ticket**, which gives you free access to the region's public transportation network (buses, trains, and boats) and discounts on cable cars and local attractions. This is a great way to explore Ticino without worrying about individual ticket costs.

Booking Tickets:

You can buy train tickets at any station, online through the **SBB** website, or using the **SBB Mobile App**. It's best to buy tickets in advance during peak travel seasons (summer and holidays), but for shorter routes, you can purchase them on the day of travel.

Buses in Ticino

Buses in Ticino complement the train network and are ideal for reaching smaller towns, villages, and remote hiking trails. The **Autopostale** bus service runs frequent routes throughout the region, and buses are punctual, clean, and comfortable.

Key Bus Routes:

- **Lugano to Gandria**: A scenic bus ride along **Lake Lugano** to the quaint village of Gandria. This bus runs every hour and costs around **CHF 5-8** one way.
- **Bellinzona to Verzasca Valley**: Buses from Bellinzona take you into the stunning **Verzasca Valley**, where you can hike or explore villages like **Lavertezzo**. The journey takes about 40 minutes and costs **CHF 8-12**.
- **Locarno to Cardada-Cimetta**: This bus route takes you from **Locarno** to the base of the **Cardada-Cimetta** cable car, where you can hike or enjoy panoramic views of **Lake Maggiore**. Tickets are around **CHF 6-10**.

Ticket Prices:

- A single bus ticket typically costs between **CHF 2.50-6**, depending on the distance. Most buses have ticket machines on board, or you can buy tickets from the station or **SBB Mobile App**.

Passes:

- The **Ticino Ticket** is valid for bus travel, so if you have one from your accommodation, you can use it on all public buses in the region.

Schedules:

Buses in Ticino generally run from early morning (around 6:00 AM) until late evening (11:00 PM), though services to more remote areas may be less frequent. Check schedules online or at the bus station for the most up-to-date information.

Boat Travel on Ticino's Lakes

One of the most scenic ways to travel in Ticino is by boat. Ferries and boat cruises operate on both **Lake Lugano** and **Lake Maggiore**, connecting towns along the lakes and offering visitors stunning views of the surrounding mountains and landscapes.

Lake Lugano Boats:

- Ferries run between **Lugano** and **Gandria**, **Morcote**, and other lakeside villages. You can hop on a boat for a quick trip or enjoy a longer lake cruise.
- **Cost**: Prices range from **CHF 15-30**, depending on the route. The **Ticino Ticket** gives you a discount on boat trips, making this a cost-effective way to enjoy the lake.

Lake Maggiore Boats:

- Ferries on **Lake Maggiore** run between **Locarno**, **Ascona**, and the **Brissago Islands**, where you can explore botanical gardens and other attractions.
- **Cost**: A round-trip ferry from Locarno to Ascona costs around **CHF 12**, while a full-day cruise exploring the lake can cost **CHF 40-60**.

Booking:

Tickets for boat rides can be purchased at the dock or online. During the summer, boats run frequently, but it's always best to check the schedule ahead of time, especially if you're planning a longer journey.

Renting a Car: What You Need to Know

While public transportation is excellent in Ticino, renting a car gives you the freedom to explore remote areas that are harder to reach by bus or train, such as mountain passes, valleys, and smaller villages. However, there are some considerations to keep in mind when renting a car in Ticino.

Benefits of Renting a Car in Ticino:

- **Flexibility**: A car allows you to visit more remote areas, such as the **Verzasca Valley** or drive along scenic mountain roads like the **Monte Ceneri Pass**. You can also travel on your own schedule, making it easier to stop for photos or visit smaller towns that might not be served by public transport.
- **Scenic Drives**: Ticino has some beautiful driving routes, such as the road along **Lake Lugano** or the scenic drive through the **Maggia Valley**.
- **Day Trips**: Renting a car makes day trips to nearby regions like northern Italy much easier. For example, you can drive from Lugano to **Lake Como** in just under an hour.

Drawbacks of Renting a Car:

- **Parking**: Parking in Ticino's cities can be a challenge, especially in places like Lugano or Locarno, where parking spaces are limited and expensive. Street parking typically costs **CHF 2-4 per hour**, and parking garages charge around **CHF 20-30 per day**.
- **Fuel Costs**: Switzerland has some of the highest fuel prices in Europe, with gas costing around **CHF 1.90-2.10 per liter**. This can add up, especially if you're planning long road trips.
- **Toll Roads and Vignette**: To use the Swiss highways, your car needs a **vignette** (toll sticker). Rental cars usually come with the vignette, but if you're bringing a car from outside Switzerland, you'll need to purchase one for **CHF 40** at the border or at gas stations.

Car Rental Agencies in Ticino:

1. **Europcar**: Available in **Lugano** and at nearby airports, Europcar offers a wide selection of vehicles from economy cars to SUVs.

- **Address**: Via Clemente Maraini 41, 6900 Lugano
- **Cost**: Around **CHF 70-120 per day**, depending on the car type and season.

2. **Hertz**: Hertz is another reliable option with branches in Ticino and nearby **Milan Malpensa Airport**.

- **Address**: Via San Gottardo 13, 6900 Lugano
- **Cost**: From **CHF 60 per day** for a standard car.

Tips for Renting a Car:

- **Book Early**: During peak seasons (summer and holidays), it's best to book your rental car well in advance to ensure availability.
- **Automatic vs. Manual**: Most rental cars in Switzerland are manual, so if you're not comfortable driving a manual car, be sure to request an automatic when booking.
- **Insurance**: Check that your rental includes basic insurance coverage, but you might want to consider adding extra coverage for peace of mind, especially if you're planning to drive in more remote areas.

Local Driving Laws:

- **Speed Limits**: The speed limit in towns and cities is **50 km/h**, while highways are limited to **120 km/h**. On smaller rural roads, the speed limit is usually **80 km/h**.
- **Seatbelts**: Seatbelts are mandatory for all passengers, both in the front and back seats.

- **Drinking and Driving**: Switzerland has strict drink-driving laws, with a blood alcohol limit of **0.05%**. It's best to avoid alcohol altogether if you're planning to drive.

Cycling in Ticino: Bike Rentals and Scenic Routes

Where to Rent Bikes in Ticino

Bike rentals are available throughout Ticino, with options in major cities and tourist areas. Whether you're looking for a standard road bike, mountain bike, or electric bike (e-bike), you can easily find a rental option that suits your needs.

Rent a Bike Lugano: Located near the **Lugano train station**, Rent a Bike offers a variety of bicycles, including e-bikes, city bikes, and mountain bikes. They also provide helmets and maps with recommended cycling routes.

- **Address**: Via Stazione 1, 6900 Lugano
- **Cost**: CHF 25-35 per day for a standard bike, CHF 40-50 for an e-bike
- **How to Get There**: A 5-minute walk from the train station.

Locarno Bike Rental: Near the waterfront in Locarno, this rental shop specializes in road bikes and offers guided cycling tours as well. They provide everything from daily rentals to week-long packages.

- **Address**: Via della Pace 5, 6600 Locarno
- **Cost**: CHF 30-40 per day
- **How to Get There**: Close to the **Locarno train station**.

BikePort Bellinzona: A convenient option for cyclists looking to explore Bellinzona's historic castles. BikePort rents standard bikes and e-bikes, ideal for exploring the city and the surrounding areas.

- **Address**: Via Dogana 1, 6500 Bellinzona
- **Cost**: CHF 25-40 per day, with discounts for multi-day rentals.

E-Bike Rentals:

E-bikes are a popular option in Ticino, especially if you want to explore the region's hilly or mountainous terrain without exhausting yourself. E-bike rentals are available at most rental shops, with daily rates ranging from **CHF 40-60**. These electric-assisted bikes make it easy to cover long distances and tackle steep inclines, even if you're not an experienced cyclist.

Popular Cycling Routes in Ticino

Ticino offers a range of cycling routes, from easy, flat rides around the lakes to more challenging climbs through the mountains. Here are some of the best routes, categorized by skill level.

For Beginners and Families:

Lugano to Gandria Lakeside Route: This flat, easy route runs along the edge of **Lake Lugano** and is perfect for families or casual cyclists. The ride from Lugano to Gandria takes about 1-1.5 hours at a leisurely pace, offering stunning lake views along the way. There are plenty of spots to stop for a picnic or a swim.

- **Distance**: 10 km
- **Difficulty**: Easy
- **How to Get There**: Start from Lugano's city center and follow the well-marked bike path along the lake toward Gandria.

Lake Maggiore Ride (Locarno to Ascona): This short, flat ride between **Locarno** and **Ascona** is another great option for beginners. The route takes you along the shores of **Lake Maggiore**, passing beaches, parks, and cafés.

- **Distance**: 5 km

- **Difficulty**: Easy
- **How to Get There**: Start at **Locarno's Piazza Grande** and follow the lakeside bike path to Ascona.

For Intermediate Cyclists:

Verzasca Valley Route: Starting from **Locarno**, this route takes you up the **Verzasca Valley**, passing through picturesque villages and the famous **Verzasca Dam**, where you can stop to admire the view or try bungee jumping. The road is mostly uphill, but the gradient is manageable for intermediate cyclists.

- **Distance**: 25 km (one way)
- **Difficulty**: Moderate
- **How to Get There**: Begin at Locarno's train station and follow the signs for Verzasca Valley.

Monte Ceneri Pass: This route is ideal for cyclists who want a challenge without tackling high-altitude climbs. The ride from **Bellinzona** to **Lugano** via the **Monte Ceneri Pass** offers beautiful views of the surrounding countryside, and the uphill sections are followed by rewarding descents.

- **Distance**: 30 km
- **Difficulty**: Moderate
- **How to Get There**: Start from Bellinzona's train station and head south toward Monte Ceneri.

For Experienced Cyclists:

Monte Brè Loop: For more advanced cyclists, the climb to **Monte Brè** offers one of the most scenic and challenging rides in Ticino. The route starts in **Lugano** and takes you up the mountain, with steep inclines and sharp switchbacks. The view from the top is worth the effort, with panoramic views over Lake Lugano and the Alps.

- **Distance**: 15 km (one way)
- **Difficulty**: Hard
- **How to Get There**: Start from Lugano's city center and follow the road signs toward **Monte Brè**.

Centovalli Route: This long-distance ride takes you from Locarno into the **Centovalli Valley**, a remote area known for its lush forests and traditional villages. The route is hilly and requires a good level of fitness, but it offers some of the most beautiful scenery in Ticino.

- **Distance**: 40 km (one way)
- **Difficulty**: Hard
- **How to Get There**: Start from Locarno's Piazza Grande and follow the road signs for Centovalli.

Bike-Friendly Accommodations

Several hotels and guesthouses in Ticino cater specifically to cyclists, offering secure bike storage, repair kits, and even guided tours.

Hotel Federale Lugano: This bike-friendly hotel in Lugano offers secure storage for bikes and provides cycling maps of the surrounding area. The staff can also help arrange bike rentals and recommend routes for all skill levels.

- **Address**: Via Paolo Regazzoni 8, 6900 Lugano
- **Cost**: Rooms start at **CHF 150 per night**.

Casa Berno Hotel (Ascona): Located near **Lake Maggiore**, Casa Berno offers easy access to bike paths around the lake and into the mountains. The hotel provides bike storage, repair services, and can arrange e-bike rentals.

- **Address**: Via Gottardo Madonna 15, 6612 Ascona

- **Cost**: Rooms start at **CHF 180 per night**.

Ostello Montebello (Bellinzona): This budget-friendly hostel is popular with cyclists, offering affordable accommodation, bike storage, and a communal kitchen. It's located near the **Castles of Bellinzona**, making it a great base for exploring the region by bike.

- **Address**: Via Nocca 4, 6500 Bellinzona
- **Cost**: Dorm beds start at **CHF 40 per night**, private rooms from **CHF 80**.

Walking Tours: Exploring Ticino on Foot

Ticino is a fantastic region to explore on foot, with its mix of vibrant cities, historic towns, and scenic trails. Walking tours are a great way to discover the area's rich culture and natural beauty. You can choose between guided tours led by knowledgeable locals or self-guided routes for a more flexible experience.

Guided Walking Tours

Lugano City Tour: This guided walking tour takes you through the highlights of **Lugano**, including the city's historic center, **Parco Ciani**, and the beautiful lakeside promenade. The tour lasts about 2 hours and is perfect for first-time visitors who want to get a feel for the city's history and culture.

- **Cost**: CHF 25 per person
- **How to Book**: Book through the **Lugano Tourist Office** or online via their website.

Bellinzona Castles Tour: Bellinzona is home to three UNESCO World

Heritage castles, and this guided walking tour takes you through the history of these impressive fortresses. The tour includes visits to **Castelgrande**, **Montebello**, and **Sasso Corbaro**, with a guide explaining the historical significance of each castle.

- **Cost**: CHF 35 per person, includes entry to all three castles
- **How to Book**: Book at the **Bellinzona Tourist Office** or online.

Locarno Old Town Tour: Explore **Locarno's Piazza Grande**, narrow streets, and historic churches with a local guide who will take you through the city's fascinating past. The tour also includes a visit to the **Madonna del Sasso Sanctuary**, which offers panoramic views of the town and lake.

- **Cost**: CHF 20 per person
- **How to Book**: Available through the **Locarno Tourist Office**.

Self-Guided Walking Routes

For those who prefer to explore at their own pace, Ticino offers several well-marked walking routes that you can follow on your own. These self-guided routes are easy to navigate, with plenty of signage along the way.

Lugano Lakeside Promenade: This flat, easy walk takes you along the shores of **Lake Lugano**, passing through **Parco Ciani** and offering stunning views of the surrounding mountains. It's perfect for a leisurely stroll and is accessible for all ages, including families with children.

- **Distance**: 3 km
- **Difficulty**: Easy
- **How to Get There**: Start at **Piazza della Riforma** in central Lugano and follow the lakeside path.

Bellinzona to Montebello Castle: For a more challenging self-guided walk, take the trail from **Bellinzona's city center** up to **Montebello Castle**. The walk offers fantastic views over the town and the surrounding mountains, and you can explore the castle grounds at your own pace.

- **Distance**: 2 km
- **Difficulty**: Moderate
- **How to Get There**: Start from **Piazza Collegiata** in Bellinzona and follow the signs for **Montebello Castle**.

Cardada to Cimetta Hike: For a more strenuous walk, take the cable car from Locarno to **Cardada**, then hike up to **Cimetta** for panoramic views of **Lake Maggiore** and the surrounding Alps. The trail is well-marked, and there are plenty of places to stop for a picnic along the way.

- **Distance**: 5 km
- **Difficulty**: Moderate to difficult
- **How to Get There**: Take the cable car from Locarno's **Orselina station** to **Cardada**, then follow the hiking trail to Cimetta.

Family-Friendly Walking Tours

Ticino is a great destination for families, and many of the walking tours are suitable for kids. Easy, flat routes like the **Lugano Lakeside Promenade** or the **Locarno to Ascona** path are perfect for families with younger children, offering plenty of places to stop and rest along the way.

- **Bellinzona Castles for Kids**: The **Bellinzona Castles** tour offers a special family version where kids can explore the castles while learning about medieval history through interactive exhibits.
- **Cost**: CHF 15 per child, CHF 25 per adult
- **How to Book**: Available through the **Bellinzona Tourist Office**.

Family-Friendly Transportation Options in Ticino

Traveling with children in Ticino is made easy by the region's well-organized public transportation network and family-friendly driving options. Whether you choose to use buses, trains, or rent a car, you'll find plenty of accommodations for strollers, car seats, and other essentials for young children. This guide will help you navigate the best transportation choices for families, ensuring a stress-free experience.

Public Transportation for Families

Public transportation in Ticino is reliable, safe, and well-equipped to accommodate families. Buses, trains, and boats throughout the region are designed to be accessible for parents with young children, and many offer specific amenities to make your journey easier.

Buses

Buses are a convenient way to get around Ticino, especially within cities like **Lugano**, **Bellinzona**, and **Locarno**. Most buses in Ticino are low-floor vehicles, making it easy to board with a stroller or pram. Here's what you need to know about using buses with young children:

- **Stroller Access**: Nearly all buses in Ticino are equipped with ramps or low entry points, which are stroller-friendly. Once onboard, there are dedicated spaces for strollers, often located near the front of the bus.
- **Free Travel for Children**: Children under six travel for free on public buses when accompanied by an adult. Children aged 6-16 can get discounted fares, usually about half the price of a standard ticket.
- **Ticino Ticket**: If you're staying in a hotel or guesthouse, you'll receive a **Ticino Ticket**, which gives your family free access to public transportation, including buses. This is especially useful for families looking to explore different areas of Ticino without worrying about purchasing individual tickets.

Tips for Families:

- Try to board the bus from the front entrance if you're traveling with a stroller, as this is typically where stroller spaces are located.
- If your children are older, look for seats near the driver or in the priority seating areas, which are generally more spacious.

Trains

Trains in Ticino are another excellent family-friendly option, particularly for traveling between cities like Lugano, Bellinzona, and Locarno. Swiss trains are clean, spacious, and highly accessible, making them ideal for families with young children.

- **Stroller Accessibility**: All regional trains are designed to accommodate strollers and prams. Train carriages have designated spaces for strollers, and most stations have elevators or ramps to help you get to the platforms.
- **Family Discounts**: Children under six travel for free, while kids aged 6-16 can get half-price tickets. If you're traveling with more than one child, consider purchasing the **Junior Travelcard**. This card allows children to travel for free when accompanied by an adult with a valid ticket.
- **Family Coaches**: On some longer routes, such as the train from **Zurich to Lugano**, you'll find family-friendly coaches with play areas designed for children to move around safely and stay entertained.

Key Train Stations:

- **Lugano Station**: Via Clemente Maraini 10, 6900 Lugano. Well-equipped with elevators and stroller-friendly access points.
- **Bellinzona Station**: Viale Stazione 17, 6500 Bellinzona. A central hub for trains with excellent family-friendly facilities.

Tips for Families:

- Always check the train schedule ahead of time to plan your journey. Many trains have dedicated family compartments, especially during peak travel seasons, which are ideal if you're traveling with younger children who need extra space.

Boats

Boat travel on **Lake Lugano** and **Lake Maggiore** is not only scenic but also family-friendly. Many boats accommodate strollers and have plenty of space for kids to move around, making them a fun and relaxing way to explore the region.

- **Stroller Access**: Boats that run on the lakes typically have wide gangways, making it easy to board with a stroller. Once on board, there's plenty of seating, and children can move freely on deck to enjoy the views.
- **Family Discounts**: Many boat companies offer family tickets at a reduced price. Check at the docks or online for specific family-friendly packages.

Popular Boat Routes for Families:

- **Lugano to Gandria**: This short, scenic trip along the lake is perfect for families. The journey takes about 30 minutes, and Gandria offers plenty of family-friendly restaurants and walking paths.
- **Locarno to Brissago Islands**: A slightly longer trip on **Lake Maggiore**, this route is ideal for a day trip with kids. The islands have gardens and open spaces perfect for children to explore.

Tips for Families:

- Bring snacks and water for the kids, as some shorter boat trips may not

have food services on board.
- If your child enjoys being on the water, try to sit on the open deck, where they can safely take in the lake and mountain views.

Driving with Children in Ticino

Renting a car can be a great option for families, especially if you're planning to explore more remote areas of Ticino that are not easily accessible by public transport. Driving allows you to travel at your own pace, stop when necessary, and avoid crowded buses or trains. However, there are some important factors to keep in mind when driving with young children.

Car Seats

Swiss law requires that children under 12 years old or shorter than 150 cm (4'11") must use a car seat or booster seat. Rental companies in Ticino provide car seats, but it's a good idea to reserve one in advance to ensure availability.

- **Cost of Car Seats**: Car seats can be added to your rental for an additional **CHF 10-20 per day**, depending on the type (infant seat, toddler seat, or booster).
- **Types of Seats Available**: Most rental agencies offer rear-facing seats for infants, forward-facing seats for toddlers, and booster seats for older children.

Key Rental Agencies in Ticino:

- **Europcar**: Via Clemente Maraini 41, 6900 Lugano
- **Hertz**: Via San Gottardo 13, 6900 Lugano

Stroller-Friendly Vehicles

If you're traveling with a stroller, it's worth renting a larger vehicle that has enough space for both the stroller and your luggage. Compact cars may not have enough trunk space, so opt for a mid-size or SUV to ensure comfort for the whole family.

- **Car Types**: SUVs and minivans are ideal for families with strollers and car seats. Popular options like the **Volkswagen Tiguan** or **Renault Espace** offer enough space for all your gear.
- **Cost**: Expect to pay around **CHF 80-120 per day** for a family-friendly vehicle, depending on the season and availability.

Tips for Families:

- Make sure your rental car includes GPS or bring your own to navigate Ticino's roads, especially if you're venturing into more rural areas.
- Check if your rental company offers roof boxes for extra storage if you're carrying a lot of luggage.

Parking and Accessibility

Parking in Ticino's larger cities can be challenging, but there are plenty of family-friendly options if you know where to look. Many public parking garages in cities like **Lugano** and **Locarno** have spacious, well-lit parking areas that accommodate strollers and are close to elevators for easy access.

Parking Garages:

- **Autosilo Balestra** (Lugano): Via Pietro Balestra 3, 6900 Lugano. This centrally located garage is close to Lugano's city center and lakeside promenade, with elevator access for families with strollers.
- **Cost**: CHF 2.50 per hour.
- **Parking Centro** (Locarno): Via della Pace 9, 6600 Locarno. This parking facility is near Locarno's Piazza Grande, with easy access to the lakeside area and elevators for stroller access.
- **Cost**: CHF 2 per hour.

Road Safety and Traffic

Swiss roads are known for being well-maintained and safe, with clear signage and efficient traffic systems. However, some rural roads, especially in mountainous areas, can be narrow and winding, so extra caution is required when driving with children.

- **Speed Limits**: Be mindful of speed limits, especially when driving through villages or residential areas where children may be present. Speed limits in cities are typically **50 km/h**, while highways allow speeds up to **120 km/h**.
- **Rest Stops**: If you're driving longer distances, Switzerland has well-maintained rest stops along major highways, many of which have clean facilities, picnic areas, and playgrounds for children.

Tips for Families:

- Always make sure children are securely buckled into their car seats before starting your journey.
- Plan for regular breaks during longer drives, especially if traveling with infants or toddlers who may need to stretch or feed.

Where to Stay in Ticino

Luxury Hotels and Resorts for a Lavish Stay

For those looking to indulge in the finest comforts, Ticino is home to several world-class luxury hotels that offer 5-star amenities, exceptional service, gourmet dining, and breathtaking views. These high-end accommodations are perfect for travelers seeking the ultimate in relaxation and sophistication.

Grand Hotel Villa Castagnola (Lugano)
  Grand Hotel Villa Castagnola is a 5-star luxury resort located on the shores of **Lake Lugano**. Set in a former noble residence surrounded by lush subtropical gardens, this hotel offers stunning views of the lake and the surrounding mountains. The hotel's standout feature is its blend of old-world elegance with modern amenities, making it a favorite among discerning travelers.

- **Amenities**: The hotel boasts two gourmet restaurants, a luxurious spa, an indoor swimming pool, a tennis court, and a private lakeside beach. The spa offers a range of treatments, including massages, facials, and hydrotherapy.
- **Dining**: **Restaurant Le Relais**, located within the hotel, has been awarded a Michelin star and serves Mediterranean-inspired cuisine using fresh, seasonal ingredients.

- **Rooms**: Spacious and elegantly decorated rooms feature large windows that open to lake or garden views. Many of the suites come with private terraces.
- **Cost**: Rooms start at **CHF 400-500 per night**, with suites ranging from **CHF 700-1,200** depending on the season and availability.

Address: Viale Castagnola 31, 6900 Lugano

How to Get There: A 5-minute taxi ride from Lugano's city center or a 15-minute walk along the lakefront.

Hotel Splendide Royal (Lugano)

This 5-star property lives up to its name with grand interiors and exceptional service. Located in the heart of **Lugano**, the **Hotel Splendide Royal** offers elegant accommodations overlooking **Lake Lugano** and the surrounding mountains. Known for its refined atmosphere, the hotel is a favorite for those seeking a romantic and luxurious stay.

- **Amenities**: The hotel features a state-of-the-art wellness center, an indoor swimming pool, a fully equipped gym, and several conference rooms for business travelers. The wellness center offers personalized spa treatments, including Swiss beauty rituals and massages.
- **Dining**: La Veranda is the hotel's fine dining restaurant, serving Italian and Mediterranean dishes prepared with the finest local ingredients. For a more casual experience, the **Belle Epoque Bar** offers light bites and cocktails with live piano music.
- **Rooms**: The rooms are elegantly decorated with rich fabrics and antique furnishings. Many have balconies with lake views, and all come equipped with modern conveniences like Nespresso machines and marble bathrooms.
- **Cost**: Room rates range from **CHF 350-600** per night, with suites starting from **CHF 800**.

Address: Riva Antonio Caccia 7, 6900 Lugano

How to Get There: A 10-minute walk from Lugano's city center or a short taxi ride from the train station.

The View Lugano (Paradiso)

For those seeking a more contemporary luxury experience, **The View Lugano** is an ultra-modern 5-star hotel located in the upscale Paradiso district, just outside **Lugano**. The hotel is known for its sleek design, high-tech amenities, and breathtaking views over Lake Lugano.

- **Amenities**: The hotel features a full-service spa, an infinity pool, a fitness center, and electric cars available for guest use. Guests can also enjoy personalized yoga and meditation sessions.
- **Dining**: The **The View Fine Dining Restaurant** offers an innovative menu with dishes that emphasize local and organic ingredients. The hotel's rooftop bar is perfect for enjoying cocktails with panoramic lake views.
- **Rooms**: Each suite is designed with modern, minimalist décor and features floor-to-ceiling windows that open to private terraces. The rooms are equipped with smart-home technology, allowing guests to control lighting, temperature, and entertainment systems with the touch of a button.
- **Cost**: Rooms start at **CHF 450 per night**, with suites ranging from **CHF 800-1,200**.

Address: Via Guidino 29, 6900 Lugano-Paradiso

How to Get There: A 10-minute drive from Lugano's city center.

Mid-Range and Boutique Hotels: Where Comfort Meets Charm

If you're looking for comfortable accommodations with a bit of character and charm, Ticino's mid-range hotels and boutique properties won't disappoint. These options offer great value without sacrificing comfort, and many have their own unique stories to tell.

Hotel Federale (Lugano)

Located just a few steps from **Lugano's train station, Hotel Federale** is a charming mid-range hotel with a long history. Established in 1923, this family-run property offers warm hospitality and a central location, perfect for exploring the city on foot.

- **Amenities**: The hotel offers a small fitness center, a sauna, and a garden terrace where guests can enjoy breakfast in the summer. There's also a cozy restaurant serving Ticinese and Mediterranean dishes.
- **Rooms**: The rooms are simply but comfortably furnished, with modern bathrooms and free Wi-Fi. Some rooms have balconies with views of the city or lake.
- **Cost**: Rates range from **CHF 150-250 per night**, depending on the room type and season.

Address: Via Paolo Regazzoni 8, 6900 Lugano

How to Get There: A 5-minute walk from the train station or a 10-minute walk to **Piazza della Riforma**.

Boutique Hotel La Rocca (Ascona)

Nestled on the hills above **Lake Maggiore, Boutique Hotel La Rocca** offers stunning lake views and a more intimate experience. This boutique hotel has a Mediterranean-inspired design, with colorful gardens, cozy terraces, and a peaceful ambiance.

- **Amenities**: The hotel features an outdoor swimming pool, a wellness area with a sauna, and a private beach on the lake. Guests can also take advantage of the free shuttle service to Ascona's town center.
- **Dining**: The on-site restaurant offers regional cuisine, with many dishes featuring fresh seafood from the lake. You can dine on the terrace with panoramic views of Lake Maggiore.

- **Rooms**: Rooms are bright and airy, with Mediterranean-inspired décor. Most rooms come with private balconies or terraces overlooking the lake.
- **Cost**: Room rates start at **CHF 200-300 per night**.

Address: Via Ronco 61, 6614 Ascona
How to Get There: A 5-minute drive from **Ascona's town center**.

Grotto Flora (Bigogno)

If you're looking for something a bit more off the beaten path, **Grotto Flora** is a delightful boutique hotel located in the small village of **Bigogno**, just a short drive from Lugano. The property is housed in a historic 18th-century building and features rustic charm combined with modern comforts.

- **Amenities**: The hotel has a lovely garden and terrace where guests can relax, as well as an on-site **grotto** restaurant serving traditional Ticinese dishes.
- **Rooms**: The rooms are simple but comfortable, with exposed wooden beams and stone walls that give them a cozy, rustic feel. Free Wi-Fi is available in all rooms.
- **Cost**: Rooms are affordable, starting at **CHF 120-180 per night**.

Address: Via Cantonale 86, 6917 Bigogno
How to Get There: A 15-minute drive from **Lugano**.

Hotel Belvedere (Locarno)

This historic hotel in **Locarno** combines modern comfort with a rich heritage. **Hotel Belvedere** has been welcoming guests since 1898 and offers a mix of old-world charm and contemporary amenities. Perched on a hillside, the hotel offers beautiful views of **Lake Maggiore** and is just a short walk from the town center.

- **Amenities**: The hotel features an indoor swimming pool, a wellness center with a sauna and steam bath, and a large garden. Guests can also rent e-bikes to explore the area.
- **Dining**: The hotel's restaurant serves a combination of Swiss and Italian cuisine, and there's a terrace for outdoor dining with lake views.
- **Rooms**: The rooms have been recently renovated and offer a mix of modern décor and classic touches. Many rooms come with balconies overlooking the lake.
- **Cost**: Rates range from **CHF 200-350 per night**, depending on the season.

Address: Via ai Monti della Trinità 44, 6600 Locarno
How to Get There: A 10-minute walk from **Locarno's Piazza Grande**.

Unique Stays: Special Themes and Historical Significance

For travelers looking for something a little different, Ticino offers several unique accommodations that stand out for their historical significance, design, or special themes.

Castello del Sole (Ascona)

This luxurious 5-star resort is set in a historic castle on the shores of **Lake Maggiore**. **Castello del Sole** offers a mix of historical architecture and modern luxury, with sprawling gardens, a private beach, and a world-class spa.

- **Amenities**: The hotel features a 2,500-square-meter spa, tennis courts, an 18-hole golf course, and several swimming pools. Guests can also enjoy exclusive access to the **Terreni alla Maggia**, a working farm where they produce wine, rice, and honey.
- **Dining**: **Ristorante Locanda Barbarossa**, the hotel's Michelin-starred restaurant, serves gourmet dishes made from ingredients grown

on the property.
- **Rooms**: Rooms are spacious and elegantly furnished, with large windows offering views of the lake or gardens. Suites come with private terraces or balconies.
- **Cost**: Rates start at **CHF 600 per night** for standard rooms, with suites costing up to **CHF 1,500**.

Address: Via Muraccio 142, 6612 Ascona
How to Get There: A 5-minute drive from Ascona's town center.

Villa Principe Leopoldo (Lugano)

Perched on a hill overlooking **Lake Lugano**, **Villa Principe Leopoldo** is a former royal residence that has been transformed into a luxury hotel. The villa combines historic charm with modern elegance, offering guests a unique stay in one of Ticino's most iconic properties.

- **Amenities**: The hotel features a full-service spa, an outdoor swimming pool, tennis courts, and beautifully manicured gardens. Guests can also take advantage of the hotel's personal concierge service for planning day trips or activities.
- **Dining**: The **Principe Leopoldo Restaurant** serves haute cuisine in a refined setting, with an extensive wine list that includes rare bottles from around the world.
- **Rooms**: Rooms are decorated in a classic, elegant style, with high ceilings, antique furnishings, and large balconies with views of the lake and mountains.
- **Cost**: Rooms start at **CHF 400 per night**, with suites starting at **CHF 800**.

Address: Via Montalbano 5, 6900 Lugano
How to Get There: A 10-minute drive from Lugano's city center.

Budget-Friendly Stays and Hostels for the Savvy Traveler

Ticino isn't just for luxury travelers—there are plenty of affordable places to stay, whether you're looking for hostels, guesthouses, or budget hotels. These budget-friendly accommodations offer the essentials like clean rooms, good locations, and sometimes even a few extra perks like free breakfast or Wi-Fi.

Youth Hostel Lugano Savosa

Located in a quiet residential area just outside of **Lugano**, the **Youth Hostel Lugano Savosa** is one of the best budget-friendly options in the region. It offers both dormitory-style rooms and private rooms, making it a great choice for solo travelers, couples, and families.

- **Amenities**: Free Wi-Fi, a swimming pool, a large garden, and a communal kitchen where guests can cook their own meals. There's also a playground for kids and a ping-pong table for a bit of fun.
- **Cost**: Dormitory beds start at **CHF 40 per night**, while private rooms begin at **CHF 85**. Breakfast is included in the price.
- **Address**: Via Cantonale 13, 6942 Savosa, Lugano
- **How to Get There**: A 10-minute bus ride from Lugano's main train station, or a 25-minute walk.

What to Expect: Clean and comfortable rooms, friendly staff, and a laid-back atmosphere. The hostel is located in a quiet area, making it a peaceful retreat while still being close to Lugano's main attractions.

Ostello Montebello (Bellinzona)

For travelers looking to explore the historic city of **Bellinzona**, **Ostello Montebello** offers an affordable and centrally located option. This hostel is situated close to Bellinzona's famous castles and is a great base for exploring the area.

- **Amenities**: Free Wi-Fi, shared kitchen facilities, and bike rentals. There's also a small garden area where you can relax after a day of sightseeing.
- **Cost**: Dormitory beds start at **CHF 35 per night**, and private rooms are available from **CHF 75**.
- **Address**: Via Nocca 4, 6500 Bellinzona
- **How to Get There**: A 10-minute walk from Bellinzona's train station or a short bus ride.

What to Expect: Simple but comfortable rooms, a friendly atmosphere, and easy access to Bellinzona's historic sites. The staff can help arrange tours and provide recommendations for local attractions.

Locarno Youth Hostel

Located near **Lake Maggiore** in **Locarno**, this youth hostel is ideal for travelers who want to enjoy the natural beauty of Ticino without spending a fortune. The hostel is just a short walk from the lakefront and the town center, making it a great option for budget travelers.

- **Amenities**: Free Wi-Fi, free breakfast, a large outdoor terrace, and communal kitchen facilities. The hostel also has laundry services and bike rentals.
- **Cost**: Dormitory beds start at **CHF 38 per night**, while private rooms are available from **CHF 85**.
- **Address**: Via B. Varenna 18, 6600 Locarno
- **How to Get There**: A 15-minute walk from Locarno's train station or a 5-minute bus ride.

What to Expect: A laid-back atmosphere with friendly staff, comfortable rooms, and easy access to the lake and town center. This is a great spot for backpackers or anyone looking to explore the Locarno region on a budget.

Finding the Best Deals on Budget Accommodations

If you're looking to save even more money on accommodations in Ticino, here are a few tips:

- **Book in Advance**: Hostels and budget hotels can fill up quickly, especially during the summer months. Booking a few months ahead will not only ensure you get a room, but you'll often find better deals.
- **Use Hostel Aggregators**: Websites like **Hostelworld** or **Booking.com** often have deals or discounts on hostels and budget hotels. You can compare prices and read reviews from other travelers to find the best option.
- **Consider Guesthouses**: In smaller towns and rural areas, guesthouses or family-run inns can be an affordable and more intimate alternative to hotels. Many guesthouses offer comfortable rooms at lower rates than hotels, and you may even get a home-cooked breakfast included.

Family-Friendly Accommodations: Hotels with Pools, Kids Clubs, and Babysitting Services

Traveling with children requires a bit more planning, but Ticino has plenty of hotels that cater to families, offering amenities like pools, kids' clubs, babysitting services, and family suites. These hotels make family vacations easier and more enjoyable by offering fun activities for kids and relaxing options for parents.

Parco San Marco Lifestyle Beach Resort (Cima di Porlezza)
Located on the shores of **Lake Lugano**, **Parco San Marco** is one of the most family-friendly resorts in Ticino. The resort offers a wide range of activities for kids, along with plenty of amenities to keep parents happy.

- **Amenities**: The resort has a private beach, several swimming pools, a spa, a kids' club, and playgrounds. There are also daily organized

activities for children, including arts and crafts, sports, and nature walks.
- **Kids Club and Babysitting**: The **Bim Bam Bino Club** caters to children aged 2 to 12, with a range of supervised activities throughout the day. Babysitting services are also available for an additional fee.
- **Family Suites**: The resort offers spacious family suites with separate living areas and balconies overlooking the lake or gardens.
- **Cost**: Family suites start at **CHF 300 per night**, with special family packages available that include meals and activities for children.
- **Address**: Via Privata San Marco 1, 22018 Cima di Porlezza
- **How to Get There**: A 15-minute drive from Lugano's city center.

What to Expect: A luxurious yet family-friendly atmosphere, with plenty of activities for kids and relaxation options for parents. The private beach and lakeside setting make it perfect for families who love the outdoors.

Hotel Belvedere (Locarno)

Hotel Belvedere in **Locarno** is a great option for families looking for a mix of luxury and kid-friendly amenities. Set on a hill overlooking **Lake Maggiore**, the hotel is close to the town center and offers plenty of activities for children.

- **Amenities**: The hotel features an indoor swimming pool, a large garden, a wellness center, and a restaurant that serves kid-friendly meals. There's also a family games room where kids can play table tennis, foosball, and board games.
- **Family Suites and Discounts**: The hotel offers spacious family rooms and suites, as well as family discounts on stays of three nights or more.
- **Kids Club**: During the summer, the hotel runs a kids' club with organized activities, including treasure hunts, arts and crafts, and outdoor games.
- **Cost**: Family rooms start at **CHF 250 per night**, with packages available during peak seasons.

- **Address**: Via ai Monti della Trinità 44, 6600 Locarno
- **How to Get There**: A 10-minute walk from Locarno's Piazza Grande.

What to Expect: A family-friendly hotel with a mix of modern amenities and a relaxing atmosphere. The indoor pool and wellness center make it easy for parents to unwind while the kids stay entertained.

Resort Collina d'Oro (Agra)

Resort Collina d'Oro is a 5-star luxury hotel just outside of **Lugano**, offering a peaceful retreat for families. While the hotel is known for its wellness center and spa, it also caters to families with young children.

- **Amenities**: The resort has an outdoor pool, a large garden, a wellness center with a sauna and steam bath, and an on-site restaurant offering kid-friendly meals. There's also a cinema room where families can enjoy movie nights together.
- **Babysitting Services**: The hotel offers professional babysitting services, allowing parents to enjoy some time at the spa or a romantic dinner.
- **Family Suites**: Spacious family suites are available, with two bedrooms, a living area, and private terraces with stunning views of the surrounding countryside.
- **Cost**: Family suites start at **CHF 350 per night**, with discounts available for longer stays.
- **Address**: Via Roncone 22, 6927 Agra
- **How to Get There**: A 10-minute drive from Lugano's city center.

What to Expect: A tranquil setting that's perfect for families looking to relax and enjoy the natural beauty of Ticino. The hotel's wellness center and babysitting services make it easy for parents to enjoy some downtime while the kids are well taken care of.

Villa Sassa Hotel, Residence & Spa (Lugano)

Located in the heart of **Lugano**, **Villa Sassa Hotel, Residence & Spa** is a popular choice for families looking for both comfort and convenience. The hotel offers a range of family-friendly amenities, including a large outdoor pool and easy access to Lugano's main attractions.

- **Amenities**: The hotel has an outdoor pool with a dedicated children's area, a large wellness center, a fitness center, and a restaurant with a kids' menu. There's also a play area for younger children.
- **Family Rooms and Discounts**: Villa Sassa offers family suites with separate living areas and balconies. Families staying for three nights or more can enjoy discounted rates and special packages that include meals and access to the wellness center.
- **Babysitting Services**: Babysitting services are available upon request.
- **Cost**: Family rooms start at **CHF 280 per night**, with discounts for extended stays.
- **Address**: Via Tesserete 10, 6900 Lugano
- **How to Get There**: A 10-minute walk from Lugano's city center.

What to Expect: A family-friendly hotel with a central location, making it easy to explore Lugano. The outdoor pool and wellness center provide plenty of options for both parents and children to relax and enjoy their stay.

Unique Stays: From Agriturismos to Chalets and Bed & Breakfasts

Agriturismos: Farm Stays in Ticino

An agriturismo stay, or farm stay, is a wonderful way to experience the countryside of Ticino while enjoying the region's agricultural traditions. Many of these family-run farms offer cozy accommodations, delicious home-cooked meals, and the opportunity to see daily farm life up close. If you love the idea of waking up to fresh air, green pastures, and homegrown breakfasts, an agriturismo stay is a perfect option.

Agriturismo Al Saliciolo (Magliaso)

Tucked away in the quiet village of **Magliaso**, **Agriturismo Al Saliciolo** offers a peaceful retreat on a working farm. Guests can enjoy simple yet comfortable rooms with views of the surrounding hills and farmland. The farm produces fresh vegetables, fruits, and dairy products, which are served in the on-site restaurant.

- **Amenities**: Guests can explore the farm, meet the animals, and even participate in seasonal activities like fruit picking. There's a farm shop where you can purchase local products such as honey, cheese, and homemade jams.
- **Cost**: Rooms start at **CHF 80-120 per night**, including breakfast.
- **Address**: Via Monte Rosa 5, 6983 Magliaso
- **How to Get There**: A 20-minute drive from Lugano's city center.

What to Expect: A down-to-earth experience where you can unwind in nature and enjoy farm-fresh meals. It's ideal for travelers who appreciate rural life and want a slower, more relaxed pace.

Agriturismo Cantina Carrara (Lugano)

Located just outside **Lugano**, **Agriturismo Cantina Carrara** is a winery and farm offering rustic accommodations and an unforgettable farm-to-table experience. The property is surrounded by vineyards and olive groves, and guests can take part in wine tastings, olive oil production tours, and enjoy home-cooked meals made from locally sourced ingredients.

- **Amenities**: The farm offers guided vineyard tours, wine tastings, and cooking classes. The rooms are simple but cozy, with traditional decor and views of the surrounding countryside.
- **Cost**: Prices start at **CHF 100 per night** for a double room, with breakfast included.
- **Address**: Strada delle Vigne 10, 6900 Lugano
- **How to Get There**: A 15-minute drive from Lugano city center.

What to Expect: A perfect blend of countryside relaxation and culinary indulgence, especially for wine lovers. The intimate atmosphere and personal touch from the hosts make it feel like a home away from home.

Charming Bed & Breakfasts

For those who prefer a cozy, intimate setting with a personal touch, Ticino has many charming bed & breakfasts. These accommodations often feature warm hospitality, homemade breakfasts, and rooms with a lot of character. B&Bs are an excellent choice for travelers who want to experience Ticino like a local.

B&B Villa Carlotta (Ascona)

Nestled near the shores of **Lake Maggiore**, **Villa Carlotta** is a beautifully restored historic villa offering a blend of old-world charm and modern comfort. This B&B features spacious rooms, a lush garden, and a peaceful atmosphere just a short walk from the town center.

- **Amenities**: A large breakfast is served each morning with fresh bread, local cheeses, and homemade jams. There's also a sun terrace where you can relax with a book or a glass of wine.
- **Cost**: Rooms start at **CHF 150-180 per night**, including breakfast.
- **Address**: Via San Gottardo 12, 6612 Ascona
- **How to Get There**: A 10-minute walk from Ascona's lakeside promenade.

What to Expect: A charming B&B with personal service and beautiful surroundings. Ideal for couples looking for a romantic getaway or travelers wanting to explore Ascona on foot.

B&B Casa Concerto (Brissago)

Overlooking **Lake Maggiore**, **B&B Casa Concerto** is a hidden gem offering spectacular views and a peaceful setting. This small B&B features a few well-decorated rooms with private terraces, perfect for enjoying the lake and mountain scenery.

- **Amenities**: Guests can relax in the garden, enjoy a hearty breakfast on the terrace, or walk down to the nearby lakefront. The B&B also offers free use of bicycles, making it easy to explore the surrounding area.
- **Cost**: Rooms start at **CHF 120-160 per night**, with breakfast included.
- **Address**: Via Ronco di Sopra 5, 6614 Brissago
- **How to Get There**: A 15-minute drive from Locarno.

What to Expect: A tranquil retreat with jaw-dropping views. It's perfect for travelers looking for a quiet place to unwind and take in the natural beauty of Ticino.

Mountain Chalets

For those who want to experience the Alpine side of Ticino, a stay in a mountain chalet is a unique way to enjoy the region's scenic beauty and outdoor activities. Chalets often provide rustic charm, and they are the perfect base for hiking, skiing, or just soaking in the mountain atmosphere.

Chalet Bellavista (Sonogno)

Located in the picturesque **Verzasca Valley**, **Chalet Bellavista** is a traditional stone chalet offering cozy accommodations with stunning views of the surrounding mountains and valleys. This secluded retreat is ideal for nature lovers looking to escape the city and experience the tranquility of the Swiss Alps.

- **Amenities**: The chalet features a wood-burning fireplace, a fully equipped kitchen, and a private terrace with panoramic views. Hiking trails start right from the doorstep, and the village of **Sonogno** is just a short walk away.
- **Cost**: The chalet rents for **CHF 200-250 per night**, with a two-night minimum stay.
- **Address**: Strada Verzasca 45, 6637 Sonogno

- **How to Get There**: A 40-minute drive from Locarno.

What to Expect: A peaceful, rustic escape where you can disconnect from the hustle and bustle. The perfect choice for hikers, couples, or small families who want to immerse themselves in nature.

Camping and Glamping: Outdoorsy Stays in Ticino

For travelers who want to fully embrace Ticino's natural beauty, camping and glamping offer a chance to stay in the great outdoors without sacrificing comfort. Whether you prefer traditional camping or a more luxurious glamping experience, Ticino has several excellent options with scenic views and top-notch facilities.

Camping Tamaro (Rivera)

Camping Tamaro is one of Ticino's most popular campsites, offering a wide range of amenities and activities. Located near **Monte Tamaro**, this family-friendly campsite provides easy access to hiking and outdoor adventures, making it a great base for nature lovers.

- **Amenities**: The campsite features clean, modern facilities, including showers, a swimming pool, a playground, and a restaurant. There are pitches for tents, campervans, and caravans, as well as small bungalows for rent. Organized activities, such as guided hikes and kids' programs, are available during the summer.
- **Cost**: Tent pitches start at **CHF 25-30 per night**, and bungalows are available from **CHF 80**.
- **Address**: Via Cantonale 2, 6802 Rivera
- **How to Get There**: A 20-minute drive from Lugano or a short walk from Rivera-Bironico train station.

What to Expect: A well-equipped campsite with plenty of activities for families. It's the perfect spot for those who want to explore Monte Tamaro and enjoy a relaxed outdoor vacation.

Glamping at Campeggio Monte Generoso (Mendrisio)

For a more luxurious outdoor experience, **Campeggio Monte Generoso** offers glamping options that combine the beauty of nature with the comforts of a hotel. Located near **Monte Generoso**, this campsite provides stunning views and upscale amenities for a unique stay.

- **Amenities**: Glamping tents are equipped with real beds, private bathrooms, and a small kitchenette. The campsite also has a swimming pool, a spa area, and a restaurant serving local dishes. Guests can take part in yoga sessions, guided nature walks, or simply relax by the campfire.
- **Cost**: Glamping tents start at **CHF 150 per night**, depending on the season.
- **Address**: Via Generoso 78, 6850 Mendrisio
- **How to Get There**: A 15-minute drive from Mendrisio's town center.

What to Expect: A luxurious take on camping, with all the benefits of being in nature without sacrificing comfort. Ideal for couples or families looking for a unique and relaxing outdoor experience.

Camping Piccolo Paradiso (Avegno)

For those who prefer a more traditional camping experience, **Camping Piccolo Paradiso** offers a peaceful setting along the **Maggia River**. Surrounded by nature, this campsite is a favorite among hikers and outdoor enthusiasts.

- **Amenities**: The campsite has all the essentials, including clean bathrooms, hot showers, and a small café. It's also located right on the river, so guests can swim or relax by the water. There are pitches for tents, caravans, and campervans.

- **Cost**: Tent pitches start at **CHF 20 per night**, and campervan spots are available from **CHF 35**.
- **Address**: Via al Fiume 3, 6670 Avegno
- **How to Get There**: A 10-minute drive from Locarno.

What to Expect: A simple, quiet campsite perfect for nature lovers. The riverfront location provides a scenic backdrop, and the proximity to hiking trails makes it a great base for outdoor activities.

Itineraries for Every Traveler

3 Days in Ticino: A Perfect Introduction

Day 1: Exploring Lugano

Start your trip in **Lugano**, the heart of Ticino, known for its elegant streets, lakeside views, and lively piazzas.

Morning: Stroll through Parco Ciani and Visit Lugano's Old Town

- Begin your day with a peaceful walk through **Parco Ciani**, Lugano's largest park, located right by the lake. The park offers scenic paths along the lakefront, gardens filled with colorful flowers, and playgrounds for children.
- After your walk, head into **Lugano's Old Town**, where you can explore its charming streets lined with boutique shops, cafés, and historic buildings. Be sure to visit **Piazza della Riforma**, the city's main square, which is surrounded by colorful buildings and outdoor cafés.

Lunch: Grotto della Salute

- For lunch, stop by **Grotto della Salute**, a traditional Ticinese restaurant that offers local specialties like risotto, polenta, and fresh lake fish. It's located in a peaceful garden, making it a perfect spot to relax before

continuing your day.
- **Address**: Via al Grotto 10, 6900 Lugano
- **Cost**: CHF 20-30 per person

Afternoon: Funicular Ride to Monte Brè

- In the afternoon, take the funicular from **Cassarate** up to **Monte Brè**, one of the best viewpoints in Lugano. From the top, you'll get stunning panoramic views of **Lake Lugano**, the surrounding mountains, and even as far as the Swiss Alps. If you're feeling adventurous, there are hiking trails that lead down the mountain through charming villages like **Brè** and **Gandria**.
- **Funicular Cost**: CHF 25 round trip

Dinner: Antica Osteria del Porto

- After descending from Monte Brè, enjoy dinner at **Antica Osteria del Porto**, a lakeside restaurant known for its fresh seafood and traditional Ticinese dishes.
- **Address**: Riva Caccia 3, 6900 Lugano
- **Cost**: CHF 40-60 per person

Day 2: Lake Maggiore and Ascona

On your second day, explore the charming towns around **Lake Maggiore**, particularly **Locarno** and **Ascona**, known for their Mediterranean feel and stunning lake views.

Morning: Discover Locarno's Piazza Grande

- Start your day in **Locarno** with a visit to **Piazza Grande**, the town's main square, famous for its open-air events, including the annual **Locarno Film Festival**. Stroll through the narrow streets lined with

colorful buildings and visit the **Madonna del Sasso Sanctuary**, which offers excellent views of the town and lake.
- **How to Get There**: A 40-minute train ride from Lugano

Lunch: Osteria Chiara

- For lunch, head to **Osteria Chiara** in Locarno, where you can try delicious homemade pasta and local specialties.
- **Address**: Via alla Motta 7, 6600 Locarno
- **Cost**: CHF 25-35 per person

Afternoon: Relax in Ascona

- After lunch, take a short bus ride or boat to **Ascona**, one of Ticino's most picturesque lakeside towns. Ascona's waterfront promenade is lined with pastel-colored houses and outdoor cafés, making it the perfect place for a relaxing afternoon stroll. If you're up for some history, visit the **Museo Comunale d'Arte Moderna**, which showcases works by modern artists like Paul Klee.
- **Cost**: CHF 10 entry to the museum

Dinner: Al Pontile

- End your day with dinner at **Al Pontile**, a lakeside restaurant in Ascona offering beautiful views of the lake and mountains. Their menu features Mediterranean-inspired dishes with fresh local ingredients.
- **Address**: Via Lido 9, 6612 Ascona
- **Cost**: CHF 35-50 per person

Day 3: Bellinzona and the Castles

Spend your final day in Ticino exploring the medieval town of **Bellinzona**, home to three UNESCO-listed castles.

Morning: Visit Bellinzona's Three Castles

- Bellinzona is famous for its three castles—**Castelgrande**, **Montebello**, and **Sasso Corbaro**—all connected by a series of walls and towers. Begin your visit at **Castelgrande**, the largest and oldest of the three. From here, you can either walk or take a shuttle to the other two castles.
- **Entry Cost**: CHF 12 for a combined ticket to all three castles

Lunch: Ristorante Castelgrande

- After exploring the castles, enjoy lunch at **Ristorante Castelgrande**, located within the castle walls. The restaurant offers local Ticinese cuisine with a modern twist, and dining in such a historic setting is a unique experience.
- **Address**: Piazza Nosetto, 6500 Bellinzona
- **Cost**: CHF 30-50 per person

Afternoon: Explore Bellinzona's Old Town

- In the afternoon, stroll through **Bellinzona's Old Town**, where you'll find quaint shops, traditional cafés, and the **Piazza Collegiata**, which is home to the beautiful **Collegiata dei SS Pietro e Stefano** church. If you visit on a Saturday, you can also explore the weekly market that fills the town's squares with stalls selling local products, crafts, and food.

Dinner: Grotto San Michele

- End your day with dinner at **Grotto San Michele**, located near

Montebello Castle. The restaurant offers authentic Ticinese dishes in a cozy setting.
- **Address**: Via Orico 8, 6500 Bellinzona
- **Cost**: CHF 35-45 per person

5-Day Family-Friendly Itinerary

Day 1: Arrival in Lugano

Morning: Explore Parco Ciani

- Upon arrival, start your family adventure with a visit to **Parco Ciani**, where children can run around and play while parents enjoy the peaceful surroundings. The park has a large playground, and the lakeside paths are ideal for a family stroll.

Lunch: Pizza at La Tinèra

- For lunch, head to **La Tinèra**, a family-friendly pizzeria in Lugano's Old Town, known for its wood-fired pizzas and welcoming atmosphere.
- **Address**: Via dei Gorini 2, 6900 Lugano
- **Cost**: CHF 15-20 per person

Afternoon: Visit the Swissminiatur Park

- After lunch, take a short drive to **Swissminiatur**, an open-air museum featuring miniature replicas of Switzerland's most famous landmarks. The park is fun for kids, who can enjoy the train rides that loop around the miniatures.
- **Entry Cost**: CHF 19 for adults, CHF 12 for children
- **Location**: Via Cantonale, 6815 Melide (15 minutes by car from Lugano)

Day 2: Fun at Monte Tamaro

Morning: Cable Car Ride to Monte Tamaro

- Start your day by taking the cable car from **Rivera** up to **Monte Tamaro**, a family-friendly mountain with plenty of activities for kids. Once at the top, you'll find adventure parks, hiking trails, and zip lines.
- **Cable Car Cost**: CHF 27 for adults, CHF 14 for children

Lunch: Picnic at Monte Tamaro

- Pack a picnic lunch and enjoy it at the top of Monte Tamaro while taking in the stunning views of the surrounding mountains.

Afternoon: Toboggan Run and Adventure Park

- After lunch, let the kids have fun at the **Alpine Coaster Toboggan Run** or the **Adventure Park**, which features rope courses and climbing activities suitable for children.
- **Toboggan Cost**: CHF 5 per ride

Day 3: Bellinzona and the Castles

Morning: Visit Bellinzona's Castles

- Spend the morning exploring **Castelgrande** and **Montebello Castle**. Kids will love running through the castle grounds, climbing the towers, and imagining life as a medieval knight.

Lunch: Grotto San Michele

- Stop for lunch at **Grotto San Michele**, located near **Montebello Castle**, where you can try local Ticinese dishes in a relaxed setting.

- **Cost**: CHF 25-35 per person

Afternoon: Bellinzona Market

- If it's a Saturday, head to **Bellinzona's market** where families can sample local cheeses, breads, and sweets.

Day 4: Day Trip to Locarno

Morning: Visit the Falconeria Locarno

- Start your day with a visit to the **Falconeria Locarno**, where kids can watch bird of prey shows and learn about falconry.
- **Entry Cost**: CHF 20 for adults, CHF 12 for children
- **Location**: Via delle Scuole 12, 6600 Locarno

Lunch: Lunch at Osteria Borghese

- Have lunch at **Osteria Borghese**, which offers a kid-friendly menu with pasta, pizza, and local specialties.
- **Cost**: CHF 20-30 per person
- **Address**: Via Borghese 3, 6600 Locarno

Afternoon: Splash & Spa Tamaro

- Spend the afternoon at **Splash & Spa Tamaro**, an indoor water park with pools, slides, and a spa for parents. It's a great way to relax while the kids have fun.
- **Cost**: CHF 33 for adults, CHF 27 for children

Day 5: Lugano's Lido and Funicular to Monte Brè

Morning: Swim at Lido di Lugano

- Start your last day with a trip to **Lido di Lugano**, a lakeside beach area with pools, water slides, and playgrounds that are perfect for families. Relax by the lake while the kids enjoy the water.
- **Entry Cost**: CHF 6 for adults, CHF 4 for children
- **Address**: Viale Castagnola 3, 6900 Lugano

Lunch: Grotto della Salute

- For lunch, enjoy traditional Ticinese fare at **Grotto della Salute**.
- **Cost**: CHF 20-30 per person
- **Address**: Via al Grotto 10, 6900 Lugano

Afternoon: Funicular to Monte Brè

- In the afternoon, take the funicular up **Monte Brè** for stunning views of Lake Lugano and the Alps. There are also easy walking paths suitable for kids.
- **Cost**: CHF 25 round trip

Adventure Seeker's 7-Day Itinerary

Day 1: Arrival in Lugano and Introduction to the Outdoors

Morning: Lugano City and Lake Kayaking

- Start your adventure by exploring **Lake Lugano** with a morning kayaking session. You can rent a kayak from **Lugano Rent a Boat**,

located near the lakefront, and paddle along the calm waters while enjoying views of Monte Brè and the surrounding mountains.
- **Gear Rental**: Kayaks are available for **CHF 20 per hour**.
- **Address**: Via Foce, 6900 Lugano
- **How to Get There**: A short walk from Lugano's city center.

Lunch: La Cucina di Alice

- After kayaking, grab lunch at **La Cucina di Alice**, a lakeside restaurant offering a variety of fresh salads, pasta, and grilled fish.
- **Cost**: CHF 25-35 per person
- **Address**: Riva Albertolli 5, 6900 Lugano

Afternoon: Hike to Monte Brè

- In the afternoon, take the funicular to **Monte Brè** and hike along one of the several well-marked trails. The hike to the summit takes about 2-3 hours and rewards you with stunning views of the lake and mountains.
- **Funicular Cost**: CHF 25 round trip
- **How to Get There**: Funicular departs from **Cassarate** in Lugano.

Day 2: Explore Valle Verzasca

Morning: Hike in the Verzasca Valley

- Head to the **Verzasca Valley** for a scenic hike along the **Sentiero Verzasca** trail. Start at **Lavertezzo**, a village known for its iconic stone bridge, **Ponte dei Salti**, and emerald-green waters. The trail follows the river and passes by waterfalls and crystal-clear swimming spots.
- **Distance**: 12 km round trip
- **Difficulty**: Moderate
- **How to Get There**: A 40-minute drive from Lugano or take a bus from Bellinzona.

Lunch: Grotto al Ponte

- Enjoy lunch at **Grotto al Ponte** in Lavertezzo, a traditional Ticinese grotto offering local dishes like polenta and risotto.
- **Cost**: CHF 20-30 per person
- **Address**: Via Valle Verzasca 12, 6633 Lavertezzo

Afternoon: Cliff Jumping and Swimming

- In the afternoon, head to one of the natural pools along the river for some cliff jumping and swimming. The area around Lavertezzo is perfect for thrill-seekers, with cliffs ranging from 5 to 10 meters high.
- **Gear Rental**: No gear needed, but be cautious of water depth and currents.

Day 3: Rock Climbing in Ponte Brolla

Morning: Rock Climbing

- **Ponte Brolla**, near Locarno, is one of the best spots for rock climbing in Ticino. The area offers routes for all levels, from beginners to experienced climbers. If you're new to climbing, consider booking a session with a guide through the local climbing school.
- **Gear Rental**: Climbing gear can be rented at **ClimbPoint** in Locarno for around **CHF 50** per day.
- **How to Get There**: A 15-minute drive from Locarno or accessible by train.

Lunch: Grotto America

- After a morning of climbing, refuel at **Grotto America**, a cozy restaurant near Ponte Brolla serving Ticinese specialties.
- **Cost**: CHF 25-35 per person

- **Address**: Via Cappella 2, 6605 Locarno

Afternoon: Relax at the Maggia River

- Spend the afternoon relaxing by the **Maggia River**, located nearby. The riverbanks are perfect for a refreshing swim and lounging by the water after a day of climbing.

Day 4: Canyoning in the Maggia Valley

Morning: Canyoning Adventure

- For a real thrill, book a canyoning trip in the **Maggia Valley**. Ticino is known for its world-class canyoning routes, with options ranging from easy to advanced. **Valle Maggia Canyoning** offers guided tours through narrow gorges, waterfalls, and natural slides.
- **Cost**: CHF 120-160 per person, depending on the difficulty level.
- **Gear Rental**: All equipment is provided by the tour company.

Lunch: Grotto Pozzasc

- After your canyoning adventure, enjoy lunch at **Grotto Pozzasc**, located in the picturesque village of **Peccia**. This rustic grotto serves homemade pasta and fresh local cheeses.
- **Cost**: CHF 20-30 per person
- **Address**: Via della Valle 3, 6670 Peccia

Day 5: Monte Tamaro and Adventure Park

Morning: Hike to Monte Tamaro

- Take the cable car to **Monte Tamaro** for a day filled with adventure. Start with a hike to the summit of **Monte Tamaro** for panoramic views

of Ticino's lakes and mountains.
- **Cable Car Cost**: CHF 25 round trip
- **How to Get There**: Cable car departs from **Rivera**.

Lunch: Packed Picnic

- Bring a picnic lunch to enjoy at the top of Monte Tamaro, where you'll find several scenic spots with tables.

Afternoon: Adventure Park

- After lunch, challenge yourself at the **Adventure Park**, which offers zip lines, rope courses, and climbing walls. The park is family-friendly but has plenty of advanced courses for thrill-seekers.
- **Cost**: CHF 20-30 per person for the Adventure Park

Day 6: Paragliding and Mountain Biking

Morning: Paragliding from Monte Lema

- For a bird's-eye view of Ticino, book a tandem paragliding flight from **Monte Lema**. Soar over the lush valleys and lakes as you glide through the air with a professional guide.
- **Cost**: CHF 150-200 for a tandem flight
- **How to Get There**: A 30-minute drive from Lugano

Lunch: Chalet di Breggia

- After your flight, head to **Chalet di Breggia** for a hearty lunch of local mountain cuisine.
- **Cost**: CHF 20-30 per person
- **Address**: Via Monte Generoso 8, 6830 Chiasso

Afternoon: Mountain Biking at Monte Tamaro

- In the afternoon, rent a mountain bike from **MTB Ticino** and hit the trails on **Monte Tamaro**. The area offers several trails ranging from easy to difficult, with stunning views along the way.
- **Bike Rental Cost**: CHF 35-45 per day
- **How to Get There**: Start from **Rivera**.

Day 7: Kayaking on Lake Maggiore and Farewell Dinner

Morning: Kayaking on Lake Maggiore

- Spend your final morning kayaking on **Lake Maggiore**. Rent a kayak from **Verbano Rentals** and paddle along the lake's clear waters, exploring the shores of **Ascona** and nearby islands.
- **Kayak Rental Cost**: CHF 20 per hour
- **How to Get There**: Rentals available near **Ascona's Lido**.

Lunch: Lido Ascona

- After kayaking, enjoy lunch at the **Lido Ascona**, a lakeside restaurant offering Mediterranean cuisine.
- **Cost**: CHF 30-40 per person
- **Address**: Via Lido 9, 6612 Ascona

Afternoon: Relax by the Lake

- Spend the afternoon relaxing by **Lake Maggiore**, either swimming at the lido or lounging on the beach.

Dinner: Farewell at Grotto Baldoria

- End your adventure-packed week with a farewell dinner at **Grotto**

Baldoria, a traditional Ticinese grotto in **Ascona** that serves delicious local dishes in a cozy setting.
- **Cost**: CHF 35-50 per person
- **Address**: Via Borgo 31, 6612 Ascona

Luxury 4-Day Escape

If you're looking for a luxurious and relaxing getaway, Ticino is the perfect destination. This 4-day luxury itinerary is designed to indulge your senses with private yacht tours, fine dining, and exclusive spa treatments, all while enjoying Ticino's breathtaking landscapes.

Day 1: Arrival and Spa Day

Morning: Check into The View Lugano

- Begin your luxury escape by checking into **The View Lugano**, a sleek and modern 5-star hotel offering panoramic views of **Lake Lugano**. The hotel's private suites feature floor-to-ceiling windows and personal terraces.
- **Cost**: CHF 500-1,000 per night, depending on the suite.
- **Address**: Via Guidino 29, 6900 Lugano-Paradiso

Afternoon: Spa Treatment

- After settling in, head to the hotel's spa for an afternoon of relaxation. The **Private Spa Experience** includes a sauna, steam bath, and personalized treatments such as a deep tissue massage or Swiss facial.
- **Cost**: CHF 200-300 for a half-day spa package

Dinner: Ristorante Principe Leopoldo

- Enjoy an elegant dinner at **Ristorante Principe Leopoldo**, one of Ticino's most luxurious fine dining spots. The restaurant offers a tasting menu featuring local and Mediterranean flavors, paired with fine wines from the hotel's cellar.
- **Cost**: CHF 120-180 per person for the tasting menu
- **Address**: Via Montalbano 5, 6900 Lugano

Day 2: Private Yacht Tour and Wine Tasting

Morning: Private Yacht Tour on Lake Lugano

- Start your day with a private yacht tour on **Lake Lugano**. Rent a luxury yacht through **Lugano Boat Rental** and enjoy a few hours cruising the lake with champagne and a personal guide.
- **Cost**: CHF 600-800 for a half-day yacht tour
- **How to Book**: Book directly through the hotel or Lugano Boat Rental.

Lunch: Ristorante Arté al Lago

- After your boat tour, have lunch at **Ristorante Arté al Lago**, a Michelin-starred restaurant located right on the lake. The restaurant specializes in seafood, with dishes made from freshly caught lake fish.
- **Cost**: CHF 100-150 per person
- **Address**: Via Cortivo 10, 6900 Lugano

Afternoon: Wine Tasting at Tenuta Bally & von Teufenstein

- In the afternoon, visit **Tenuta Bally & von Teufenstein**, a prestigious winery near Lugano, for a private wine tasting. You'll sample Ticino's finest Merlot wines while learning about the winemaking process from the vineyard's owners.

- **Cost**: CHF 60-100 per person for a private tasting
- **Address**: Via Municipio 30, 6927 Agra

Day 3: Shopping and Helicopter Tour

Morning: Shopping in Lugano

- Spend your morning shopping in Lugano's upscale boutiques. Visit **Via Nassa**, the city's most famous shopping street, where you'll find designer brands, Swiss watches, and luxury goods.

Lunch: Grand Café Al Porto

- For lunch, stop at **Grand Café Al Porto**, one of Lugano's oldest and most elegant cafés, known for its historic setting and refined menu.
- **Cost**: CHF 40-60 per person
- **Address**: Via Pessina 3, 6900 Lugano

Afternoon: Private Helicopter Tour

- In the afternoon, take a private helicopter tour over **Lake Lugano** and the surrounding Alps. **Swiss Helicopter** offers personalized tours that provide stunning aerial views of Ticino's landscapes.
- **Cost**: CHF 1,200-1,500 for a 60-minute flight
- **How to Book**: Book directly with Swiss Helicopter.

Day 4: Day Trip to Ascona and Farewell Dinner

Morning: Relax in Ascona

- On your final day, take a private car to **Ascona**, where you can spend the morning relaxing by **Lake Maggiore**. Ascona's waterfront promenade is the perfect spot to stroll or sit at an outdoor café and enjoy the view.

Lunch: Ristorante da Enzo

- Have lunch at **Ristorante da Enzo**, a fine dining restaurant in Ascona offering exquisite Italian cuisine in a beautiful garden setting.
- **Cost**: CHF 100-150 per person
- **Address**: Via Collegio 8, 6612 Ascona

Afternoon: Explore Brissago Islands

- Take a private boat to the **Brissago Islands** for a leisurely afternoon exploring the botanical gardens and relaxing by the water.
- **Cost**: CHF 200 for a private boat transfer
- **Location**: Lake Maggiore, near Ascona

Dinner: La Palma au Lac

- End your luxury escape with a farewell dinner at **La Palma au Lac**, a lakeside restaurant offering elegant Mediterranean cuisine and breathtaking views of **Lake Maggiore**.
- **Cost**: CHF 120-150 per person
- **Address**: Viale Verbano 29, 6600 Locarno

Top Attractions in Ticino

Lake Lugano: A Perfect Spot for Water Sports and Relaxation

Lake Lugano is a breathtaking lake bordered by both Switzerland and Italy, with clear blue waters and towering mountains providing the perfect setting for water activities. It's an ideal destination for those seeking both adventure and tranquility. The lake is dotted with charming lakeside villages, making it easy to combine water activities with a bit of cultural exploration.

Kayaking on Lake Lugano

One of the best ways to experience the beauty of Lake Lugano is by kayak. Kayaking allows you to glide along the peaceful waters, taking in views of nearby mountains like **Monte Brè** and **Monte San Salvatore**. Kayaks can be rented from several locations around the lake, and the water is generally calm, making it ideal for both beginners and experienced kayakers.

Where to Rent Kayaks:
  1. **Lugano Rent a Boat**: Located near the **Lido di Lugano**, this rental shop offers single and double kayaks for **CHF 15-25 per hour**.

- **Address**: Via Foce 14, 6900 Lugano
- **Contact**: +41 91 923 72 72

2. **Ceresio Fun**: Another great option, especially for beginners. Ceresio

Fun also offers short kayaking lessons for those who need a quick refresher.

- **Cost**: CHF 20 per hour
- **Address**: Viale Castagnola, 6900 Lugano

Best Spots for Kayaking:

- **Gandria**: Kayak from **Lugano** to the charming fishing village of **Gandria**. This quiet corner of the lake offers stunning views and peaceful surroundings.
- **San Rocco**: A scenic paddle destination with views of Monte Brè and Monte San Salvatore.

Paddleboarding on Lake Lugano

Paddleboarding is a popular activity on Lake Lugano, especially during the summer months when the lake's waters are calm and inviting. It's a great way to enjoy the lake at a slower pace while getting some exercise. You can rent paddleboards from several lakeside vendors.

Where to Rent Paddleboards:

- **Lugano Rent a Boat**: In addition to kayaks, this shop offers paddleboard rentals for **CHF 20 per hour**.
- **Lido di Lugano**: The **Lido** is not only a great place for swimming but also for paddleboarding. Boards are available for rent, and the calm waters near the Lido make it an ideal spot for beginners.
- **Address**: Viale Castagnola 6, 6900 Lugano

Best Paddleboarding Spots:

- **Morcote**: Paddleboard around the charming village of **Morcote**, known for its beautiful architecture and scenic surroundings.

- **Bissone**: A quieter area of the lake, perfect for paddleboarding if you prefer fewer people and a more relaxed experience.

Scenic Boat Tours on Lake Lugano

If you prefer to take in the sights without breaking a sweat, a boat tour is the way to go. Several companies offer boat trips that take you around the lake, stopping at key villages and scenic spots. You'll get to see the lake from a new perspective, and many tours offer commentary on the history and geography of the region.

Popular Boat Tours:

Grand Tour of Lake Lugano: This 2-3 hour tour departs from **Lugano** and covers the key sights around the lake, including **Monte Brè**, **Gandria**, and **Morcote**. The tour also crosses into the Italian side of the lake, offering a view of the Swiss-Italian border.

- **Cost**: CHF 40-50 per person
- **Departure Location**: Lugano Pier

Lugano to Gandria: For a shorter experience, take a boat trip from Lugano to **Gandria**, a quaint lakeside village. The ride takes about 30 minutes, and you can explore the village before heading back.

- **Cost**: CHF 15-20 round trip
- **Best Time for Boat Tours**: Late spring and early summer are the best times for boat tours. The weather is warm, and the views are clear without the peak tourist crowds.

Lakeside Dining and Relaxation by Lake Lugano

After a day on the water, head to one of the many lakeside restaurants to relax and enjoy some local cuisine. Lake Lugano's waterfront is lined with eateries offering everything from traditional Ticinese dishes to Italian-inspired fare.

Top Lakeside Dining Spots:

Ristorante La Cucina di Alice: Known for its fresh, locally sourced dishes, this lakeside restaurant offers Mediterranean cuisine with a focus on fish from the lake.

- **Cost**: CHF 30-50 per person
- **Address**: Riva Albertolli 1, 6900 Lugano

Grotto Morchino: Located in the nearby hills, this rustic grotto serves Ticinese specialties like **risotto** and **polenta** in a cozy setting with views of the lake.

- **Cost**: CHF 25-35 per person
- **Address**: Via Carona 8, 6900 Lugano

Lake Maggiore: A Blend of Adventure and Tranquility

Lake Maggiore, shared by both Switzerland and Italy, offers a slightly different atmosphere compared to Lake Lugano. With its larger size, Mediterranean climate, and stunning views, it's a favorite for those seeking a blend of relaxation and outdoor adventure. **Locarno** and **Ascona**, two towns located on the Swiss side of the lake, serve as hubs for water activities, while the Italian side offers more opportunities to explore charming lakeside villages.

Kayaking on Lake Maggiore

Kayaking on Lake Maggiore offers more open waters compared to Lake Lugano, making it ideal for longer paddles and exploring hidden coves. You can rent kayaks from **Ascona** or **Locarno** and paddle along the Swiss shores before crossing into Italy for a full day of exploration.

Where to Rent Kayaks:

- **Verbano Rentals**: Located in **Locarno**, this shop offers kayak rentals and guided tours. You can rent single or double kayaks starting at **CHF 20 per hour**.
- **Address**: Via B. Varenna 6, 6600 Locarno
- **Ascona Watersports**: Another option for kayak rentals, with easy access to some of the quieter parts of the lake.
- **Cost**: CHF 20-30 per hour
- **Address**: Via Lido 9, 6612 Ascona

Best Kayaking Routes:

- **Brissago Islands**: Paddle to the **Brissago Islands**, home to a beautiful botanical garden. The islands are a peaceful destination and offer a great stop for a picnic.
- **Ascona to Brissago**: Paddle along the shoreline from **Ascona** to the town of **Brissago**, passing by luxury villas and scenic viewpoints.

Paddleboarding on Lake Maggiore

Lake Maggiore's calm waters and wide open spaces make it a perfect spot for paddleboarding. You can paddle in the more sheltered bays near Ascona or venture out further to explore the islands and small beaches along the shore.

Where to Rent Paddleboards:

- **Ascona Watersports**: In addition to kayaks, this shop also rents paddleboards, with boards starting at **CHF 20 per hour**.
- **Address**: Via Lido 9, 6612 Ascona

Best Paddleboarding Spots:

- **Ascona Bay**: The waters near **Ascona** are calm and ideal for paddle-boarding, especially for beginners. You can paddle past luxury villas and enjoy views of the mountains in the distance.
- **Locarno**: Paddle along the shores near Locarno for a more scenic experience, with views of the town and surrounding hills.

Scenic Boat Tours on Lake Maggiore

Boat tours on Lake Maggiore allow you to explore both the Swiss and Italian sides of the lake, with stops at picturesque villages and islands along the way. The **Brissago Islands** and the Italian town of **Stresa** are popular stops for those looking to combine nature and culture.

Popular Boat Tours:

Ascona to Brissago Islands: This 30-minute boat ride takes you from **Ascona** to the **Brissago Islands**, where you can explore the lush botanical garden.

- **Cost**: CHF 15 per person round trip
- **Departure Location**: Ascona Pier

Full-Day Tour of Lake Maggiore: Departing from **Locarno**, this full-day tour takes you across the lake, with stops at **Isola Bella** and **Isola Madre** in Italy. You'll have time to explore the gardens and palaces on the islands before returning to Switzerland.

- **Cost**: CHF 60-80 per person
- **Departure Location**: Locarno Pier

Lakeside Dining and Relaxation by Lake Maggiore

Lake Maggiore's lakeside towns offer some of the best dining options in Ticino, with restaurants featuring Italian and Mediterranean-inspired dishes. After a day on the water, enjoy a meal at one of the many waterfront restaurants.

Top Lakeside Dining Spots:
Ristorante da Enzo: Located in **Ascona**, this fine dining restaurant offers a mix of Italian and Swiss cuisine with beautiful views of the lake.

- **Cost**: CHF 40-60 per person
- **Address**: Via Collegio 8, 6612 Ascona

Ristorante Lago: In **Locarno**, this casual lakeside restaurant serves fresh seafood and pasta dishes, with outdoor seating right by the water.

- **Cost**: CHF 30-45 per person
- **Address**: Via Lido 2, 6600 Locarno

Practical Tips for Visiting Lake Lugano and Lake Maggiore
- **Best Time to Visit**: The best time to visit **Lake Lugano** and **Lake Maggiore** for water sports and boat tours is from May to September, when the weather is warm and the lakes are calm.
- **Costs**: Kayak and paddleboard rentals range from **CHF 15-30 per hour**, while boat tours cost **CHF 15-80** depending on the length of the tour.
- **How to Get There**: Both lakes are easily accessible by train or car. **Lugano** is a central hub for Lake Lugano, while **Locarno** and **Ascona** serve as starting points for exploring Lake Maggiore. Regular trains and buses connect these towns to major Swiss cities like **Zurich** and **Milan**.

Bellinzona's Castles - UNESCO World Heritage Sites

Bellinzona, the capital of Ticino, is best known for its impressive medieval castles, which have been recognized as **UNESCO World Heritage Sites** since the year 2000. These three castles—**Castelgrande, Montebello,** and **Sasso Corbaro**—are key landmarks that played a crucial role in the region's history. Originally built to defend against invaders and control trade routes between the Alps and the Po Valley, these castles still stand tall, offering visitors a glimpse into Ticino's past.

Exploring the castles of Bellinzona is like stepping back in time, and it's easy to imagine the days when soldiers stood guard on these very ramparts. Whether you're a history enthusiast or just someone who appreciates a stunning view, visiting Bellinzona's castles is a must. Here's what you need to know about each castle, what to expect during your visit, and practical tips on how to see all three in one day.

Castelgrande: The Largest and Oldest Fortress

Castelgrande, located in the heart of Bellinzona, is the oldest and largest of the three castles. Its foundations date back to the 1st century BC, though much of the structure as it stands today was built during the medieval period. Castelgrande dominates the landscape from a rocky hill, offering panoramic views of Bellinzona and the surrounding valleys. Historically, this castle was the main fortification protecting the town and its strategic location between northern and southern Europe.

What to Expect at Castelgrande

- **Exploring the Castle**: Castelgrande features two impressive towers—the **Torre Bianca** (White Tower) and **Torre Nera** (Black Tower). Visitors can climb both towers for excellent views of the city and surrounding mountains. The castle's courtyards, stone walls, and well-

preserved ramparts give you a sense of the castle's original grandeur.
- **Museum**: Castelgrande also houses a museum that traces the history of the castle and Bellinzona itself. Exhibits include archaeological finds from the site, medieval weaponry, and detailed models of the castles as they evolved over the centuries.
- **Entry Fee**: CHF 5 for adults, CHF 2.50 for children. Entry to the museum is included in the combined ticket for all three castles.

Highlights of Castelgrande

- **The View**: The views from Castelgrande are some of the best in Ticino. You can see the entire city of Bellinzona, the other two castles, and the surrounding valleys from the castle's ramparts.
- **The Walls**: Castelgrande's thick stone walls are still intact and give you a sense of the scale of this massive fortress.
- **History**: As you explore the castle, you'll see plaques and exhibits that explain how the fortress was used to protect Bellinzona from invasions, particularly during conflicts with the Swiss Confederacy and Milanese forces.

Getting to Castelgrande

- **Location**: Piazza Nosetto, 6500 Bellinzona
- **How to Get There**: Castelgrande is located right in the center of Bellinzona and is easily accessible by foot. From the main square, **Piazza Nosetto**, you can either walk up a steep path to the castle or take an elevator from **Piazza del Sole**, which is located at the base of the hill.

Montebello Castle: A Picture-Perfect Medieval Fortress

Montebello Castle, perched on a hill just above Bellinzona's old town, is often considered the most picturesque of the three castles. Built in the 13th century, it served as a secondary fortification to Castelgrande and was expanded over the years to bolster the town's defenses. Montebello offers a more intimate experience than Castelgrande, with its narrow corridors, stone archways, and wooden bridges giving it a true medieval atmosphere.

What to Expect at Montebello Castle

- **Exploring the Castle**: The inner courtyard is surrounded by high stone walls and towers, and visitors can walk along the ramparts to get a better sense of how the castle defended the town. Montebello also has a small museum displaying medieval artifacts, including armor, weapons, and everyday objects used by the people who once lived here.
- **Entry Fee**: Included in the combined ticket for all three castles (CHF 12 for adults, CHF 6 for children).

Highlights of Montebello

- **The Towers**: Montebello's towers are smaller than Castelgrande's, but they offer a more personal look at medieval military architecture. Climbing the towers gives you sweeping views of Bellinzona, Castelgrande, and the surrounding hills.
- **Medieval Festivals**: Montebello often hosts medieval-themed events and festivals, particularly during the summer months. These events feature reenactments, traditional food, and demonstrations of medieval crafts and skills.
- **The Walk**: The walk from the town center up to Montebello is a highlight in itself. Though it's uphill, the path is scenic, and you'll pass through charming streets as you make your way to the castle.

Getting to Montebello Castle

- **Location**: Via Artore, 6500 Bellinzona
- **How to Get There**: Montebello is about a 10-minute walk uphill from Castelgrande. There are well-marked paths leading to the castle, and while the walk is a bit steep, it's manageable for most visitors. You can also drive up to Montebello or take a short taxi ride from the city center.

Sasso Corbaro Castle: The Highest and Most Secluded Castle

Sasso Corbaro Castle, built in 1479, is the smallest and most isolated of the three castles, but it offers the best views. Located high above Bellinzona, Sasso Corbaro was designed to be the final line of defense for the town. Unlike the other two castles, which were built on natural rock formations, Sasso Corbaro was constructed entirely by human hands on a steep hilltop. While it's a bit further from the city center, it's well worth the visit for the panoramic views of the Alps and the valley below.

What to Expect at Sasso Corbaro Castle

- **Exploring the Castle**: Sasso Corbaro feels more remote and peaceful than the other two castles. The castle walls, towers, and inner courtyard have been well-preserved, and there is a small museum inside the castle that focuses on the history of Bellinzona and the strategic importance of the three castles.
- **Entry Fee**: Included in the combined ticket for all three castles (CHF 12 for adults, CHF 6 for children).

Highlights of Sasso Corbaro

- **The Views**: Sasso Corbaro's main attraction is the view. From the

castle's ramparts, you can see all three castles, the town of Bellinzona, and the surrounding mountains. On clear days, the view stretches far into the distance, offering a truly breathtaking panorama.
- **Seclusion**: Unlike Castelgrande and Montebello, which are closer to the town, Sasso Corbaro offers a more tranquil experience. The lack of crowds makes it a great spot for quiet reflection and photography.

Getting to Sasso Corbaro Castle

- **Location**: Via Sasso Corbaro, 6500 Bellinzona
- **How to Get There**: Sasso Corbaro is located about a 20-minute walk uphill from Montebello. The path is steep, so if you prefer not to walk, you can take a taxi or drive up to the castle. There is parking available near the entrance.

How to Visit All Three Castles in One Day

Visiting all three castles in one day is entirely possible and highly recommended for those interested in medieval history and architecture. Here's how to make the most of your day:

1. **Start Early**: Begin your day at **Castelgrande**, as it's the largest and will take the most time to explore. Plan to spend about 1.5 to 2 hours here, including time to climb the towers and visit the museum.
2. **Walk to Montebello**: After visiting Castelgrande, take the scenic walk to **Montebello Castle**. Spend about an hour here exploring the courtyard, towers, and museum.
3. **Lunch in Bellinzona**: Take a break for lunch at one of the local restaurants in Bellinzona. **Ristorante Internazionale** near the train station is a good option for traditional Ticinese cuisine.

- **Address**: Viale Stazione 35, 6500 Bellinzona
- **Visit Sasso Corbaro**: After lunch, either walk or drive up to **Sasso Corbaro Castle**. Spend about an hour here enjoying the views and exploring the museum.

Special Events: If your visit coincides with one of the medieval festivals held at the castles, be sure to stay for the reenactments and demonstrations. These events usually take place during the summer months.

Practical Tips for Visiting Bellinzona's Castles
- **Combined Ticket**: A combined ticket for all three castles costs **CHF 12 for adults** and **CHF 6 for children**. It's valid for the entire day and allows access to all the museums and towers.
- **Opening Hours**: The castles are generally open from **10:00 AM to 5:00 PM** (March through October) and **11:00 AM to 4:00 PM** (November through February). It's best to check the exact times before your visit, as they can vary depending on the season.
- **How to Get There**: Bellinzona is easily accessible by train from **Lugano**, **Locarno**, or **Zurich**. From the Bellinzona train station, it's a short walk to the base of **Castelgrande**. Taxis and buses are also available if you prefer not to walk to **Montebello** or **Sasso Corbaro**.

Ascona: A Lakeside Gem with a Mediterranean Vibe

Ascona, often referred to as Ticino's most elegant town, is a small, picturesque place that exudes a Mediterranean charm. With its brightly colored buildings lining the lakeside promenade, its relaxed atmosphere, and its strong artistic presence, Ascona is a must-visit for anyone traveling to Ticino.

Lakeside Promenade

The highlight of Ascona is undoubtedly its **Lungolago**, the lakeside promenade that runs along **Lake Maggiore**. Palm trees, flower gardens, and outdoor cafés line the promenade, creating the perfect environment for a leisurely stroll. The lake's calm waters and the surrounding mountains provide stunning views, especially at sunset when the light reflects off the lake's surface.

- **Best Time for a Stroll**: Early evening is ideal for a relaxing walk along the promenade, when the cafés and restaurants start to fill up and the town comes to life.
- **Scenic Photography Spots**: The promenade offers numerous spots for photography, with the pastel-colored buildings and the lake's tranquil waters providing a perfect backdrop. Try capturing the scene at **Piazza Giuseppe Motta**, where the combination of the square and the waterfront creates a postcard-worthy shot.

Vibrant Cultural Life

Ascona is well-known for its strong connection to the arts. The town has been an artist's haven since the early 20th century, and that artistic influence is still evident today in its numerous galleries and cultural events.

Museo Comunale d'Arte Moderna: Art lovers should not miss the **Museo Comunale d'Arte Moderna**, which houses works by famous modern artists like Paul Klee and Julius Bissier. The museum is a centerpiece of Ascona's art scene, offering exhibitions that rotate throughout the year.

- **Address**: Via Borgo 34, 6612 Ascona
- **Entry Cost**: CHF 10 for adults, CHF 5 for children
- **How to Get There**: A short 5-minute walk from **Piazza Giuseppe Motta**.

JazzAscona Festival: Ascona is home to the annual **JazzAscona Festival**, one of Europe's premier jazz events. Held every summer, this 10-day festival draws jazz musicians from around the world and features open-air concerts along the promenade. The festival has a relaxed, joyful atmosphere, making it a highlight of Ascona's cultural calendar.

- **When**: Late June to early July
- **Cost**: Free for most outdoor concerts, with some ticketed performances ranging from CHF 30-100

Dining and Shopping

Ascona's elegant vibe is reflected in its dining scene, which offers everything from traditional Ticinese dishes to international cuisine.

- **Ristorante Al Pontile**: Located right on the lake, this restaurant is known for its fresh fish and risotto. The outdoor terrace offers stunning views, making it one of the best places in town to enjoy a meal by the water.
- **Cost**: CHF 35-50 per person
- **Address**: Via Al Lago 4, 6612 Ascona

For shopping, the streets near **Piazza Giuseppe Motta** are filled with boutique shops offering local handicrafts, art, and luxury goods. It's a great place to find unique souvenirs or just enjoy window shopping.

Locarno: A Blend of History and Culture

Just a short distance from Ascona lies **Locarno**, a larger town that is equally charming but offers a more bustling vibe. Known for its historic architecture, cultural events, and stunning piazzas, Locarno has something to offer every traveler, from history buffs to festival-goers.

Piazza Grande

The heart of Locarno is **Piazza Grande**, one of the largest squares in

Switzerland. This grand piazza is a lively hub, surrounded by cafés, shops, and restaurants. It's a great place to relax, people-watch, and enjoy the local atmosphere.

- **Locarno Film Festival**: Every August, **Piazza Grande** transforms into an open-air cinema for the **Locarno Film Festival**, one of the oldest and most prestigious film festivals in the world. The festival showcases independent and international films, and watching a movie under the stars in such a stunning setting is an unforgettable experience.
- **When**: Early to mid-August
- **Cost**: Tickets range from CHF 15-30 per screening
- **Tip**: Arrive early to grab a good seat, as the outdoor screenings can get crowded.
- **Best Time to Visit**: Even when the festival isn't in town, **Piazza Grande** is a great spot to explore. During the day, you can enjoy a coffee at one of the square's cafés, and in the evenings, the square often hosts live music or small cultural events.

Cultural Landmarks

Locarno's rich history is reflected in its architecture and cultural landmarks.

Castello Visconteo: This medieval castle, located just off **Piazza Grande**, dates back to the 12th century. Visitors can explore its courtyards, towers, and small museum, which displays archaeological finds from the region. It's a must-see for history enthusiasts.

- **Address**: Piazza Castello, 6600 Locarno
- **Entry Cost**: CHF 10 for adults, CHF 5 for children

Madonna del Sasso Sanctuary: Perched on a hill overlooking Locarno, the **Madonna del Sasso Sanctuary** is one of Ticino's most important religious sites. The sanctuary offers breathtaking views of the town and **Lake Maggiore**, and it's easily reached by funicular from Locarno's city center.

- **Cost**: CHF 8 round-trip funicular ride
- **Address**: Via Santuario, 6600 Locarno

Markets and Local Life

Locarno hosts several markets throughout the year, giving visitors a chance to experience local life and pick up fresh produce or handmade goods.

- **Weekly Market**: Every Thursday, **Piazza Grande** fills with stalls selling local food, flowers, and crafts. It's a lively scene where you can find everything from fresh cheeses to handwoven baskets.
- **When**: Every Thursday from 9:00 AM to 1:00 PM

Dining in Locarno

Locarno's dining options reflect its blend of Swiss and Italian influences. Whether you're in the mood for a pizza, pasta, or traditional Swiss dishes, you'll find something to satisfy your appetite.

- **Ristorante Cittadella**: Located near **Piazza Grande**, this cozy restaurant offers a mix of Italian and Swiss dishes. Their homemade pasta is particularly popular, and the outdoor seating area is perfect for people-watching.
- **Cost**: CHF 40-60 per person
- **Address**: Via della Motta 3, 6600 Locarno

Visiting During Festival Season

Both **Ascona** and **Locarno** are best experienced during their respective festival seasons. The **JazzAscona Festival** and the **Locarno Film Festival** are highlights of Ticino's cultural calendar, and visiting during these events adds an extra layer of excitement to your trip.

- **JazzAscona Tips**: If you're visiting during the **JazzAscona Festival**, make sure to check the festival schedule in advance. Many of the concerts are free and take place outdoors along the lakeside promenade, but there are also ticketed events that may sell out.
- **Best Time to Visit**: Late June to early July
- **Locarno Film Festival Tips**: During the **Locarno Film Festival**, Piazza Grande is the main venue for outdoor screenings, but there are also smaller screenings held in local theaters. To make the most of your experience, consider purchasing a day pass, which allows access to multiple screenings.
- **Best Time to Visit**: Early to mid-August

Scenic Spots for Photography and Relaxation

Both towns offer numerous scenic spots where you can relax and take in the natural beauty of **Lake Maggiore**.

- **Best Photography Spots**: In Ascona, the lakeside promenade is the ideal place to capture the town's colorful buildings and peaceful waters. In Locarno, the view from the **Madonna del Sasso Sanctuary** is unbeatable, with panoramic views of the town, lake, and mountains.
- **Quiet Relaxation**: If you're looking for a quiet spot to relax, head to one of the town's lakeside parks. **Parco delle Camelie** in Locarno is a peaceful garden filled with blooming flowers, and **Lido Ascona** offers a quiet stretch of beach where you can swim or simply relax by the water.

Natural Beauty of Valle Verzasca

The defining feature of Valle Verzasca is its **Verzasca River**, which runs through the valley in a series of pools, waterfalls, and rapids. The water is a striking shade of green, thanks to the unique composition of the surrounding rocks, and the clarity of the river allows you to see straight to the bottom. The valley itself is surrounded by towering mountains and dotted with small villages, each offering a glimpse into traditional Ticinese life.

- **Ponte dei Salti**: One of the valley's most iconic landmarks is the **Ponte dei Salti**, a double-arched stone bridge that dates back to the 17th century. The bridge spans the Verzasca River near the village of **Lavertezzo**, and it's a popular spot for photography, cliff diving, and swimming in the natural pools below.
- **Best Time to Visit**: Early morning or late afternoon provides the best lighting for photos, and the crowds are usually thinner during these times.
- **Safety Tip**: While cliff diving from the bridge into the deep pools below is a popular activity, it's essential to be cautious. The river's currents can be strong, and diving is only recommended for experienced swimmers.

Outdoor Activities in Valle Verzasca

Valle Verzasca offers a wide range of outdoor activities, from gentle hikes along the river to more adventurous pursuits like canyoning and rock climbing. The valley's rugged terrain and pristine waters make it a perfect destination for those looking to explore Ticino's wild side.

Hiking in Valle Verzasca

The valley is crisscrossed by several well-marked hiking trails that range in difficulty from easy walks suitable for families to more challenging routes that take you high into the mountains. The most popular trail is the **Sentiero

Verzasca, which runs alongside the river from the dam at **Vogorno** to the village of **Sonogno**.

- **Sentiero Verzasca Trail**: This scenic 12 km trail is one of the best ways to experience the valley. It follows the river, passing through picturesque villages, ancient stone houses, and the famous Ponte dei Salti. The trail is relatively easy, making it suitable for hikers of all levels.
- **Start Point**: Vogorno Dam
- **End Point**: Sonogno
- **Distance**: 12 km
- **Duration**: 3-4 hours (one way)
- **Safety Tip**: Parts of the trail can be slippery, especially after rain. Sturdy hiking shoes are recommended.
- **Sonogno Village**: At the end of the Sentiero Verzasca trail lies the charming village of **Sonogno**, where time seems to stand still. The village is known for its traditional stone houses and the **Casa Genardini Museum**, which showcases the local history and crafts of the valley.
- **Entry Cost (Museum)**: CHF 3 per person
- **Address**: Via Sonogno 19, 6637 Sonogno

Swimming in Natural Pools

The Verzasca River's natural pools are a highlight for visitors, especially during the summer months when the water provides a refreshing escape from the heat. The most popular swimming spot is near the Ponte dei Salti, where the deep, clear pools are perfect for a quick dip.

- **Best Swimming Spots**: The pools near **Lavertezzo** are the most accessible, and the water here is calm enough for swimming. However, be aware that the water can be quite cold, even in summer.
- **Safety Tip**: Always check the water's depth and current before swimming. The river's currents can be deceptive, especially after rain.

Canyoning and Adventure Sports

For those seeking more adventure, Valle Verzasca offers some of the best canyoning in Ticino. Canyoning involves descending through the river's gorges, jumping into pools, sliding down waterfalls, and navigating narrow rock passages. It's a thrilling way to experience the valley's rugged landscape up close.

- **Canyoning Tours**: Several local companies offer guided canyoning tours, which include all necessary equipment and expert guidance. These tours cater to different experience levels, from beginners to advanced adventurers.
- **Cost**: CHF 100-150 per person, depending on the difficulty level and duration of the tour
- **Recommended Company**: **Ticino Outdoor Canyoning**

How to Get to Valle Verzasca

Valle Verzasca is easily accessible by both car and public transport from **Locarno**.

- **By Car**: The drive from Locarno to the valley takes about 30 minutes. Follow the road along the river, passing the impressive **Verzasca Dam**, one of the highest dams in Europe, where you can stop to admire the views.
- **By Public Transport**: From Locarno, take bus route 321 towards **Sonogno**, which stops at key points along the valley, including **Lavertezzo** and **Vogorno**. Buses run frequently, and the journey takes about 45 minutes.
- **Bus Cost**: CHF 5-10 one way, depending on the stop

The Sacred Monte Madonna del Sasso

The **Madonna del Sasso Sanctuary** is one of Ticino's most important religious and cultural landmarks. Perched high above **Locarno**, the sanctuary offers stunning views of **Lake Maggiore** and the surrounding mountains, making it a popular pilgrimage site and a must-visit for those exploring the region.

Religious and Historical Significance

The **Madonna del Sasso** (Our Lady of the Rock) Sanctuary was founded in the late 15th century after a local friar, **Fra Bartolomeo**, had a vision of the Virgin Mary at the site. Since then, the sanctuary has been a significant place of pilgrimage, attracting visitors who come to pay their respects and admire its spiritual and architectural beauty.

The sanctuary complex includes the main church, several chapels, and a small museum. The interior of the church is adorned with beautiful frescoes and artwork, including a painting of the **Assumption of the Virgin Mary** by renowned Italian artist **Antonio Ciseri**.

- **Main Church**: The interior of the church is richly decorated with frescoes and stucco work. The highlight is **Ciseri's painting**, which dominates the altar and is considered one of his finest works.
- **Chapel Walk**: Along the path leading up to the sanctuary are several small chapels, each with its own unique artwork depicting scenes from the life of Christ and the Virgin Mary.

What to Expect at the Top

Visitors to the sanctuary are rewarded with panoramic views of **Locarno**, **Lake Maggiore**, and the surrounding mountains. The sanctuary's elevated position makes it one of the best viewpoints in the region, especially at sunset when the lake glows in the fading light.

- **Best Time to Visit**: For the best views, visit in the late afternoon or early evening. The light at this time is perfect for photography, and the sanctuary is usually quieter.

How to Reach Madonna del Sasso

The sanctuary is accessible by funicular from **Locarno**'s city center, making the journey both easy and scenic. The funicular ride takes about 5 minutes and offers views over the town as you ascend.

- **Funicular Details**:
- **Cost**: CHF 8 round trip
- **Departure Point**: **Piazza Castello**, Locarno
- **Operating Hours**: Daily from 8:00 AM to 6:00 PM

For those who prefer to walk, there is also a well-marked footpath that leads up to the sanctuary. The walk takes about 20-30 minutes, depending on your pace, and passes several chapels along the way.

Nearby Attractions

Once you've visited the **Madonna del Sasso**, there are several other nearby attractions that are worth exploring:

- **Locarno Old Town**: Just a short walk or funicular ride back into town, Locarno's old town is filled with charming streets, historic buildings, and cafés where you can relax after your visit.
- **Castello Visconteo**: This medieval castle is located near **Piazza Grande** and offers a glimpse into Ticino's history with its small museum and well-preserved towers.
- **Entry Fee**: CHF 10 for adults, CHF 5 for children
- **Address**: Piazza Castello, 6600 Locarno

Tips for Visiting Valle Verzasca and Madonna del Sasso
- **Best Time to Visit**: Valle Verzasca is best visited in late spring to early autumn when the weather is warm and the river is at its most beautiful. The Madonna del Sasso is open year-round, but the best views are on clear days, particularly at sunset.
- **What to Bring**: If you're hiking in the valley, sturdy shoes and plenty of water are essential. For those visiting the sanctuary, consider bringing a camera to capture the incredible views from the top.
- **Guided Tours**: Several companies offer guided tours of both Valle Verzasca and the Madonna del Sasso. These tours typically include transportation, a local guide, and in some cases, entry fees to the sanctuary or museums.

Religious and Historical Significance of Madonna del Sasso

The sanctuary's origins date back to 1480 when a local Franciscan friar, **Fra Bartolomeo**, experienced a vision of the Virgin Mary on the rocky hillside above Locarno. In honor of this divine event, the sanctuary was built, and it has since become a major pilgrimage site. Over the centuries, the sanctuary has been expanded and beautified, now standing as a symbol of faith and devotion in the region.

The site's religious significance is reflected in its artwork, architecture, and the reverence with which it is treated by locals and visitors alike. The name itself, **Madonna del Sasso**, translates to "Our Lady of the Rock," which speaks to the sacredness of the location, resting on a high rock that overlooks the town and **Lake Maggiore**. The peaceful setting and the sanctuary's connection to religious history make it a place of quiet contemplation for pilgrims and tourists.

What Visitors Can See and Experience at the Sanctuary

Visitors to the **Madonna del Sasso** Sanctuary can expect a rich cultural and spiritual experience, with the sanctuary's impressive architecture, religious artworks, and panoramic views being the key highlights.

The Church of Madonna del Sasso

At the heart of the sanctuary is the main church, a beautiful structure that showcases a blend of Renaissance and Baroque styles. The church's interior is richly decorated with **frescoes**, **stucco** work, and religious paintings that reflect the deep spiritual significance of the site.

- **Art and Architecture**: One of the most important pieces in the church is the **Assumption of the Virgin Mary**, a painting by the Italian artist **Antonio Ciseri**, which adorns the altar. The frescoes inside the church depict various biblical scenes, and the craftsmanship seen in the intricate stucco work is breathtaking.
- **Chapel of the Pietà**: Located within the church is a smaller chapel dedicated to the Pietà, which contains a moving statue of the Virgin Mary holding the body of Jesus after his crucifixion. This chapel is a quiet space for personal reflection and prayer.

Surrounding Chapels

Along the path leading up to the sanctuary are several small chapels that were built to depict different events in the life of Christ and the Virgin Mary. These chapels, adorned with frescoes and sculptures, offer an opportunity to explore the religious journey that has made the site so sacred to many.

- **Way of the Cross**: The chapels are part of a **Way of the Cross**, where pilgrims traditionally walk and pray at each station. Even for those not on a religious pilgrimage, walking this path provides a peaceful and reflective experience, enhanced by the beauty of the surrounding nature.

Panoramic Views

One of the main draws of the Madonna del Sasso Sanctuary, aside from its religious importance, is the spectacular view it offers. From the top, visitors are treated to a panoramic view of **Locarno, Lake Maggiore,** and the surrounding mountains. The view is especially striking in the late afternoon when the light casts a golden hue over the lake and the town below.

- **Best Time for Views**: The late afternoon and early evening are ideal times to visit for the best lighting and a quieter atmosphere. Sunset from the sanctuary is particularly breathtaking, as the colors of the sky reflect on the lake's surface.

The Sanctuary Museum

The sanctuary is also home to a small museum that houses a collection of religious artifacts, paintings, and sculptures from the history of the sanctuary. The museum provides insight into the sanctuary's past and the significance of the artworks housed here.

- **Entry Cost**: Entry to the museum is included in the general admission to the sanctuary.

How to Reach Madonna del Sasso

There are several ways to reach the **Madonna del Sasso** Sanctuary, depending on how much time and energy you want to invest in getting there.

By Funicular

The most popular and scenic way to reach the sanctuary is by **funicular**. The funicular ride from **Locarno**'s city center to the sanctuary takes about

5 minutes and offers sweeping views of the town and lake as you ascend the hill. It's a quick and easy option for visitors who want to experience the journey with minimal physical effort.

- **Cost**: CHF 8 for a round-trip ticket
- **Operating Hours**: Daily from 8:00 AM to 6:00 PM
- **Departure Location**: **Piazza Castello**, Locarno

On Foot

For those who prefer a more active approach, there is a walking path from the town that leads up to the sanctuary. The path takes about 20-30 minutes, depending on your pace, and passes by the small chapels that are part of the **Way of the Cross**. Walking to the sanctuary allows for a more immersive experience, as you can stop at each chapel along the way and enjoy the surrounding nature.

- **Walking Time**: 20-30 minutes from Locarno city center
- **Difficulty**: Moderate; the path is uphill but well-maintained.

By Car

There is also the option to drive up to the sanctuary, though parking can be limited, especially during busy times of the year. If you are traveling by car, it's best to arrive early to secure a parking spot.

- **Parking**: A small parking lot is available near the sanctuary, but spaces are limited.

When to Visit Madonna del Sasso for the Best Experience

While the **Madonna del Sasso** Sanctuary is open year-round, the best time to visit is during the **spring** and **autumn** months when the weather is mild and the surrounding landscape is at its most beautiful. Springtime brings blooming flowers and greenery, while autumn offers colorful foliage and clear skies for great views.

- **Spring and Autumn**: These seasons are ideal for visiting, as the weather is comfortable for walking, and the views are clear. Spring, in particular, brings a sense of renewal and is a wonderful time to experience the sanctuary in a peaceful setting.
- **Avoiding Crowds**: If you want to avoid the busiest times, it's best to visit early in the morning or late in the afternoon, particularly during the summer months when tourists flock to Locarno.

Nearby Attractions to Combine with Your Visit

Locarno and its surroundings offer several other attractions that can be combined with a visit to the **Madonna del Sasso**.

Locarno Old Town

Once you descend from the sanctuary, take a stroll through **Locarno's Old Town**, which is filled with narrow streets, historic buildings, and charming cafés. **Piazza Grande**, the town's main square, is a great place to relax with a coffee or explore local shops.

- **Best Time to Visit**: Early afternoon, when the square is lively with people but not too crowded.

Castello Visconteo

Just a short walk from **Piazza Grande** is **Castello Visconteo**, a medieval castle that offers visitors a glimpse into the region's history. The castle's towers and walls are well-preserved, and the museum inside displays artifacts from Ticino's past.

- **Entry Cost**: CHF 10 for adults, CHF 5 for children
- **Location**: Piazza Castello, 6600 Locarno

Lake Maggiore

If you have time, consider taking a boat tour on **Lake Maggiore** after your visit to the sanctuary. Boat tours depart regularly from Locarno's pier and offer a scenic way to explore the lake and its surrounding towns.

- **Cost**: CHF 15-40 depending on the length of the tour
- **Departure Point**: Locarno Pier, near Piazza Grande

Practical Tips for Visiting Madonna del Sasso

- **Dress Modestly**: As the Madonna del Sasso is a religious site, visitors are expected to dress modestly when entering the church. Shoulders and knees should be covered out of respect for the sanctuary.
- **Bring a Camera**: The views from the top of the sanctuary are some of the best in Ticino, so don't forget to bring a camera to capture the stunning panoramas of **Lake Maggiore** and the surrounding mountains.
- **Guided Tours**: If you're interested in learning more about the history and significance of the sanctuary, consider joining a guided tour. Several local companies offer tours that include transportation, a visit to the sanctuary, and an exploration of Locarno's other attractions.
- **Guided Tour Costs**: Typically range from CHF 25-50, depending on the length of the tour and the inclusions (e.g., museum entry, transportation).

Exploring the Brissago Islands: A Botanical Paradise

Nestled in the heart of **Lake Maggiore**, the **Brissago Islands** consist of two islands: **Isola Grande** and **Isola Piccola**. The larger of the two, **Isola Grande**, is open to the public and is home to one of the most diverse and stunning botanical gardens in Switzerland. **Isola Piccola** is privately owned and not accessible, but **Isola Grande** alone makes for an unforgettable visit.

Beauty and Tranquility of the Brissago Islands

The **Brissago Islands** are renowned for their serene atmosphere and natural beauty, making them a favorite destination for nature lovers and garden enthusiasts. The islands offer a unique microclimate due to their location on **Lake Maggiore**, allowing for the growth of plants from all over the world. The **Botanical Garden of Ticino**, situated on **Isola Grande**, features over 1,700 species of plants from subtropical regions, including palms, bamboo, magnolias, and a variety of exotic flowers.

The garden is laid out in carefully maintained sections, each representing different regions of the world, such as South America, Asia, and Africa. Visitors can stroll through lush greenery, passing by rare plants like the **Chilean Wine Palm** and **New Zealand Flax**, while enjoying the tranquil sounds of the lake in the background.

- **Best Time to Visit**: The best time to visit the **Brissago Islands** is between **April and October**, when the garden is in full bloom. Spring and early summer are particularly beautiful, with many plants flowering and the weather being pleasant for walking. During these months, the vibrant colors of the garden come alive, and the island's atmosphere is most inviting.

What Makes the Brissago Islands Unique?

The uniqueness of the **Brissago Islands** lies in their combination of natural beauty and rare plant species. The garden's diversity is a testament to Ticino's rich botanical heritage, and the islands' peaceful atmosphere provides a welcome escape from the busier towns along the lake. For those interested in plants, architecture, or simply relaxing in nature, the islands offer an unparalleled experience.

- **Villa Emden**: Another highlight of the islands is the elegant **Villa**

Emden, a grand 19th-century villa that now houses an art gallery. The villa's architecture adds to the charm of the island, and its terraces offer stunning views of **Lake Maggiore** and the surrounding mountains.

How to Get to the Brissago Islands

The **Brissago Islands** are accessible by boat from several points along **Lake Maggiore**, with the most common departure points being **Locarno**, **Ascona**, and **Brissago**. Regular ferries run throughout the day, and the journey takes around 30 minutes from Locarno and 20 minutes from Ascona.

- **Cost of Ferry Ride**: The ferry ride typically costs between **CHF 15-25** for a round trip, depending on the departure point. Most boat operators also offer combination tickets that include entry to the botanical garden.
- **Address and Ferry Departure Points**:
- **Locarno Pier**: Piazzale Stazione, 6600 Locarno
- **Ascona Pier**: Lungolago Motta, 6612 Ascona

Entry Fees and Practical Information

Once on the islands, visitors are required to pay an entrance fee to access the botanical garden.

- **Entry Fee to Botanical Garden**: CHF 8 for adults, CHF 3 for children.
- **Opening Hours**: The garden is open daily from **9:00 AM to 6:00 PM** during the tourist season (April to October).

Combining a Visit with Other Activities

A visit to the **Brissago Islands** can easily be combined with other activities along **Lake Maggiore**. After exploring the islands, consider taking a boat tour of the lake or visiting nearby towns like **Ascona** or **Brissago** for a relaxing lakeside lunch.

- **Boat Tours**: Several companies offer scenic boat tours that include

stops at various points along the lake, such as the **Brissago Islands**, **Ascona**, and **Cannobio** (on the Italian side of the lake). These tours provide a perfect opportunity to see the lake from a different perspective and explore multiple towns in one day.
- **Cost of Boat Tours**: CHF 20-40, depending on the length of the tour and stops included.

Swissminiatur: A Family Favorite in Ticino

For families and those curious about Switzerland's most famous landmarks, **Swissminiatur** offers a fun and educational experience. Located in **Melide**, just a short distance from **Lugano**, this open-air park features miniature replicas of Switzerland's most iconic buildings, landmarks, and landscapes, all set in a beautifully landscaped garden.

Why Swissminiatur is a Must-Visit for Families

Swissminiatur is particularly popular with families because it offers an engaging way to learn about Switzerland's history, culture, and geography in one place. The park spans over **14,000 square meters** and contains more than **120 miniature models**, all built to a scale of 1:25. Visitors can walk through the park and see tiny versions of famous Swiss castles, churches, mountains, and even working trains that travel between the models on mini railways.

Key Exhibits:

- **Château de Chillon**: One of Switzerland's most famous castles, located near **Montreux**, is faithfully recreated in miniature form at **Swissminiatur**. The model includes the surrounding lake and mountainous landscape, giving visitors a sense of the castle's real-life grandeur.
- **Matterhorn**: The iconic **Matterhorn** mountain, perhaps Switzerland's most recognizable peak, is another highlight of the park. Visitors

can marvel at the detailed reproduction of the mountain and even see miniature cable cars that "carry" passengers up the slopes.
- **Swiss Railways**: The park features several working trains that wind their way through the miniature landscape, passing by famous landmarks and towns. This feature is especially popular with children, who enjoy watching the trains make their way around the park.

How to Navigate the Park

Swissminiatur is designed to be easily navigable, with wide paths leading visitors from one exhibit to the next. The park is family-friendly, with plenty of benches for rest and shaded areas for picnics.

- **Audio Guides**: For those interested in learning more about each exhibit, **Swissminiatur** offers audio guides in several languages, which provide detailed explanations of the landmarks and their significance.
- **Playground and Activities for Kids**: In addition to the miniatures, **Swissminiatur** has a small playground for children and several activities, such as remote-controlled boats and a mini train ride that circles the park.

Practical Tips for Visiting Swissminiatur

- **Entry Fees**: CHF 19 for adults, CHF 12 for children aged 6-15, and free for children under 6.
- **Opening Hours**: The park is open daily from **9:00 AM to 6:00 PM** during the tourist season (April to November).
- **How to Get There from Lugano**: **Swissminiatur** is easily accessible from **Lugano** by car or public transport. The park is located in **Melide**, just 15 minutes from Lugano by car or a short ride on the **S10** train (Lugano-Melide). There is also a ferry service that runs from **Lugano** to **Melide**, offering a scenic way to reach the park.
- **Train Cost**: CHF 4-6 one way from Lugano to Melide.
- **Ferry Cost**: CHF 10-15 one way.

Nearby Dining and Family-Friendly Activities

After a day at **Swissminiatur**, there are several nearby options for dining and other activities that families can enjoy.

- **Ristorante Al Boccalino**: Located just a short walk from **Swissminiatur**, this family-friendly restaurant offers a range of traditional Ticinese dishes, such as **risotto** and **polenta**, along with pizza and pasta. It's a great spot for lunch or dinner after exploring the park.
- **Cost**: CHF 25-40 per person
- **Address**: Via Cantonale 28, 6815 Melide
- **Lido di Melide**: Just a short distance from the park, **Lido di Melide** is a lakeside beach with a swimming area, making it a perfect spot to cool off in the summer months. There's also a playground and picnic area, making it ideal for families looking to relax by the lake.
- **Entry Fee**: CHF 5 per person for beach access.

Outdoor Adventures and Activities

Best Hiking Trails for All Levels

Ticino's varied landscape provides a wide range of hiking opportunities, with trails that cater to all skill levels. Whether you're looking for a gentle stroll through picturesque valleys or a more challenging mountain ascent, Ticino has something for everyone. Here's a breakdown of the best hiking routes, organized by difficulty.

Easy Hiking Trails: Family-Friendly and Scenic Walks

For those looking for a more leisurely outdoor experience or those hiking with children, Ticino offers a number of easy, scenic trails that are accessible to everyone.

Sentiero dell'Olivo (Olive Path)

This easy, family-friendly hike is one of the most scenic in the Lugano area. The **Sentiero dell'Olivo** winds along the shores of **Lake Lugano**, offering beautiful views of the water and passing through olive groves.

- **Distance**: 3.5 km
- **Duration**: 1-1.5 hours
- **Difficulty**: Easy
- **Highlights**: The views of Lake Lugano are stunning, and the path is well-marked and mostly flat, making it perfect for families and

casual walkers. Along the way, there are information panels about the cultivation of olives in the region.
- **Best Time to Visit**: Spring and autumn are ideal, with mild temperatures and blooming flowers. Summer is also fine, but the path can get crowded.
- **How to Get There**: The trail starts at **Gandria**, a short bus ride from Lugano, and finishes near **Castagnola**.

Sentiero Verzasca

The **Sentiero Verzasca** is an easy trail that follows the emerald-green waters of the **Verzasca River** through the beautiful **Valle Verzasca**. This scenic hike passes by quaint villages, stone houses, and historic bridges.

- **Distance**: 12 km
- **Duration**: 3-4 hours (one way)
- **Difficulty**: Easy to moderate (mostly flat, but longer distance)
- **Highlights**: The **Ponte dei Salti**, a 17th-century stone bridge in **Lavertezzo**, is a must-see. There are also several natural pools along the way that are perfect for swimming in the summer.
- **Best Time to Visit**: Spring, summer, and early autumn are great for hiking this trail. The valley is particularly beautiful in the spring when the flowers bloom.
- **How to Get There**: Take a bus from **Locarno** to **Vogorno**, where the trail begins, and hike towards **Sonogno**. Public transport is available at both ends of the trail.

Moderate Hiking Trails: A Bit More Adventure

For those looking to get more of a workout while enjoying spectacular views, Ticino has several moderate trails that are still manageable for most hikers but offer a bit more challenge.

Monte Brè

A moderately challenging hike, **Monte Brè** offers panoramic views over

Lugano, **Lake Lugano**, and the surrounding mountains. It's one of the most popular hiking destinations in the region.

- **Distance**: 6 km (from **Cureggia** to the summit)
- **Duration**: 2-3 hours
- **Difficulty**: Moderate (steep in places)
- **Highlights**: The views from the top are breathtaking, and you can see all the way to the **Monte Rosa** massif and the **Bernese Alps** on clear days. The hike also takes you through charming mountain villages.
- **Best Time to Visit**: Late spring to early autumn is best, as the weather is pleasant and the trails are in good condition.
- **How to Get There**: Take a bus from **Lugano** to **Cureggia** and hike up to Monte Brè. Alternatively, you can take the funicular from Lugano to **Monte Brè** for an easier ascent.

Maggia Valley Waterfall Hike

This hike through the **Valle Maggia** is a favorite among nature lovers. The trail takes you through a forested valley, past beautiful waterfalls and along the **Maggia River**.

- **Distance**: 8 km
- **Duration**: 2.5-3 hours
- **Difficulty**: Moderate
- **Highlights**: The **Cascata del Salto**, a stunning waterfall, is the main attraction. The trail also offers plenty of opportunities to stop for a picnic or take a dip in the river.
- **Best Time to Visit**: Summer is perfect for this hike, as the cool waters provide a refreshing break from the heat.
- **How to Get There**: The hike starts at **Bignasco**, accessible by bus from **Locarno**.

Challenging Hiking Trails: For Experienced Hikers

For more experienced hikers looking for a challenge, Ticino has several demanding trails that reward your effort with incredible views and a sense of accomplishment.

Sentiero Cristallina

This multi-day trek through the **Cristallina Valley** is a challenging hike for seasoned adventurers. The trail passes through remote alpine landscapes, glaciers, and high mountain passes.

- **Distance**: 32 km (multi-day)
- **Duration**: 2-3 days
- **Difficulty**: Challenging
- **Highlights**: The **Cristallina Hut** (Rifugio Cristallina) offers a stunning overnight stop with incredible views of the surrounding glaciers. The hike also offers the chance to spot alpine wildlife like ibex and marmots.
- **Best Time to Visit**: Summer, when the snow has melted and the trails are clear.
- **How to Get There**: The trail starts at **Bedretto**. You can take a bus from **Airolo** to **Bedretto**.

Monte Tamaro to Monte Lema Ridge Hike

This ridge hike is one of Ticino's most famous, connecting the peaks of **Monte Tamaro** and **Monte Lema**. It's a tough but rewarding hike with incredible views of the Alps and **Lake Maggiore**.

- **Distance**: 13 km
- **Duration**: 5-6 hours
- **Difficulty**: Challenging (steep sections and exposed ridges)
- **Highlights**: The ridge walk between the two peaks offers some of the best views in Ticino. On a clear day, you can see as far as the **Matterhorn**.
- **Best Time to Visit**: Late spring to early autumn, when the weather is clear and stable.

- **How to Get There**: Take the cable car from **Rivera** to **Monte Tamaro**. After finishing at **Monte Lema**, you can take a cable car down to **Miglieglia** and catch a bus back to Lugano.

Hiking Tips and Safety

- **Gear**: Always wear proper hiking shoes with good traction, especially for more challenging trails. Bring a backpack with water, snacks, and a map. Sunscreen, a hat, and a light jacket are also essential, even in summer, as weather conditions can change quickly.
- **Trail Safety**: Stick to marked trails and pay attention to signs. Some trails, especially at higher elevations, can become dangerous in bad weather. Always check the weather forecast before heading out and let someone know your hiking plans.
- **Best Seasons for Hiking**: Spring and early autumn are the best times to hike in Ticino, as the temperatures are cooler, and the trails are less crowded. Summer can be hot, but it's still a great time to hike if you start early in the morning.

Water Sports: Kayaking, Paddleboarding, and Boating in Ticino

Ticino's lakes and rivers offer excellent opportunities for water sports, from kayaking to paddleboarding and boating. Whether you're looking to explore the calm waters of **Lake Lugano** or paddle down the more adventurous **Verzasca River**, Ticino has plenty of options for water enthusiasts.

Kayaking in Ticino

Kayaking is one of the most popular water sports in Ticino, offering a peaceful way to explore the region's lakes and rivers. Both **Lake Lugano** and **Lake Maggiore** are perfect for beginner and experienced kayakers, with calm waters and stunning scenery.

- **Lake Lugano Kayaking**: Kayaking on **Lake Lugano** allows you to explore the quiet bays, hidden beaches, and the stunning natural landscape that surrounds the lake. Several rental stations along the lake provide kayaks for hourly or daily use.

Best Kayaking Spots:

- **Gandria** to **San Rocco**: This route offers stunning views of the mountains and the lakeside villages.
- **Morcote**: A quieter area of the lake with beautiful, calm waters ideal for beginners.
- **Rental Costs**: CHF 15-30 per hour or CHF 60-80 per day, depending on the location and type of kayak.
- **Guided Kayak Tours**: Guided tours are available for those who want to explore the lake with a knowledgeable guide. These tours typically last 2-3 hours and include all equipment.
- **Cost of Guided Tours**: CHF 50-100 per person.
- **River Kayaking on the Verzasca River**: For more experienced kayakers, the **Verzasca River** offers thrilling whitewater kayaking, with rapids and challenging sections. This is not recommended for beginners, but guided tours are available for those with intermediate or advanced skills.
- **Safety Tip**: Always wear a helmet and life jacket, and ensure you are confident in your skills before attempting river kayaking.

Paddleboarding

Paddleboarding has become increasingly popular in Ticino, thanks to the calm waters of **Lake Lugano** and **Lake Maggiore**. This relaxing activity allows you to glide across the water while enjoying the beautiful scenery.

Best Spots for Paddleboarding:

- **Lake Maggiore**: Paddleboarding is particularly popular near **Ascona**, where the water is calm, and the views are stunning.

- **Lake Lugano**: The area around **Paradiso** and **Morcote** is ideal for paddleboarding, with easy access to the water and rental stations nearby.
- **Rental Costs**: CHF 20-40 per hour for paddleboard rentals.
- **Lessons for Beginners**: If you're new to paddleboarding, lessons are available at various locations around the lakes. These lessons usually last an hour and cover basic paddling techniques and safety.
- **Cost of Lessons**: CHF 50-70 per hour.

Boating on Ticino's Lakes

Exploring Ticino's lakes by boat is a wonderful way to take in the stunning views and visit lakeside towns. You can rent motorboats, sailboats, or take a guided boat tour to see the area's best sights from the water.

- **Boat Rentals**: Motorboats and sailboats can be rented from several locations along **Lake Lugano** and **Lake Maggiore**. No boating license is required for smaller boats with limited horsepower.
- **Cost of Boat Rentals**: CHF 50-100 per hour, depending on the size and type of boat.

Best Boating Routes:

- On **Lake Lugano**, a popular route is from **Lugano** to the picturesque village of **Gandria**, where you can stop for lunch at a lakeside restaurant.
- On **Lake Maggiore**, explore the **Brissago Islands** or head to **Ascona** for a day of sightseeing and dining.

Safety Tips for Water Sports

- **Weather Awareness**: Always check the weather forecast before heading out on the water. Winds can pick up quickly, making kayaking and paddleboarding more difficult.
- **Life Jackets**: Always wear a life jacket, even if you're an experienced swimmer. Conditions on the lakes can change rapidly.

- **Best Times for Water Sports**: Early mornings or late afternoons are the best times for kayaking and paddleboarding, as the water is usually calmer and there are fewer boats on the lakes.

Mountain Biking in Ticino's Stunning Landscapes

Key Mountain Biking Routes

Ticino boasts a variety of mountain biking routes that take you through some of the most breathtaking landscapes in Switzerland. Here are a few must-ride trails:

Monte Tamaro to Monte Lema Trail One of the most popular and scenic mountain biking trails in Ticino is the route from **Monte Tamaro** to **Monte Lema**. This route is known for its stunning ridge-line views, challenging terrain, and rewarding downhill sections. It's best suited for intermediate to advanced riders, as it involves steep climbs and descents.

- **Distance**: 17 km
- **Duration**: 3-4 hours
- **Difficulty**: Intermediate to advanced
- **Highlights**: The ride offers spectacular views of **Lake Maggiore**, the **Lugano Prealps**, and, on clear days, even the **Matterhorn**. The trail is mostly single-track, with a mix of rocky and smooth sections, making it an exciting ride for experienced bikers.
- **Best Time to Ride**: Late spring to early autumn, when the trails are dry and the weather is mild.

Maggia Valley Trails The **Valle Maggia** is a paradise for bikers who love exploring remote valleys and charming mountain villages. The valley offers a network of trails that range from easy, family-friendly rides along the river to more challenging routes that take you up into the mountains.

- **Distance**: Varies by trail, ranging from 10-30 km
- **Difficulty**: Easy to moderate
- **Highlights**: The valley is known for its peaceful atmosphere, with trails passing by traditional stone houses, waterfalls, and lush forests. One of the most popular routes takes you from **Locarno** to the picturesque village of **Cevio**, where you can enjoy a relaxing break before continuing.
- **Best Time to Ride**: Spring and summer are the best seasons, with pleasant temperatures and blooming wildflowers.

Lugano Bike Route For those looking for a mix of urban and rural biking, the **Lugano Bike Route** offers a fantastic way to explore the area around **Lake Lugano**. This route is perfect for beginners and families, as it follows mostly paved paths and offers stunning views of the lake, surrounding mountains, and charming lakeside villages.

- **Distance**: 25 km
- **Difficulty**: Easy
- **Highlights**: The route starts in **Lugano** and takes you through peaceful parks, past historic villas, and along the lakefront, making it an ideal ride for those who want to combine sightseeing with a leisurely bike ride.
- **Best Time to Ride**: Year-round, though spring and autumn offer the most pleasant weather for biking.

Renting Mountain Bikes and Guided Tours

If you don't have your own bike, renting one in Ticino is easy. Several shops and rental stations are located in the major towns and near popular biking routes. Many also offer e-bikes, which can make climbing the region's steep hills much more manageable.

Where to Rent Bikes:

BikePort Lugano: Located in the center of **Lugano**, this shop offers a wide range of mountain bikes, e-bikes, and road bikes for rent.

- **Address**: Via Maggio 1, 6900 Lugano
- **Cost**: CHF 35-50 per day for standard bikes, CHF 60-90 for e-bikes.

Funivie Monte Tamaro: You can rent bikes directly at the **Monte Tamaro** cable car station, making it convenient if you're planning to ride the **Tamaro-Lema** trail.

- **Cost**: CHF 45-70 per day.

Guided Mountain Biking Tours: For those new to mountain biking or looking to explore more remote areas, guided tours are a great option. Local guides can show you the best routes, provide technical advice, and ensure a safe and enjoyable ride.

- **Mountain Bike Ticino Tours** offers guided trips throughout the region, including custom routes based on your skill level.
- **Cost**: CHF 100-150 per person for a half-day tour, including bike rental.

Accommodation and Bike-Friendly Facilities

Many hotels and lodges in Ticino cater specifically to mountain bikers, offering secure bike storage, repair stations, and even guided tours.

1. Hotel Vezia (Lugano): This bike-friendly hotel is located just outside of **Lugano** and offers secure bike storage, a repair workshop, and easy access to nearby trails.

- **Cost**: CHF 120-180 per night.

2. Ostello Monte Tamaro (Monte Tamaro): A budget-friendly option for bikers riding the **Monte Tamaro** trail, this hostel offers basic accommodations with bike storage and on-site bike rentals.

- **Cost**: CHF 80-100 per night.

Paragliding and Zip-lining: Ticino for Thrill Seekers

For those looking to take their outdoor adventures to the next level, Ticino offers some of the best paragliding and zip-lining opportunities in Switzerland. Soaring above the valleys, lakes, and mountains of Ticino is an unforgettable experience, providing breathtaking views and an adrenaline rush like no other.

Paragliding in Ticino

Ticino's varied topography makes it a prime spot for paragliding, offering perfect conditions for both beginners and experienced fliers. There are several launch sites across the region, but **Monte Lema** and **Monte Tamaro** are two of the most popular.

Monte Lema Paragliding Monte Lema is one of the top spots for paragliding in Ticino, thanks to its high altitude and spectacular views. From the launch point, you'll glide over the **Malcantone** hills, with views of **Lake Maggiore**, **Lake Lugano**, and the surrounding mountains.

- **Tandem Flights**: If you've never paraglided before, you can book a tandem flight with an experienced pilot who will guide you through the entire process. No experience is necessary, and all equipment is provided.
- **Cost of Tandem Flights**: CHF 180-250 per person.
- **Best Time for Paragliding**: Spring and summer are the best seasons for paragliding, with stable weather and clear skies.

- **How to Get There**: Take the cable car from **Miglieglia** to the summit of **Monte Lema**. Tandem flight companies often meet at the base of the cable car.

Monte Tamaro Paragliding Paragliding from **Monte Tamaro** offers a unique perspective of the **Ticino Alps**, with views stretching from the **Lugano** region to **Italy**. The thermals at **Monte Tamaro** make it a great spot for long, scenic flights.

- **Tandem Flights**: Several local operators offer tandem flights from **Monte Tamaro**. Flights typically last 20-40 minutes, depending on the wind conditions.
- **Cost of Tandem Flights**: CHF 200-250 per person.
- **How to Get There**: Take the cable car from **Rivera** to the summit of **Monte Tamaro**.

Zip-lining in Ticino

If you prefer to stay a bit closer to the ground but still want an adrenaline rush, **zip-lining** is a thrilling way to experience Ticino's landscapes. **Monte Tamaro Adventure Park** offers one of the best zip-lining experiences in the region.

Monte Tamaro Adventure Park Located near **Lugano, Monte Tamaro Adventure Park** is home to several zip lines that take you flying over the forest canopy and along mountain ridges. The park's most famous zip line spans over **400 meters** and provides breathtaking views of the surrounding valleys and lakes.

- **Cost**: CHF 35-45 per person, depending on the package.
- **Safety Requirements**: All participants must wear helmets and harnesses provided by the park. The minimum age is usually 8 years, with a minimum weight requirement of 30 kg.

OUTDOOR ADVENTURES AND ACTIVITIES

- **How to Get There**: Take the cable car from **Rivera** to **Monte Tamaro**.

Trekking Monte Carasso and Zip-lining For a more immersive adventure, combine zip-lining with hiking at **Monte Carasso**. After a short hike up the mountain, participants can take a thrilling ride down the zip line, which offers panoramic views of the **Bellinzona** region.

- **Cost**: CHF 40 per person.
- **Best Time for Zip-lining**: The best time for zip-lining in Ticino is during the summer months when the weather is stable and the skies are clear.

Practical Tips for First-Timers

- **What to Wear**: For both paragliding and zip-lining, wear comfortable clothing that allows for movement. Sturdy shoes (no sandals or flip-flops) are a must. Bring a light jacket, as temperatures can drop at higher altitudes.
- **Weather Conditions**: Paragliding and zip-lining are weather-dependent activities. Always check the forecast before booking, as strong winds or storms can lead to cancellations.
- **What to Expect**: If it's your first time paragliding or zip-lining, expect a rush of adrenaline as you take off, followed by a feeling of weightlessness as you soar through the air. Tandem flights and zip lines are safe and guided by experienced professionals.

Rock Climbing in Ticino's Valleys

Ticino is one of Switzerland's best-kept secrets for rock climbers. Known for its smooth granite cliffs, dramatic gorges, and well-maintained routes, the region attracts climbers of all skill levels. Two of the most popular climbing areas are **Ponte Brolla** and the **Verzasca Valley**, both offering a range of routes that suit beginners as well as experienced climbers.

Key Rock Climbing Spots in Ticino

Ponte Brolla Ponte Brolla, located just outside of **Locarno**, is one of the most popular climbing destinations in Ticino. The area is known for its beautiful granite walls and offers routes that range from easy to difficult. Climbers enjoy this spot not just for the quality of the climbs but for the stunning surroundings, with the **Maggia River** running through the area.

- **Climbing Levels**: Beginners to advanced

Best Routes:

- For beginners, the **Ponte Brolla Slabs** are a perfect starting point, with routes graded from **3 to 5** on the difficulty scale.
- For advanced climbers, there are multi-pitch routes that go up to **7a**, offering a more challenging ascent with spectacular views of the river and valley below.
- **Best Time to Climb**: Spring and autumn are ideal for climbing in **Ponte Brolla**, as the temperatures are mild, and the rock is less likely to be slippery from rain or heat.

Verzasca Valley The **Verzasca Valley** is famous for its clear, emerald-green river, but it's also a hidden gem for climbers. The granite walls here offer some of the best climbing in the region, with routes that vary from easy slabs to more technical climbs.

- **Climbing Levels**: Intermediate to advanced

Best Routes:

- The **Lavertezzo** area has routes that start at a moderate level, making it great for climbers with some experience.
- The multi-pitch routes at **Cugnasco** provide a challenge for more advanced climbers, with technical routes reaching up to **7b+**.
- **Scenic Highlights**: In addition to the climbs, the views of the **Verzasca River** and the famous **Ponte dei Salti** stone bridge make this area especially beautiful. Many climbers cool off with a swim in the river after a day on the cliffs.
- **Best Time to Climb**: Spring and summer are ideal, but avoid the height of summer when temperatures can rise significantly.

Gear Rentals, Climbing Schools, and Guided Tours

If you're new to climbing or need equipment, there are plenty of rental shops, climbing schools, and guided tours in the region.

Gear Rental: Many outdoor shops in **Locarno** and **Lugano** offer gear rentals, including climbing shoes, harnesses, ropes, and helmets. **Alpstation Lavizzara** in **Locarno** is a popular choice for renting climbing gear.

- **Cost**: CHF 15-30 for full-day rentals
- **Address**: Via Cittadella 7, 6600 Locarno

Climbing Schools: If you're a beginner or want to improve your skills, consider booking a session with a climbing school. **Ticino Outdoor Adventures** offers both beginner courses and advanced technique workshops in **Ponte Brolla** and the **Verzasca Valley**.

- **Cost**: CHF 80-120 per person for half-day lessons

- **Website**: www.ticinooutdoor.ch

Guided Climbing Tours: For those looking to explore the best spots with an expert guide, **Vertical Joy** offers guided multi-pitch climbing tours. These are great for intermediate to advanced climbers looking to tackle some of Ticino's most challenging routes.

- **Cost**: CHF 150-250 per person for a full-day tour
- **Contact**: +41 91 751 63 84

Safety Tips for Rock Climbing

- **Weather Conditions**: Always check the weather before heading out, as rain can make granite surfaces slippery and dangerous. Avoid climbing after heavy rainfall.
- **Bring Plenty of Water**: Especially in summer, temperatures can rise, so staying hydrated is key.
- **Rock Climbing Insurance**: Ensure your travel insurance covers rock climbing, as it's considered an extreme sport by many insurers.
- **Gear Check**: Always inspect your gear, especially ropes and harnesses, for any wear or damage before using them.

Where to Stay and Dine After a Climbing Day

After a day of climbing, you'll want a comfortable place to rest and recharge. Luckily, the **Locarno** and **Valle Verzasca** areas have a range of accommodations and restaurants perfect for tired climbers.

Ostello Cresciano: A budget-friendly option for climbers, this hostel offers simple, clean rooms and is located near some of the best climbing areas. It also has a shared kitchen for preparing meals.

- **Cost**: CHF 50-80 per night

- **Address**: Via alle Cantine 10, 6705 Cresciano

Ristorante Grotto Ponte Brolla: After a long day of climbing in **Ponte Brolla**, head to this traditional Ticinese grotto for a hearty meal. Try the local specialties like **polenta** and **braised beef**, perfect for refueling.

- **Cost**: CHF 25-40 per person
- **Address**: Via Cantonale 1, 6652 Ponte Brolla

La Stalla, Lavertezzo: Located in the heart of the **Verzasca Valley**, this rustic restaurant serves local dishes, including fresh trout from the river.

- **Cost**: CHF 30-50 per person
- **Address**: Via Cantonale, 6633 Lavertezzo

Scenic Drives Through Ticino's Alpine Roads

While rock climbing offers an up-close experience with Ticino's natural beauty, scenic drives through the region's alpine roads provide a broader view of its breathtaking landscapes. From high mountain passes to winding valley roads, these routes showcase Ticino's diverse geography and cultural landmarks.

Key Scenic Routes in Ticino

Gotthard Pass One of the most famous Alpine passes in Switzerland, the **Gotthard Pass** connects the northern part of the country to Ticino and offers an unforgettable driving experience. The road twists and turns through dramatic mountain landscapes, with panoramic views around every corner.

- **Distance**: 64 km from **Andermatt** to **Airolo**

- **Driving Time**: 1.5 hours (without stops)
- **Highlights**: The **Tremola Road**, a cobblestone stretch of the old **Gotthard Pass**, is one of the most iconic sections. Stop at the **Gotthard Hospice**, a historic building located at the top of the pass, where you can visit a museum dedicated to the history of the **Gotthard Pass**.
- **Best Time to Drive**: Late spring to early autumn, as the pass is closed in winter due to snow.
- **Driving Tip**: The road can be narrow and steep in places, so drive cautiously, especially when going downhill.

Valle Leventina The **Valle Leventina** offers a more relaxed drive through Ticino's alpine valleys. This route takes you from **Airolo** down to **Biasca**, passing through charming villages, forests, and alongside the **Ticino River**.

- **Distance**: 40 km
- **Driving Time**: 1 hour
- **Highlights**: Stop in the village of **Faido**, known for its beautiful waterfalls, or visit the Romanesque church of **San Nicolao** in **Giornico**, which dates back to the 12th century.
- **Best Time to Drive**: Year-round, but spring and autumn are particularly beautiful when the valley is lush and green.

Lukmanier Pass For those looking for a quieter alternative to the Gotthard, the **Lukmanier Pass** offers equally stunning views with less traffic. The pass connects **Disentis** in **Graubünden** to **Biasca** in Ticino and takes you through peaceful alpine meadows and past serene lakes.

- **Distance**: 45 km
- **Driving Time**: 1.5 hours
- **Highlights**: The **Santa Maria Monastery** in **Disentis** is a must-see before you begin your drive, and there are several scenic viewpoints along the pass where you can stop for photos.
- **Best Time to Drive**: Summer and early autumn. The pass is typically

closed from November to May due to snow.

Practical Information for Scenic Drives

- **Road Conditions**: While the roads in Ticino are generally well-maintained, some mountain passes can be narrow and winding. Make sure to check the weather and road conditions before heading out, as snow or rain can make driving difficult.

Driving Tips:

- Always keep an eye on your speed, especially on steep descents.
- Be prepared for sudden weather changes, particularly in the higher passes.
- Make sure your car is in good condition, with tires suitable for mountain driving.

Where to Stop for Food and Sightseeing:
Ristorante Tremola San Gottardo (Gotthard Pass): Located at the top of the pass, this restaurant offers traditional Swiss dishes with a view of the surrounding mountains.

- **Cost**: CHF 25-40 per person
- **Address**: Via Tremola 1, 6780 Airolo

Grotto dei Pescatori (Valle Leventina): A cozy spot in **Faido** serving local Ticinese dishes, including **risotto** and **minestrone**.

- **Cost**: CHF 20-35 per person
- **Address**: Via alla Stazione, 6760 Faido

Best Times for Scenic Drives

- **Spring and Autumn**: These are the best times for scenic drives, as the weather is mild and the landscapes are at their most vibrant. In spring, you'll see the valleys come alive with wildflowers, while autumn offers brilliant foliage and crisp, clear skies.
- **Winter**: Many high-altitude passes, like the **Gotthard Pass**, are closed in winter, but lower routes like **Valle Leventina** remain open. Be prepared for snowy conditions and always carry chains if driving in winter.

Parco Ciani: Lugano's Favorite Family Park

One of the most beautiful parks in Ticino, **Parco Ciani** is located in the heart of **Lugano**, right on the shores of **Lake Lugano**. This expansive green space is perfect for families looking for a relaxing day outdoors, offering plenty of activities to keep kids entertained while parents enjoy the scenery.

What to Expect

Parco Ciani is often referred to as the "green lung" of Lugano, covering over **63,000 square meters**. The park is a mix of manicured lawns, shady trees, colorful flower beds, and walking paths that meander along the lakefront. For children, the park features an extensive **playground** area equipped with swings, slides, and climbing frames.

- **Playground Area**: The playground is a favorite among locals, with well-maintained equipment that caters to children of all ages. There's plenty of seating nearby for parents to relax while keeping an eye on their kids.
- **Picnic Areas**: There are several picnic spots throughout the park, many with tables and benches under large trees for shade. Families can bring

their own food, or grab a bite from nearby cafés and restaurants.
- **Walking Paths**: The park's paved walking paths are ideal for families with strollers or young children on scooters. The paths wind through the park, offering scenic views of the lake, the surrounding mountains, and the historic **Villa Ciani**.

Practical Details

- **Entry**: Free
- **Opening Hours**: Open daily from sunrise to sunset.
- **Facilities**: Public restrooms are available near the playground and main entrance. The park is stroller-friendly with wide, flat paths.
- **Nearby Dining**: If you don't want to pack a picnic, there are several family-friendly restaurants near the park, including **Ristorante La Cucina di Alice**, located right on the lakeshore.
- **Cost**: CHF 20-40 per person for a casual lunch.
- **Address**: Via Al Lago, 6900 Lugano

Al Maglio Zoo: A Fun Day with Animals

Located in **Magliaso**, about 15 minutes from **Lugano, Al Maglio Zoo** is a popular destination for families looking to spend a day with animals. The zoo is home to a variety of species, including exotic animals such as lions, tigers, monkeys, and birds, as well as local farm animals.

What to Expect

Al Maglio Zoo offers a fun and educational experience for children, who can learn about different animals and their habitats. The zoo is well-organized, with shaded paths that lead visitors through the various enclosures. Kids especially love the petting zoo area, where they can interact with friendly goats, sheep, and ponies.

- **Animal Encounters**: The zoo has a variety of animals from around

the world, including big cats, reptiles, and tropical birds. There are also several feeding times throughout the day, where visitors can watch the zookeepers interact with the animals.
- **Petting Zoo**: For younger children, the petting zoo is always a highlight. Here, kids can feed and pet farm animals like goats and rabbits. The staff is friendly and knowledgeable, making it a fun and safe experience.
- **Playground**: After exploring the zoo, families can take a break at the on-site playground, which has slides, swings, and climbing structures.

Practical Details

- **Entry Fee**: CHF 12 for adults, CHF 6 for children (3-12 years old). Children under 3 enter free.
- **Opening Hours**: Open daily from **9:00 AM to 6:00 PM** (spring and summer). The zoo closes at **5:00 PM** during autumn and winter.
- **Facilities**: The zoo offers picnic areas, restrooms, and a small café that serves snacks, sandwiches, and ice cream.
- **How to Get There**: **Al Maglio Zoo** is located at **Via Stazione 1, 6983 Magliaso**, and can be easily reached by car or public transport. Parking is available on-site, and there's a train station nearby, with trains running from **Lugano** to **Magliaso**.
- **Website**: www.zooalmaglio.ch

Swissminiatur: A Family Favorite in Melide

Though not a zoo or playground, **Swissminiatur** in **Melide** is another must-visit for families. This open-air park features miniature models of famous Swiss landmarks, castles, and towns, all built to scale. It's an educational and fun way for children to learn about Switzerland's geography and culture.

- **Entry Fee**: CHF 19 for adults, CHF 12 for children (6-15 years old). Children under 6 enter free.
- **Opening Hours**: Open daily from **9:00 AM to 6:00 PM** (April to

October).
- **Facilities**: The park includes picnic areas, a playground, and a small restaurant.
- **Location**: Via Cantonale, 6815 Melide, a 15-minute drive from **Lugano**.

Monte Tamaro Adventure Park: A Full Day of Family Fun

For families with older children looking for more adventurous activities, **Monte Tamaro Adventure Park** offers a variety of exciting options. Located just a short drive from **Lugano**, **Monte Tamaro** is a mountain-top park that features zip lines, mountain biking, and a large outdoor playground.

What to Expect

- **Outdoor Playground**: The playground at **Monte Tamaro** is perfect for kids to burn off energy. It's located at the top of the **Monte Tamaro** cable car and includes climbing structures, slides, and swings.
- **Zip Line Adventure**: For older children and parents looking for a thrill, the park's **zip line** is a must-try. The zip line runs 400 meters down the mountain, offering spectacular views and an adrenaline-pumping experience.
- **Mountain Biking**: The park also offers mountain biking trails suitable for families with older children. Bikes can be rented at the top of the mountain.
- **Parco Avventura**: A ropes course with different levels of difficulty that's perfect for active families. The course includes bridges, nets, and zip lines among the trees.

Practical Details

- **Entry Fee**: Free to enter the park, but additional costs apply for zip-lining and other activities.
- Zip line: CHF 35 per person
- Ropes course: CHF 20-35 depending on the course
- **Cable Car Fee**: CHF 20 for adults, CHF 10 for children (round trip)
- **Opening Hours**: Open daily from **9:00 AM to 5:00 PM** during the summer months.
- **Facilities**: There are picnic areas, public restrooms, and a restaurant at the top of the mountain, offering traditional Swiss meals and snacks.
- **How to Get There**: Take the cable car from **Rivera**, located about 15 minutes from **Lugano**, to the top of **Monte Tamaro**. Parking is available at the cable car station.
- **Website**: www.montetamaro.ch

Special Events and Seasonal Activities

Ticino's parks and outdoor attractions often host special events and activities for families, especially during school holidays and the summer season.

Nature Walks at Parco Ciani: During the spring and summer, **Parco Ciani** offers guided nature walks for families. These walks are designed to teach children about the local flora and fauna in a fun and engaging way.

- **Cost**: Free
- **Dates**: Typically held on weekends; check the local tourist office for schedules.

Educational Programs at Al Maglio Zoo: The zoo offers seasonal educational programs for children, such as animal feeding demonstrations and behind-the-scenes tours with the zookeepers. These programs are available during the summer months and provide a more interactive experience.

- **Cost**: CHF 5 per child, in addition to regular zoo entry.

Family Days at Monte Tamaro: In the summer, **Monte Tamaro** hosts special family days, featuring discounted rates for zip-lining and biking, along with free entertainment for kids like face painting and scavenger hunts.

- **Cost**: Varies depending on activities.

Beaches and Lakeside Fun

Best Beaches on Lake Maggiore and Lake Lugano

Both **Lake Maggiore** and **Lake Lugano** have many beaches where you can relax, swim, and enjoy the sunshine. Here's a guide to the top beaches around these lakes, highlighting those with the best water quality, scenic views, and facilities.

Lido di Locarno – Lake Maggiore

Lido di Locarno is one of the most popular beach spots on **Lake Maggiore**. It's a well-maintained lido that offers plenty of activities for both adults and children, along with beautiful views of the surrounding mountains.

- **Water Quality and Beach Conditions**: The water at **Lido di Locarno** is known for being clear and calm, making it a great place for swimming. The beach is a mix of sand and pebbles, with a large grassy area for sunbathing.
- **Facilities**: This lido has everything you need for a comfortable beach day. There are swimming pools, including a heated outdoor pool, water slides for kids, and a wellness center with a sauna. The beach also has changing rooms, showers, and shaded areas.
- **Food and Drink**: There's a café on-site serving snacks, drinks, and light meals, perfect for a quick bite between swims.

- **Lifeguards**: Lifeguards are on duty during the summer season, ensuring a safe environment for everyone.
- **Entry Fees**: CHF 10-15 for adults, CHF 6-10 for children, depending on the season.
- **Location**: Via Gioacchino Respini 11, 6600 Locarno
- **How to Get There**: Easily accessible by foot from **Locarno** town center or by car, with parking available on-site.

Lido di Lugano – Lake Lugano

For those looking for a beautiful beach near the city, **Lido di Lugano** is an excellent choice. Located within walking distance from **Lugano's** town center, this beach is ideal for anyone looking to mix a day of swimming with some city exploration.

- **Water Quality and Beach Conditions**: The water is clean and inviting, and the beach area consists of fine sand, making it a favorite for sunbathers. There's also a large grassy area where you can spread out and relax.
- **Facilities**: **Lido di Lugano** has a variety of pools, including an Olympic-size pool, diving boards, and a special area for children with water features. There are also showers, changing rooms, and sunbeds available for rent.
- **Food and Drink**: The on-site restaurant offers a wide range of Italian dishes, including pizza, pasta, and salads, as well as snacks like ice cream and drinks.
- **Lifeguards**: Lifeguards are present during opening hours.
- **Entry Fees**: CHF 10 for adults, CHF 5 for children.
- **Location**: Via Lido, 6900 Lugano
- **How to Get There**: A short walk from **Lugano's** town center or by public transport (bus stop: **Lugano Lido**).

Lido di Ascona – Lake Maggiore

Lido di Ascona is a stunning beach with one of the longest sandy shorelines on **Lake Maggiore**. The soft sand and clear waters make it one of the most relaxing places to spend a day.

- **Water Quality and Beach Conditions**: The water here is incredibly clear, and the beach is sandy, making it ideal for swimming and sunbathing. The view across the lake is spectacular, especially at sunset.
- **Facilities**: **Lido di Ascona** has excellent facilities, including changing rooms, showers, and beach chairs available for rent. There's also a large grassy area if you prefer to set up on the lawn. The lido also offers boat and pedal boat rentals for those who want to explore the lake further.
- **Food and Drink**: A beach café serves fresh, local dishes, as well as light snacks and cold drinks throughout the day.
- **Lifeguards**: Lifeguards are on duty throughout the summer.
- **Entry Fees**: CHF 10 for adults, CHF 5 for children.
- **Location**: Via Lido, 6612 Ascona
- **How to Get There**: A short walk from **Ascona** town center, or by car with parking available nearby.

Family-Friendly Beach Spots with Shallow Waters

When traveling with young children, it's important to find beaches that are safe and family-friendly. The following spots offer calm, shallow waters, making them ideal for families with young kids. Many of these beaches also offer playgrounds, shaded areas, and picnic spots for a full day of fun.

Lido San Domenico – Lake Lugano

Lido San Domenico is a quieter, family-friendly beach located just outside the busy center of **Lugano**. The calm, shallow waters make it perfect for families with small children who want a safe spot to swim.

- **Water Quality and Beach Conditions**: The water is clean and clear,

with a shallow area that's ideal for kids to splash around safely. The beach is a mix of sand and small pebbles, but there are plenty of grassy spots for picnicking.
- **Facilities**: While smaller than some of the other lidos, **Lido San Domenico** offers basic amenities such as changing rooms, showers, and a small snack bar. There's also a playground nearby, so kids can switch between swimming and playing.
- **Family-Friendly Features**: The beach has shallow waters and plenty of shade from nearby trees, making it comfortable for families to relax.
- **Entry Fees**: Free
- **Location**: Via San Domenico, 6900 Lugano
- **How to Get There**: By car or public transport (bus stop: **Lugano San Domenico**), with limited parking available nearby.

Lido di Brissago – Lake Maggiore

Another great option for families is **Lido di Brissago**, located on the quiet eastern shore of **Lake Maggiore**. Known for its peaceful atmosphere and shallow waters, this is a perfect beach for families with young kids.

- **Water Quality and Beach Conditions**: The water here is shallow for a long distance, making it a safe place for children to swim. The beach is mostly grassy, with some sandy areas near the shore.
- **Facilities**: The beach has good amenities, including changing rooms, showers, and picnic tables. There's also a playground for children and a large shaded area for parents who want to relax out of the sun.
- **Family-Friendly Features**: The beach offers pedal boat rentals, which are always a hit with families, and there are plenty of open spaces for kids to run around.
- **Entry Fees**: Free
- **Location**: Via Lido 18, 6614 Brissago
- **How to Get There**: Easily accessible by car, with parking available nearby.

Lido di Caslano – Lake Lugano

Lido di Caslano is located in a picturesque setting near **Caslano** village and is a popular spot for families looking for a quieter beach experience. The beach is surrounded by trees and offers plenty of shade and grassy areas for picnics.

- **Water Quality and Beach Conditions**: The water here is shallow and calm, making it perfect for children to swim safely. The beach is sandy with a large grassy area where families can relax and set up picnic blankets.
- **Facilities**: There are basic facilities available, including changing rooms, showers, and a snack bar that serves drinks, ice cream, and sandwiches. The nearby park also has a playground, which is ideal for young kids.
- **Family-Friendly Features**: In addition to the playground, the lido offers family-friendly events during the summer, including outdoor movie nights and kids' entertainment programs.
- **Entry Fees**: Free
- **Location**: Via Cantonale, 6987 Caslano
- **How to Get There**: By car, with parking available nearby, or by train (Caslano station is a short walk from the beach).

Special Events and Seasonal Activities at the Beaches

Ticino's lakeside beaches often host special events and activities during the summer months, which can be especially fun for families. Here are a few seasonal highlights:

- **Lido di Lugano Summer Events**: During the summer, **Lido di Lugano** often hosts beach volleyball tournaments and family-friendly festivals. These events usually include live music, games for kids, and food stalls serving local specialties.
- **Outdoor Movie Nights at Lido di Caslano**: In July and August, **Lido di Caslano** organizes outdoor movie nights for families. These

screenings take place right on the beach, and children can enjoy a movie under the stars while parents relax with a drink from the beach bar.
- **Paddleboarding Lessons at Lido di Ascona**: **Lido di Ascona** offers family-friendly paddleboarding lessons during the summer. These lessons are a great way for families to learn a new sport together in a safe, supervised environment.

Water Sports: Swimming, Boating, and More

Ticino's lakes are a playground for water sports enthusiasts. From paddleboarding on serene waters to jet skiing at thrilling speeds, there's something for everyone, no matter your skill level. Below are some of the best beaches for water sports, along with companies that offer rentals, lessons, and guided tours.

Paddleboarding and Kayaking on Lake Lugano

If you're looking for a peaceful yet invigorating water sport, **paddleboarding** and **kayaking** on **Lake Lugano** are perfect activities. The calm waters make it ideal for beginners, while the stunning views of the surrounding mountains add a touch of serenity to your adventure.

Best Beaches for Paddleboarding:

- **Lido di Lugano**: This lido offers an easy entry point to the water and is one of the best places to rent a paddleboard or kayak. The waters near **Lugano** are generally calm, providing a smooth ride, and you can paddle out to get views of the city from the water.
- **Gandria**: If you prefer a quieter spot, head to the village of **Gandria**, where you can rent paddleboards and explore the beautiful inlets around this historic lakeside village.

Rental and Lesson Information:

SUP Lugano offers rentals and paddleboarding lessons for beginners. Their experienced instructors ensure that you're confident before heading out on the water.

- **Cost**: CHF 20-30 per hour for rentals; lessons start at CHF 50.
- **Location**: Via Lido, 6900 Lugano
- **Contact**: +41 91 922 95 25

Kayak Lugano provides kayak rentals and guided tours around **Lake Lugano**.

- **Cost**: CHF 15-30 per hour, with guided tours starting at CHF 60 per person.
- **Location**: Lido di Lugano, Via Lido, 6900 Lugano
- **Website**: www.kayaklugano.ch

Windsurfing and Sailing on Lake Maggiore

For those seeking more wind-powered fun, **Lake Maggiore** is the go-to spot for **windsurfing** and **sailing**. The lake's size and occasional breezes create ideal conditions for these activities, whether you're a beginner or an experienced sailor.

Best Beaches for Windsurfing:

- **Lido di Ascona**: With good winds, **Lido di Ascona** is one of the most popular spots for windsurfing. The lido also has plenty of space for relaxing after a session on the water.
- **Brissago**: The waters around **Brissago** are slightly more challenging, making it a favorite among experienced windsurfers.

Sailing Schools and Rentals:

Ascona Sailing Club offers lessons for beginners and more advanced sailors. You can rent small sailboats for a few hours or take a course to improve your skills.

- **Cost**: CHF 40-60 per hour for rentals; sailing lessons start at CHF 80.
- **Location**: Via Lido, 6612 Ascona
- **Website**: www.asconasailingclub.ch

Windsurf Maggiore in **Brissago** provides windsurfing rentals and lessons. Whether you're just starting or looking to practice your skills, their instructors will help you master the basics.

- **Cost**: CHF 25 per hour for windsurf rentals; CHF 50 for a one-hour lesson.
- **Location**: Via Lido, 6614 Brissago
- **Contact**: +41 91 793 12 34

Jet Skiing and Speed Boating

For adrenaline seekers, **jet skiing** and **speed boating** are exciting ways to experience Ticino's lakes. The feeling of zooming across the water with the wind in your hair is an unforgettable thrill.

Best Beaches for Jet Skiing:

- **Lido di Lugano**: If you're looking for the excitement of jet skiing, **Lido di Lugano** offers rentals for those looking to add a little speed to their day on the lake.
- **Morcote**: For a more peaceful location, **Morcote**, a beautiful lakeside village on **Lake Lugano**, offers jet ski rentals with views of the lush hills and charming buildings.

Jet Ski Rentals:

Jet Ski Lugano offers hourly rentals and guided tours around the lake. Whether you're an experienced rider or a first-timer, the instructors provide thorough safety briefings.

- **Cost**: CHF 80 per hour, with discounts for multiple hours or group bookings.
- **Location**: Via Lido, 6900 Lugano
- **Contact**: +41 91 950 34 56

Speedboat Lugano: For those who prefer something a little more relaxed but still fast-paced, **Speedboat Lugano** rents motorboats for an exciting day out on the water.

- **Cost**: CHF 100 per hour (no boating license required for small boats).
- **Location**: Porto di Lugano, 6900 Lugano
- **Website**: www.speedboatlugano.ch

Swimming and Snorkeling

While paddleboarding and jet skiing are thrilling, sometimes all you want to do is swim in the refreshing lake waters. Ticino's beaches offer excellent opportunities for a day of **swimming**, with some spots even ideal for **snorkeling**.

Best Beaches for Swimming:

- **Lido di Ascona**: Known for its sandy shores and clear, shallow waters, **Lido di Ascona** is one of the best places for a refreshing swim. The water here is usually calm, making it perfect for all ages.
- **San Nazzaro**: Located on **Lake Maggiore**, **San Nazzaro** is a quieter beach that offers crystal-clear water, perfect for both swimming and snorkeling. You can explore underwater rock formations and spot a

variety of fish near the shore.
- **Snorkeling**: While **Lake Lugano** is not known for tropical marine life, the waters are clear enough in some areas for a bit of fun snorkeling. **Gandria** is a top spot for snorkeling, with rocky shores and shallow waters where you can observe the underwater world.

Lakeside Dining: Cafés and Restaurants with a View

After a day on the water, there's nothing better than enjoying a delicious meal or a refreshing drink while taking in the views of **Lake Lugano** or **Lake Maggiore**. From casual cafés to fine dining, there's no shortage of places to eat, and many of these spots offer picturesque lakeside settings.

Cafés for a Quick Bite

For a casual meal or snack after a swim or paddleboarding session, head to one of these lakeside cafés.

Rivetta Tell – Lake Lugano Situated right by the lake in **Lugano**, **Rivetta Tell** is a perfect spot for a light lunch or coffee break. The outdoor terrace offers stunning views of **Lake Lugano**, making it a great place to unwind after a busy day of water sports.

- **Recommended Dishes**: Try their fresh **bruschetta** or **homemade gelato**.
- **Cost**: CHF 15-30 per person
- **Location**: Via Lungo Lago, 6900 Lugano
- **Contact**: +41 91 921 25 47

Bar Lido Ascona – Lake Maggiore Located on the beach at **Lido di Ascona**, this café serves simple but delicious meals like salads, sandwiches, and ice cream. It's the perfect place to grab a bite in between swimming and sunbathing.

- **Recommended Dishes**: Their **pizza** is a local favorite, and the homemade **lemon sorbet** is refreshing on a hot day.
- **Cost**: CHF 10-25 per person
- **Location**: Via Lido, 6612 Ascona
- **Contact**: +41 91 791 14 44

Fine Dining with a View

For a more luxurious dining experience, several restaurants offer gourmet meals with spectacular lakeside views.

Ristorante Vetta – Monte Brè, Lake Lugano Set high on **Monte Brè**, **Ristorante Vetta** offers some of the most breathtaking views of **Lake Lugano** and the surrounding mountains. After a day of water activities, this is the perfect spot to enjoy a leisurely meal while watching the sunset.

- **Recommended Dishes**: The **risotto ai funghi** (mushroom risotto) is a house specialty, and their **fresh fish** from **Lake Lugano** is always popular.
- **Cost**: CHF 40-60 per person
- **Location**: Via Brè, 6900 Lugano
- **Contact**: +41 91 971 29 72

Ristorante Seven – Ascona, Lake Maggiore For a sophisticated dining experience, head to **Ristorante Seven** in **Ascona**. Overlooking **Lake Maggiore**, this stylish restaurant offers gourmet Mediterranean cuisine with a focus on fresh, local ingredients.

- **Recommended Dishes**: Their **seafood pasta** is a must-try, and they also offer an excellent selection of local wines.
- **Cost**: CHF 50-80 per person

- **Location**: Via Moscia 2, 6612 Ascona
- **Website**: www.ristorante-seven.ch

Practical Tips for Lakeside Fun
- **Best Time for Water Sports**: Early mornings or late afternoons are ideal for paddleboarding, kayaking, and windsurfing, as the water is usually calmer, and there are fewer people on the beaches.
- **Swimming Safety**: Always check for lifeguards if you're swimming with young children or are unfamiliar with the waters. The larger lidos like **Lido di Lugano** and **Lido di Ascona** have lifeguards on duty during peak season.
- **Sun Protection**: The sun can be strong during the summer, so don't forget to pack sunscreen, sunglasses, and a hat. Many of the beaches offer shaded areas, but it's always a good idea to bring your own umbrella or find a spot with natural shade.

Dining in Ticino

Ticino's Culinary Scene: What to Expect

In Ticino, food is deeply rooted in tradition, with many recipes passed down through generations. The region's cuisine is heavily influenced by its proximity to **Italy**, so you'll find a lot of similarities with Italian food, such as the use of olive oil, fresh herbs, and pasta. At the same time, there's a distinctly Swiss touch, with dishes that celebrate the local produce, mountain herbs, and hearty, comforting ingredients.

Key Ingredients

1. **Polenta**: Made from ground cornmeal, polenta is a staple in Ticino and can be served soft or grilled. It's often paired with **braised meats** like **rabbit** or **beef**, or enjoyed as a side dish with stews.
2. **Risotto**: Unlike the creamy risotto found in other parts of Italy, Ticino's risotto tends to be a bit drier and is often made with local wine or broth. **Risotto al Merlot** is a local favorite, using Ticino's own **Merlot wine**.
3. **Freshwater Fish**: With Ticino bordered by two lakes—**Lake Lugano** and **Lake Maggiore**—freshwater fish like **perch** and **pike** are commonly featured on menus. These fish are often served grilled, with simple but flavorful accompaniments.

4. **Grotto Cuisine**: Grottos are traditional eateries where locals and tourists alike gather for hearty, rustic meals. These restaurants are often situated in shady, forested areas, providing a cozy, outdoor dining experience with dishes like **minestrone, polenta,** and **charcuterie**.

Must-Try Local Dishes: Risotto, Polenta, and More

Ticino offers a variety of iconic dishes that every visitor should try. Below, we dive into the most famous foods in the region, explain their origins, and recommend where to find the most authentic versions.

Risotto al Merlot

Risotto is a classic Italian dish, but in Ticino, it's often made with a local twist. **Risotto al Merlot** is a rich, flavorful dish that incorporates **Merlot wine** produced in the region. The wine gives the risotto a deep, earthy flavor and a vibrant color.

- **Origins**: Ticino is famous for its **Merlot wine**, which is grown in the region's many vineyards. This dish brings together the region's love of risotto with its prized local wine, creating a perfect blend of Italian and Swiss influences.

Where to Try It:
Ristorante Vetta (Monte Brè): Known for its spectacular views over **Lake Lugano**, this restaurant serves an excellent **Risotto al Merlot** with locally sourced ingredients.

- **Cost**: CHF 35-45 for a main course.
- **Location**: Via Monte Brè, 6900 Lugano

Grotto San Michele (Lugano): For a more rustic experience, try this dish at **Grotto San Michele**, located within **Parco Ciani**.

- **Cost**: CHF 25-35
- **Location**: Viale Carlo Cattaneo, 6900 Lugano

Polenta

Polenta is a versatile and essential dish in Ticino, often served as a side or main course. It can be enjoyed soft and creamy or grilled, and it pairs well with many different toppings, from melted cheese to braised meats like **coniglio (rabbit)** or **wild boar**.

- **Origins**: Polenta's origins are deeply tied to the rural communities of Ticino, where corn was historically one of the few crops that thrived in the mountainous terrain.

Where to Try It:

1. **Grotto della Salute** (Mendrisio): Known for its traditional polenta served with slow-cooked meats, this grotto is a favorite among locals.

- **Cost**: CHF 20-30
- **Location**: Via Generoso, 6850 Mendrisio

2. **Grotto Morchino** (Lugano): This hidden gem offers **polenta** served with **rabbit**, a classic pairing in Ticino.

- **Cost**: CHF 25-40
- **Location**: Via Massagno 36, 6900 Lugano

Pesce Persico (Perch)

Freshwater perch, known locally as **pesce persico**, is a delicacy in Ticino.

The fish is typically caught in **Lake Lugano** or **Lake Maggiore** and is often served **grilled** or **fried**, accompanied by simple sides like **risotto** or **sautéed vegetables**.

- **Origins**: The abundance of freshwater fish in Ticino's lakes has made **pesce persico** a staple of local cuisine. The fish is prized for its tender, delicate flavor and is often served with light seasonings that let the natural taste shine.

Where to Try It:
1. Ristorante Portovino (Morcote): Located right on the shores of **Lake Lugano**, this restaurant is famous for its perch dishes, especially **pesce persico alla griglia** (grilled perch).

- **Cost**: CHF 40-60
- **Location**: Via Cantonale, 6922 Morcote

2. Ristorante Lago (Ascona): This lakeside restaurant offers **fried perch** with a side of lemon risotto, a delicious way to enjoy local fish.

- **Cost**: CHF 35-55
- **Location**: Via Lido 17, 6612 Ascona

Luganighetta
Luganighetta is a type of pork sausage that's unique to Ticino. It's made with a mix of pork, spices, and wine, giving it a rich, savory flavor. **Luganighetta** is often grilled and served with **polenta** or as part of a mixed grill.

- **Origins**: **Luganighetta** has its roots in the rural traditions of Ticino, where pork was a key part of the diet. The sausage is named after the city of **Lugano**, where it remains a popular dish.

Where to Try It:
1. **Grotto Ticinese** (Lugano): This rustic grotto serves up **Luganighetta** with **polenta** and sautéed greens, offering a hearty taste of Ticino's countryside.

- **Cost**: CHF 20-30
- **Location**: Via San Giorgio, 6900 Lugano

2. **Ristorante Al Grottino** (Mendrisio): For a more refined take on this classic dish, **Al Grottino** offers **Luganighetta** served with local vegetables and red wine reduction.

- **Cost**: CHF 30-45
- **Location**: Piazza del Ponte, 6850 Mendrisio

Zincarlin Cheese

One of Ticino's most beloved cheeses, **Zincarlin** is a soft, creamy cheese made from cow's milk and spiced with black pepper. It's often served as part of a **charcuterie board**, paired with local wines.

- **Origins**: **Zincarlin** is produced in the valleys of **Muggio** and is deeply tied to the agricultural traditions of the region. The cheese is known for its rich, creamy texture and slightly tangy flavor.

Where to Try It:
1. **Ristorante Grand Hotel Villa Castagnola** (Lugano): This fine dining restaurant offers **Zincarlin** as part of its **degustation menu**, paired with local wines and artisanal bread.

- **Cost**: CHF 90-120 for a tasting menu.
- **Location**: Viale Castagnola 31, 6900 Lugano

2. **Grotto Pozzoni** (Mendrisio): For a more casual experience, try **Zincarlin** at this traditional grotto, where it's served with **charcuterie** and local bread.

- **Cost**: CHF 25-35
- **Location**: Via Generoso, 6850 Mendrisio

Dining Traditions and Outdoor Dining

Ticino's culinary culture is not only about the food but also about the atmosphere. Dining is often an outdoor affair, particularly in the region's many **grotto** restaurants. These open-air eateries are typically located in shaded, wooded areas and serve hearty, rustic meals that reflect the simplicity and beauty of Ticino's food culture.

- **Outdoor Dining**: Many of Ticino's restaurants take full advantage of the region's warm climate by offering outdoor seating. Dining al fresco is common, especially in the warmer months, when locals and visitors alike flock to the terraces of lakeside restaurants or the shaded gardens of grottoes.
- **Vineyard Cuisine**: Ticino's vineyards produce some of Switzerland's best wines, and many wineries offer **wine-tasting experiences** paired with local dishes. This is a great way to sample the region's food and wine in a picturesque setting.

Popular Grottos for Outdoor Dining
1. **Grotto San Rocco** (Morcote): Tucked away in the hills above **Lake**

Lugano, this grotto offers a peaceful dining experience with views of the lake. The menu includes **risotto, polenta**, and fresh fish, all served in a charming outdoor setting.

- **Cost**: CHF 30-50 per person
- **Location**: Via Grotto, 6922 Morcote

2. Grotto Bundi (Lugano): One of the most authentic **grotto** experiences in Ticino, **Grotto Bundi** serves traditional dishes like **braised rabbit** with **polenta** and **Zincarlin cheese**. The outdoor seating is shaded by trees, offering a cool respite from the summer sun.

- **Cost**: CHF 25-40 per person

Location: Via Breganzona 10, 6900 Lugano

Best Fine Dining Restaurants in Ticino

If you're looking for a luxury dining experience in Ticino, there are several high-end restaurants that offer unforgettable meals. Many of these restaurants are led by acclaimed chefs and feature tasting menus that highlight the region's local ingredients and culinary traditions. Here's a look at some of the best fine dining options in Ticino.

Ristorante Ecco – Ascona

Ristorante Ecco is one of the most prestigious fine dining establishments in Ticino, located in the five-star **Hotel Giardino** in Ascona. This two-Michelin-starred restaurant is led by **Chef Rolf Fliegauf**, known for his innovative take on modern European cuisine with a focus on local ingredients. The dining experience here is luxurious and refined, with an emphasis on seasonal tasting menus.

- **Dress Code**: Smart casual; jackets for men are recommended but not required.
- **Menu Highlights**: The tasting menu changes seasonally, but past dishes have included **foie gras with truffle**, **sea bass with citrus emulsion**, and a dessert of **Ticino chestnuts**.
- **Cost**: CHF 180-250 per person for a multi-course tasting menu.
- **Reservation Tips**: Reservations are essential, and it's recommended to book at least a month in advance for weekend dining.
- **Location**: Via del Segnale 10, 6612 Ascona
- **Website**: www.ecco-ascona.ch
- **Contact**: +41 91 785 88 88

Ristorante Arté al Lago – Lugano

For fine dining with a view, **Ristorante Arté al Lago** in Lugano offers a luxurious experience. This one-Michelin-starred restaurant is located right on the shores of **Lake Lugano** and is renowned for its seafood dishes. Chef **Frank Oerthle** combines Mediterranean flavors with fresh, local ingredients, creating an elegant dining experience that showcases the beauty of the lake and mountains.

- **Dress Code**: Elegant; smart attire is preferred.
- **Menu Highlights**: Signature dishes include **lobster with saffron sauce**, **truffle risotto**, and **octopus with citrus vinaigrette**. The restaurant also offers a vegetarian tasting menu.
- **Cost**: CHF 150-200 per person for a multi-course meal.
- **Reservation Tips**: Bookings should be made at least two weeks in advance, especially for window seats with the best views of the lake.
- **Location**: Via Cortivo 13, 6900 Lugano
- **Website**: www.arteallago.ch
- **Contact**: +41 91 973 55 00

Galleria Arté – Lugano

Galleria Arté is another top-tier dining destination in Lugano, housed within the **Villa Principe Leopoldo**, a luxury hotel and former royal residence. The restaurant offers Mediterranean-inspired cuisine with a focus on local and seasonal ingredients, all presented in an elegant setting overlooking the lake.

- **Dress Code**: Smart casual; jackets for men are appreciated.
- **Menu Highlights**: **Black truffle pasta**, **veal tenderloin**, and a decadent selection of **Swiss cheeses** for dessert are among the favorites here.
- **Cost**: CHF 160-220 for a multi-course menu.
- **Reservation Tips**: Given the popularity of the restaurant and its high demand, particularly during the summer months, it's advisable to reserve your table several weeks in advance.
- **Location**: Via Montalbano 5, 6900 Lugano
- **Website**: www.villaprincipeleopoldo.ch
- **Contact**: +41 91 985 88 55

Seven Lugano – Lugano

For those seeking a contemporary dining experience with a luxurious touch, **Seven Lugano** is an excellent choice. Located on the **Lugano waterfront**, this restaurant offers a mix of modern Mediterranean cuisine with locally sourced ingredients, all served in a stylish and elegant environment. Chef **Claudio Bollini** and his team are known for their creative tasting menus and impeccable presentation.

- **Dress Code**: Smart casual; stylish but relaxed.
- **Menu Highlights**: Signature dishes include **tuna tartare with avocado**, **ravioli with lobster**, and **risotto with Parmesan and saffron**. There's also a selection of fine wines from Ticino's best vineyards.
- **Cost**: CHF 120-180 for a multi-course menu.
- **Reservation Tips**: The restaurant is popular for its lake views, so book early to secure a table on the terrace.
- **Location**: Piazza Riforma 1, 6900 Lugano

- **Website**: www.ristorante-seven.ch
- **Contact**: +41 91 290 77 77

Family-Friendly Restaurants and Cafés

Ticino is a great destination for families, and many restaurants are welcoming to children, offering **kids' menus**, **high chairs**, and even **play areas**. Below are some of the best family-friendly spots, from casual cafés to more upscale restaurants where children are always welcome.

Ristorante Al Porto – Ascona

Ristorante Al Porto is a lovely family-friendly restaurant located in the heart of **Ascona**, just steps away from **Lake Maggiore**. The menu features a wide variety of dishes that both adults and kids will enjoy, from **wood-fired pizzas** to fresh **seafood**. The outdoor terrace is particularly popular with families, as it offers beautiful views of the lake and plenty of space for children to run around.

- **Kids' Menu**: The restaurant offers a dedicated kids' menu with favorites like **pasta with tomato sauce**, **mini pizzas**, and **grilled chicken**.
- **Play Area**: There's a small play area within the restaurant, complete with coloring books and toys to keep little ones entertained.
- **Cost**: CHF 20-40 per person; kids' meals from CHF 12-15.
- **Location**: Via Borgo 4, 6612 Ascona
- **Contact**: +41 91 791 23 24

Ristorante La Cambusa – Lugano

Ristorante La Cambusa is a family-friendly restaurant near **Lake Lugano**. Known for its casual and welcoming atmosphere, it offers a wide range of dishes, from classic Italian pastas to burgers and grilled fish. The staff are friendly and attentive, making it an easy choice for families.

- **Kids' Menu**: The kids' menu features crowd-pleasers like **spaghetti with meatballs, chicken nuggets**, and **mini burgers**.
- **Family Amenities**: The restaurant provides **high chairs, coloring materials**, and a small indoor play area for younger children.
- **Cost**: CHF 20-50 per person; kids' meals from CHF 10-15.
- **Location**: Via Carona 14, 6900 Lugano
- **Contact**: +41 91 993 77 88

Ristorante Al Grottino – Mendrisio

Located in the picturesque town of **Mendrisio, Ristorante Al Grottino** is a family-friendly eatery that specializes in **traditional Ticino dishes**. The large garden area is perfect for families, offering plenty of space for kids to play while parents enjoy a leisurely meal. The menu caters to both adults and children, with a variety of hearty dishes made from fresh, local ingredients.

- **Kids' Menu**: Options include **grilled chicken, spaghetti bolognese**, and **fish fillets** with fries.
- **Play Area**: The restaurant's outdoor garden features a play area with swings and slides, making it a popular spot for families with young children.
- **Cost**: CHF 25-40 per person; kids' meals from CHF 12-15.
- **Location**: Via Vignalunga 8, 6850 Mendrisio
- **Contact**: +41 91 647 12 34

La Fermata Café – Lugano

La Fermata Café is a cozy, family-friendly café located in the center of **Lugano**. With its laid-back atmosphere, this is a great spot for a casual meal or snack with the kids. The café offers a wide selection of sandwiches, salads, and pastries, along with freshly squeezed juices and coffee. There's also a small play corner for children, complete with toys and books.

- **Kids' Menu**: While there's no specific kids' menu, the café offers child-friendly options like **ham and cheese sandwiches**, **fruit smoothies**, and **mini croissants**.
- **Family Amenities**: The café provides **high chairs**, **coloring books**, and toys to keep younger guests entertained.
- **Cost**: CHF 10-20 per person.
- **Location**: Via della Posta 7, 6900 Lugano
- **Contact**: +41 91 922 33 44

Grotto del Parco – Bellinzona

For families visiting **Bellinzona**, **Grotto del Parco** is a great option for a casual, family-friendly meal. This restaurant is set in a beautiful park, providing plenty of space for kids to explore and play while the adults enjoy a meal. The menu focuses on local Ticinese dishes, and there are several child-friendly options available.

- **Kids' Menu**: The restaurant offers **polenta with cheese**, **mini pizzas**, and **grilled chicken** for children.
- **Outdoor Play Area**: The park surrounding the grotto includes a playground, making it an ideal spot for families to spend a leisurely afternoon.
- **Cost**: CHF 25-45 per person; kids' meals from CHF 10-15.
- **Location**: Via Parco 1, 6500 Bellinzona
- **Contact**: +41 91 821 12 45

Street Food and Market Eats: Where the Locals Go

For a true taste of Ticino, it's best to head to the vibrant markets and street food stalls scattered throughout the region. These spots are where locals go to buy fresh produce, enjoy quick bites, and sample traditional foods. You'll find everything from **salumi** (cured meats) and **formaggio** (cheeses) to fresh fruits, vegetables, and regional specialties.

Mercato di Bellinzona: A Local Favorite

Mercato di Bellinzona, held every Saturday in the historic town of **Bellinzona**, is one of the most popular markets in Ticino. The market is a hub of activity, offering everything from fresh produce to locally made cheeses and meats. Locals come here not only to shop but also to catch up with friends and enjoy a snack at one of the food stalls.

Popular Items:

- **Ticino's salumi**: Cured meats such as **salame** and **prosciutto crudo** are always in demand, perfect for a picnic or light lunch.
- **Cheeses**: Local cheeses like **Zincarlin** and **Formaggini** are favorites, often served with crusty bread and fresh olives.
- **Chestnut honey**: A local delicacy, this rich, flavorful honey is produced in the chestnut groves of Ticino and pairs wonderfully with cheeses.

Street Food Highlights:

- **Polenta e brasato** (polenta with braised beef) is often served at the market, giving you a hearty, filling meal for just a few francs.
- Freshly baked **focaccia** and **pane ticinese** (a local bread) can be found at many stalls, and they make for a great snack on the go.

Practical Information:

- **Location**: Piazza Nosetto, 6500 Bellinzona
- **Opening Hours**: Saturdays, 8:00 AM – 12:30 PM
- **How to Get There**: Easily accessible from **Bellinzona** train station, a short 10-minute walk from the market. Parking is available nearby for those driving.

Mercato di Lugano: The Bustling Heart of the City

Held in **Piazza della Riforma** in the heart of **Lugano**, this vibrant market is a must-visit for anyone wanting to dive into Ticino's food culture. The **Mercato di Lugano** is held on Tuesdays and Fridays and is known for its fresh produce, artisanal products, and street food stalls.

Popular Items:

- **Salame nostrano**: Local salami is a must-try. The slightly spicy **Salame nostrano** is often sliced thinly and served with **polenta** or bread.
- **Fresh fruit**: The market offers an abundance of fresh fruits like **figs**, **peaches**, and **apples**, which are grown in the surrounding areas.

Street Food Highlights:

- **Frittelle di mele**: Apple fritters are a sweet treat often found at the market. Lightly fried and dusted with powdered sugar, they're a favorite with both locals and tourists.
- **Porchetta panini**: These sandwiches are made with slow-roasted pork, herbs, and a crusty roll, offering a flavorful and satisfying bite.

Practical Information:

- **Location**: Piazza della Riforma, 6900 Lugano
- **Opening Hours**: Tuesdays and Fridays, 8:00 AM – 12:30 PM
- **How to Get There**: A short walk from **Lugano's** central train station. Public transport options include buses that stop near the **Piazza della Riforma**.

Wine Tasting in Ticino's Vineyards

Ticino's wine culture is deeply rooted in its history, with **Merlot** being the region's most famous wine variety. The region's vineyards, many of which are located on scenic hillsides, offer excellent opportunities for wine tasting and tours. Whether you're a wine enthusiast or a casual drinker, exploring the vineyards of Ticino provides a perfect way to sample the local **Merlot** and learn about the winemaking process.

Fattoria Moncucchetto – Lugano

Fattoria Moncucchetto is a renowned winery located in the hills above **Lugano**. The vineyard is known for its award-winning **Merlot** wines, which are crafted with care using both traditional and modern techniques. Visitors can enjoy guided tours of the vineyard and cellar, followed by a tasting of their finest wines.

- **What to Expect**: The tour includes a walk through the vineyard, where you'll learn about the grape-growing process, and a visit to the winery's modern cellar. Tastings feature several different wines, including their flagship **Moncucchetto Merlot**.

Tasting Information:

- **Cost**: CHF 25-50 per person, depending on the tasting package.
- **Booking Tips**: Tours are available in both English and Italian. Reservations are recommended, especially during the busy summer months.
- **Location**: Via Crivelli Torricelli 13, 6900 Lugano
- **Website**: www.moncucchetto.ch
- **Contact**: +41 91 960 38 38

Cantina Il Cavaliere – Contone

Located in the **Contone** region, **Cantina Il Cavaliere** offers one of the most scenic wine-tasting experiences in Ticino. The winery specializes in **Merlot** and **Bianco di Merlot**, as well as other local varieties. Visitors can take a guided tour of the vineyard, which is nestled among the rolling hills, and enjoy tastings with spectacular views of the surrounding countryside.

- **What to Expect**: The tour includes a visit to the vineyard, a look at the winemaking facilities, and a wine tasting that includes a selection of **Merlot**, **white wines**, and **rosés**. Pairings with local cheeses and charcuterie are also available.

Tasting Information:

- **Cost**: CHF 30-40 per person for a standard tasting; private tastings are available at an additional cost.
- **Booking Tips**: English-speaking tours are available, and reservations are essential. The winery also hosts private events and offers a small shop where you can purchase their wines.
- **Location**: Via Cantonale 56, 6594 Contone
- **Website**: www.ilcavaliere.ch
- **Contact**: +41 91 851 84 15

Vegetarian, Vegan, and Dietary Options

While Ticino is known for its hearty dishes like **polenta** and **risotto**, the region has also embraced a more health-conscious approach to dining, with many restaurants now catering to vegetarians, vegans, and those with dietary restrictions. Fresh, local produce is a cornerstone of Ticino's cuisine, making it easy to find delicious, plant-based meals.

BioBistrot – Lugano

BioBistrot is a popular vegetarian and vegan restaurant located in the center of **Lugano**. The menu is focused on organic, seasonal ingredients, offering a wide range of plant-based dishes that are both healthy and flavorful. The restaurant is known for its creative take on classic dishes, using fresh, local produce to craft meals that are as nutritious as they are delicious.

Menu Highlights:

- **Vegan lasagna** made with seasonal vegetables and a creamy cashew béchamel.
- **Quinoa salad** with roasted vegetables, seeds, and a lemon-tahini dressing.
- **Dietary Options**: The restaurant offers gluten-free dishes and can accommodate other dietary restrictions upon request.
- **Cost**: CHF 15-30 per person for a main course.
- **Location**: Via Maggio 1, 6900 Lugano
- **Contact**: +41 91 922 47 33

Ristorante Della Posta – Morcote

For those looking for vegetarian and vegan options with a lakeside view, **Ristorante Della Posta** in **Morcote** is an excellent choice. This restaurant focuses on using local ingredients, with a menu that offers both traditional Ticinese dishes and modern, plant-based creations.

Menu Highlights:

- **Risotto with seasonal vegetables** and fresh herbs, served with a side of grilled polenta.
- **Vegan pizza** topped with roasted vegetables, olives, and a dairy-free cheese substitute.
- **Dietary Options**: Gluten-free options are available, and the restaurant is happy to accommodate vegan or lactose-free diets upon request.
- **Cost**: CHF 20-50 per person, depending on the dish.

- **Location**: Via Cantonale 7, 6922 Morcote
- **Contact**: +41 91 996 12 34

La Radice – Bellinzona

Located in the heart of **Bellinzona**, **La Radice** is a farm-to-table restaurant that specializes in vegetarian and vegan dishes. The restaurant sources its ingredients from local farms, ensuring that every dish is fresh, seasonal, and sustainable. With a focus on plant-based cuisine, **La Radice** offers a menu that changes regularly based on the availability of ingredients.

Menu Highlights:

- **Vegetarian polenta** with wild mushrooms and local herbs.
- **Vegan gnocchi** served with a walnut and sage pesto.
- **Dietary Options**: The restaurant offers gluten-free options and can accommodate other dietary needs upon request.
- **Cost**: CHF 20-40 per person.
- **Location**: Via Bellinzona 10, 6500 Bellinzona
- **Contact**: +41 91 821 45 78

Designer Boutiques and Local Fashion Finds

Ticino, particularly **Lugano**, is known for its upscale shopping scene. The city's elegant shopping streets are home to luxury brands, Swiss designers, and high-end boutiques offering the latest in fashion and accessories. If you're looking to indulge in some retail therapy, here are the top places to explore in Lugano and beyond.

Via Nassa – The Heart of Luxury Shopping in Lugano

One of the most famous shopping streets in Ticino is **Via Nassa**, located in the heart of **Lugano**. This street is lined with luxury boutiques, offering everything from designer clothing to high-end jewelry. It's a must-visit for travelers looking for sophisticated fashion and exclusive brands.

What to Expect:

- **Designer Boutiques**: You'll find flagship stores for brands like **Louis Vuitton, Gucci,** and **Prada** along **Via Nassa**, as well as high-end Swiss fashion labels like **Akris**.
- **Jewelry and Watches**: Swiss watches are a popular purchase in Ticino, and **Via Nassa** is home to several luxury watchmakers, including **Omega** and **Patek Philippe**.
- **Accessories**: From Italian leather handbags to Swiss silk scarves, the boutiques on **Via Nassa** offer plenty of options for shoppers looking for quality accessories.

Practical Information:

- **Location**: Via Nassa, 6900 Lugano
- **How to Get There**: **Via Nassa** is centrally located in **Lugano**, easily accessible by foot from the train station or by local bus.
- **Opening Hours**: Most boutiques are open Monday to Saturday, 10:00 AM – 6:30 PM. Some may close for lunch between 12:30 PM and 2:00 PM.

Corso Elvezia – Contemporary Swiss Fashion

For those interested in more contemporary Swiss fashion, **Corso Elvezia** in **Lugano** is another key shopping area. While it's not as glamorous as **Via Nassa, Corso Elvezia** offers a more relaxed shopping experience, with boutiques that focus on modern styles and local designers.

What to Expect:

- **Swiss Brands**: Stores like **Nuna Lie** and **K Kiosk** carry trendy Swiss

clothing and accessories for both men and women. You'll also find casual wear from Swiss designers at more affordable prices compared to the luxury stores on **Via Nassa**.
- **Shoes and Accessories**: If you're looking for stylish shoes, **Corso Elvezia** has several boutiques specializing in leather footwear and custom-made accessories.

Practical Information:

- **Location**: Corso Elvezia, 6900 Lugano
- **How to Get There**: It's just a short walk from **Piazza della Riforma** and easily accessible by local transport.
- **Opening Hours**: Monday to Saturday, 10:00 AM – 6:00 PM.

Foxtown Outlet – Designer Bargains in Mendrisio

If you're a bargain hunter looking for discounted designer goods, a trip to **Foxtown** in **Mendrisio** is well worth the journey. This outlet mall is one of the largest in Switzerland and offers deep discounts on luxury brands. **Foxtown** is home to over 160 stores, featuring everything from fashion and footwear to home goods and cosmetics.

What to Expect:

- **Designer Outlets**: Major brands like **Armani, Dolce & Gabbana, Michael Kors**, and **Versace** have outlet stores at **Foxtown**, offering discounts of up to 70% off retail prices.
- **Swiss Watches**: If you're looking to buy a Swiss watch, there are several outlet stores for brands like **Tissot** and **Tag Heuer**, where you can find high-quality watches at reduced prices.

Practical Information:

- **Location**: Via Angelo Maspoli 18, 6850 Mendrisio
- **How to Get There**: **Foxtown** is located about 20 minutes by train from **Lugano**, or a 30-minute drive. Free parking is available at the mall.
- **Opening Hours**: Monday to Sunday, 11:00 AM – 7:00 PM.
- **Website**: www.foxtown.com

Artisan Crafts and Souvenirs to Bring Home

Ticino is home to a rich tradition of **artisan crafts**, and there are plenty of places to find unique, handmade products that make excellent souvenirs. From **ceramics** and **wood carvings** to **textiles** and **leather goods**, these items reflect Ticino's cultural heritage and are often crafted by local artisans. Below are some of the best places to shop for authentic Ticinese products.

Ceramics from Ceramiche Artistiche Ticinesi – Lugano

For beautiful, hand-painted ceramics, visit **Ceramiche Artistiche Ticinesi** in **Lugano**. This small shop offers a wide selection of traditional and contemporary ceramics, including plates, bowls, vases, and decorative items. Each piece is made by local artisans, ensuring that every item is unique.

Popular Items:

- Hand-painted **plates** and **bowls** featuring floral designs or landscapes of Ticino.
- **Decorative vases** and **ceramic tiles** that make perfect gifts or souvenirs.

Practical Information:

- **Location**: Via Cattedrale 2, 6900 Lugano
- **Cost**: Prices range from CHF 20 for small decorative items to CHF 150 for larger pieces.

- **How to Get There**: Located near **Piazza della Riforma**, this shop is easy to find while exploring the city center.

Traditional Wood Carvings from Al Botteghino – Bellinzona

Wood carving is another traditional craft in Ticino, and **Al Botteghino** in **Bellinzona** is a great place to find handmade wood items. This artisan shop offers everything from **wooden figurines** to **decorative bowls** and **hand-carved furniture**. The shop specializes in using local wood, such as **chestnut** and **walnut**, to create unique pieces.

Popular Items:

- **Wooden figurines** depicting local wildlife or traditional Swiss scenes.
- **Decorative bowls** and **cutting boards** made from local wood.

Practical Information:

- **Location**: Via Orico 10, 6500 Bellinzona
- **Cost**: Smaller items like figurines start at CHF 30, while larger pieces like bowls or furniture can cost several hundred francs.
- **How to Get There**: A short walk from the **Bellinzona train station**. The shop is located near the town's famous castles, making it a convenient stop during your visit.

Textiles and Leather Goods at Tessiture di Vallemaggia – Locarno

For high-quality textiles and leather goods, **Tessiture di Vallemaggia** in **Locarno** is an excellent destination. This family-run shop specializes in **handwoven textiles** made from local wool and cotton, as well as leather bags, belts, and wallets crafted by local artisans. These items make wonderful gifts or personal keepsakes.

Popular Items:

- Handwoven **wool blankets** and **scarves** in traditional Ticinese patterns.
- **Leather handbags** and **wallets** made from locally sourced materials.

Practical Information:

- **Location**: Via San Francesco 8, 6600 Locarno
- **Cost**: Prices for textiles range from CHF 50 for scarves to CHF 250 for blankets. Leather goods range from CHF 70-200.
- **How to Get There**: Located in the center of **Locarno**, near **Piazza Grande**.

Souvenirs from Mercato di Bellinzona

For a more casual shopping experience, the **Mercato di Bellinzona** is also a great place to pick up authentic souvenirs. In addition to fresh produce, the market offers a variety of locally made products, including **jams**, **honey**, and **handmade soaps**. These items make for perfect gifts or mementos of your trip.

Popular Items:

- **Chestnut honey**: A local specialty, this honey is often sold in beautifully packaged jars.
- **Handmade soaps**: Made with natural ingredients and local herbs, these soaps are a fragrant and practical souvenir.

Practical Information:

- **Location**: Piazza Nosetto, 6500 Bellinzona
- **Cost**: Prices are generally affordable, with jars of honey starting at CHF 15 and soaps from CHF 8.
- **How to Get There**: The market is a short walk from **Bellinzona's train station**, held every Saturday morning.

Markets: What to Buy and Where

Ticino is home to several local markets, offering everything from fresh produce to antiques and handmade crafts. These markets are not just a place to shop, but also a chance to experience the local culture, taste traditional foods, and meet the artisans who craft the goods. Whether you're looking for fresh cheese, vintage trinkets, or unique souvenirs, Ticino's markets are vibrant hubs of activity.

Mercato di Bellinzona: A Saturday Tradition

The **Mercato di Bellinzona**, held every Saturday morning, is one of the most famous markets in Ticino. Set in the historic center of **Bellinzona**, the market has a lively, friendly atmosphere and offers a wide range of products, from fresh local produce to artisan crafts. It's the perfect place to pick up local delicacies, such as **salumi**, **cheeses**, and **chestnut honey**, or browse for handmade items like **ceramics** and **wood carvings**.

What to Buy:

- **Fresh Produce**: Seasonal fruits and vegetables, often sourced from local farms.
- **Cheese**: Local specialties like **Zincarlin** and **Formaggini**, both of which make excellent gifts to take home.
- **Cured Meats**: **Salame nostrano** (local salami) is a must-try, along with **prosciutto crudo**.
- **Artisan Crafts**: Handmade ceramics, wood carvings, and other traditional Ticinese products are perfect for souvenirs.
- **Best Time to Visit**: The market runs from 8:00 AM to 12:30 PM every Saturday, but it's best to arrive early for the freshest produce and best selection of crafts.
- **Location**: Piazza Nosetto, 6500 Bellinzona
- **How to Get There**: A 10-minute walk from **Bellinzona's train station**, or by car with parking available nearby.

Mercato di Lugano: A Blend of Modern and Traditional

Another market worth exploring is the **Mercato di Lugano**, which takes place on Tuesdays and Fridays in **Piazza della Riforma**. While this market is smaller than Bellinzona's, it offers a good mix of fresh food, flowers, and artisan goods. The market has a slightly more modern feel, with some stalls offering contemporary designs alongside traditional crafts.

What to Buy:

- **Flowers**: Fresh bouquets and potted plants are always available at reasonable prices.
- **Local Foods**: **Ticinese cheeses**, **salami**, and **olive oil** are popular items, and some vendors even offer tastings.
- **Souvenirs**: Look for handmade jewelry, scarves, and other small gifts to bring home.
- **Best Time to Visit**: The market is open from 8:00 AM to 12:30 PM on Tuesdays and Fridays. Mornings are the best time to visit for the freshest items.
- **Location**: Piazza della Riforma, 6900 Lugano
- **How to Get There**: The market is located in central **Lugano**, a short walk from the train station or accessible by local bus.

Mercato di Mendrisio: A Hidden Gem

Less well-known but equally charming is the **Mercato di Mendrisio**, held on Thursday mornings. This smaller, more intimate market offers a quieter shopping experience and is the perfect place to find local crafts and fresh produce without the crowds of larger markets. **Mendrisio** is also known for its **wines**, and you'll often find stalls selling bottles from nearby vineyards.

What to Buy:

- **Wines**: Local **Merlot** and **Bianco di Merlot** are popular, and vendors

are usually happy to provide samples.
- **Handmade Crafts**: Local artisans sell handwoven textiles, ceramics, and leather goods.
- **Fresh Foods**: Seasonal fruits, vegetables, and flowers are in abundance, and prices are usually more reasonable than in the larger markets.
- **Best Time to Visit**: Open from 8:00 AM to 12:30 PM on Thursdays. Arriving early ensures the best selection.
- **Location**: Piazza del Ponte, 6850 Mendrisio
- **How to Get There**: Easily reachable by train, with the market located just a few minutes from **Mendrisio's train station**.

Malls and Shopping Centers: A Guide for Families

Ticino's shopping malls and centers offer more than just retail therapy—they provide a variety of family-friendly activities, making them ideal destinations for parents traveling with children. With play areas, cinemas, and food courts, these malls offer a convenient way to combine shopping with entertainment for the whole family.

Centro Lugano Sud – Grancia

Centro Lugano Sud is one of Ticino's largest shopping centers, located just outside **Lugano** in **Grancia**. It's a family-friendly destination with a wide range of shops, including clothing, electronics, and home goods. The mall also features a large **play area** where children can run around and enjoy supervised activities while parents shop.

What to Expect:

- **Shops**: Stores range from mid-range fashion brands like **H&M** and **Zara** to electronics and home stores.
- **Family Amenities**: The mall has a dedicated **children's play area**, making it easy for parents to shop while kids are entertained. The play area is located near the food court, so families can easily take a break

for lunch or a snack.
- **Dining Options**: The food court offers a variety of options, from quick bites to full meals, including family favorites like **McDonald's** and **Pizza Hut**.

Practical Information:

- **Location**: Via Cantonale 1, 6916 Grancia
- **Opening Hours**: Monday to Saturday, 9:00 AM – 7:00 PM; closed on Sundays.
- **How to Get There**: Accessible by car, with free parking available, or by bus from **Lugano**.

Foxtown Outlet – Mendrisio

While **Foxtown** is best known as a designer outlet mall, it's also a great option for families. In addition to the luxury shopping, **Foxtown** has a **cinema** and a **children's play area**, making it easy to keep the little ones entertained while you browse the shops. The mall offers discounted prices on major fashion brands, with many shops offering kid-friendly clothing and accessories.

What to Expect:

- **Shops**: Over 160 stores, including brands like **Nike**, **Adidas**, and **Gap**, offer clothing for children, while luxury brands like **Gucci** and **Armani** attract adult shoppers.
- **Family Amenities**: **Foxtown** features a small **children's play area**, as well as a **cinema** where families can catch the latest movies.
- **Dining Options**: The food court offers a range of international and Swiss cuisine, with options like **pasta**, **burgers**, and **ice cream** to satisfy all ages.

Practical Information:

- **Location**: Via Angelo Maspoli 18, 6850 Mendrisio
- **Opening Hours**: Monday to Sunday, 11:00 AM – 7:00 PM.
- **How to Get There**: About a 20-minute train ride from **Lugano**, with free parking available for those driving.

Serfontana Shopping Center – Morbio Inferiore

For a smaller, more relaxed shopping experience, **Serfontana** in **Morbio Inferiore** is a good option. This mall is geared towards families, with a **children's area**, a **cinema**, and a variety of shops and restaurants. It's a quieter alternative to **Centro Lugano Sud** or **Foxtown**, making it a nice spot for families who want to avoid large crowds.

What to Expect:

- **Shops**: Stores include **Migros**, **H&M**, and **Coop**, offering a wide range of products for the whole family.
- **Family Amenities**: The mall's **children's play area** is a big draw for families, and there's also a **cinema** showing family-friendly films.
- **Dining Options**: Several restaurants cater to families, offering casual dining options like **pizza**, **sandwiches**, and **pastries**.

Practical Information:

- **Location**: Via Serfontana 10, 6834 Morbio Inferiore
- **Opening Hours**: Monday to Saturday, 9:00 AM – 7:00 PM.
- **How to Get There**: Easily accessible by car, with free parking available, or by public transport from **Lugano**.

Tax-Free Shopping for Tourists

One of the benefits of shopping in Switzerland is the opportunity for tourists to take advantage of **tax-free shopping**. This allows non-residents to claim back the **Value Added Tax (VAT)** on purchases made in participating stores.

Here's how tax-free shopping works in Ticino and what you need to know to claim your VAT refund.

How Tax-Free Shopping Works

Switzerland's VAT rate is 7.7%, and tourists from non-EU countries are eligible for a refund on this tax for goods purchased in Switzerland. To qualify, you must meet certain conditions:

- **Minimum Purchase Amount**: The total value of your purchases must be at least CHF 300 from the same store on the same day.
- **Eligible Items**: The tax-free refund applies to most goods, such as clothing, electronics, and souvenirs, but excludes services and food.
- **Participating Shops**: Not all shops offer tax-free shopping, so look for the **Tax-Free Shopping** sign or ask at the checkout if the store participates in the scheme.

How to Claim Your VAT Refund

1. **Shop at Participating Stores**: Make sure the shop offers tax-free shopping. When you make a qualifying purchase, ask for a **tax-free form** at the checkout.
2. **Complete the Form**: Fill out your details on the form, including your passport number and address.
3. **Get Your Form Stamped at Customs**: When you leave Switzerland, present your tax-free form, receipts, and the purchased goods to customs for verification. Customs will stamp your form, confirming that the goods are being exported.
4. **Claim Your Refund**: After your form is stamped, you can claim your VAT refund at a **tax-free desk** at the airport or other refund points. Alternatively, you can mail the form to a designated tax-free refund company to receive your refund by credit card or bank transfer.

Participating Shops in Ticino

Many high-end stores in **Lugano** and **Foxtown** participate in the tax-free shopping scheme, especially those selling luxury goods like clothing, watches, and jewelry.

- **Where to Claim Your Refund**: **Lugano Airport** has a tax-free refund desk where you can claim your refund in person before leaving the country. Major train stations like **Bellinzona** and **Lugano** also offer refund services for travelers departing by train.

Nightlife and Entertainment

Bars and Nightclubs: Where to Go in Lugano

Lugano, being the nightlife hub of Ticino, offers a diverse selection of bars and nightclubs. Whether you want to enjoy cocktails with a view, dance the night away, or listen to live music, Lugano's nightlife has something for everyone. Here's a guide to some of the top spots to experience Lugano after dark.

Seven Lugano: The Place to Be

Seven Lugano is a staple of Lugano's nightlife, known for its chic vibe, modern décor, and stunning views of **Lake Lugano**. This upscale venue combines fine dining, a lounge, and a nightclub all in one. The restaurant serves Mediterranean cuisine, while the lounge and bar are popular for their extensive cocktail menu and live DJ sets on weekends.

What to Expect:

- **Rooftop Lounge**: The rooftop terrace is one of the highlights, offering sweeping views of **Lake Lugano**. It's the perfect spot to enjoy a cocktail while watching the sunset.
- **Nightclub**: Later in the evening, the venue transforms into a lively nightclub with a resident DJ, making it a favorite spot for both locals and tourists looking to dance the night away.

- **Cost**: Cocktails are around CHF 15-20, and there is often a cover charge for the nightclub after 10:00 PM.
- **Location**: Piazza Riforma 1, 6900 Lugano
- **How to Get There**: Centrally located in **Lugano**, it's easily reachable by foot from most hotels in the city center.
- **Website**: www.sevenlugano.ch
- **Contact**: +41 91 290 77 77

La Dolce Vita: A Speakeasy with Style

For something more intimate and stylish, **La Dolce Vita** is a hidden gem in the heart of **Lugano**. This speakeasy-style bar is inspired by classic Italian films and offers a sophisticated atmosphere perfect for those looking to unwind with a craft cocktail in hand. The bar is small and cozy, with leather seats, dim lighting, and a menu of inventive drinks made by expert mixologists.

What to Expect:

- **Unique Cocktails**: The menu features creative drinks made with fresh, local ingredients and Italian spirits. The **Negroni** and **Aperol Spritz** are popular choices.
- **Live Music**: On certain nights, the bar hosts live jazz or acoustic performances, adding to the cozy, relaxed vibe.
- **Cost**: Cocktails range from CHF 12-18.
- **Location**: Via Cattedrale 5, 6900 Lugano
- **How to Get There**: Located near the **Cattedrale di San Lorenzo**, this bar is tucked away from the main streets but easily reachable on foot from the city center.

Club One: Dancing in Style

If you're looking for a high-energy night out, **Club One** is the place to be. This nightclub is one of the most popular spots in **Lugano** for dancing, drawing a mix of locals and visitors. **Club One** regularly hosts top international DJs and features a spacious dance floor, VIP areas, and a modern sound system.

What to Expect:

- **Music**: You'll find a mix of electronic, house, and dance music depending on the night. Check their event schedule for special DJ nights and themed parties.
- **VIP Area**: For those looking for a more exclusive experience, the club offers VIP tables with bottle service.
- **Cost**: Entry is typically CHF 20-30, with drinks ranging from CHF 15-25.
- **Location**: Via Lucerna 1, 6900 Lugano
- **How to Get There**: Just a 10-minute walk from **Piazza della Riforma** or a quick taxi ride from the city center.

Lido Bar: Cocktails by the Lake

For a more laid-back evening with a view, head to **Lido Bar**, located right on the shore of **Lake Lugano**. This outdoor bar is popular during the summer months, offering a relaxed atmosphere with beautiful views of the lake and surrounding mountains. It's a great spot to grab a drink before or after dinner and enjoy the evening breeze.

What to Expect:

- **Outdoor Seating**: The bar has plenty of outdoor seating, making it a perfect place to watch the sunset over the lake.
- **Casual Vibe**: **Lido Bar** has a more casual vibe than some of the city's nightclubs, with a menu that includes beers, wines, and classic cocktails.
- **Cost**: Drinks are reasonably priced, with cocktails starting at CHF 10-15.
- **Location**: Viale Castagnola 6, 6900 Lugano
- **How to Get There**: A 15-minute walk from the city center or a short

bus ride from **Piazza della Riforma**.

Music Festivals and Outdoor Concerts in Ticino

Ticino is a region that loves its music, especially in the warmer months when several music festivals and outdoor concerts take place throughout the region. Whether you're a fan of jazz, classical music, or rock, there's something for everyone. Below are some of the top music events held in Ticino each year.

JazzAscona Festival: A Celebration of Jazz by the Lake

The **JazzAscona Festival** is one of the most well-known music events in Ticino and attracts thousands of visitors each summer. Held in the picturesque town of **Ascona**, right on the shore of **Lake Maggiore**, the festival features live jazz performances from both international and Swiss musicians. With a mix of traditional jazz, blues, and modern interpretations, **JazzAscona** offers something for everyone.

What to Expect:

- **Live Music**: Performances take place on outdoor stages, with many concerts being free to attend. You'll find musicians playing everything from **Dixieland jazz** to modern experimental sounds.
- **Food and Drink**: The festival also offers food stalls serving local Ticinese dishes and drinks, so you can enjoy a meal while listening to the music.
- **Ticket Information**: Many performances are free, though some headline acts may require tickets costing around CHF 30-50.
- **Location**: Various venues in Ascona
- **Dates**: Typically held in late June to early July.
- **Website**: www.jazzascona.ch

Moon&Stars Festival: Big Names in Pop and Rock

Held in **Locarno**, the **Moon&Stars Festival** is one of the biggest music events in Ticino. The festival takes place in **Piazza Grande**, Locarno's main square, and features performances by international pop, rock, and hip-hop artists. The festival is known for its impressive lineup, which has included stars like **Ed Sheeran**, **Robbie Williams**, and **Lenny Kravitz** in past years.

What to Expect:

- **Concerts in Piazza Grande**: The main square is transformed into a massive outdoor concert venue, complete with large stages and light shows.
- **Festival Vibe**: The atmosphere is electric, with food and drink stands offering festival-goers everything from snacks to cocktails.
- **Ticket Information**: Tickets for headlining acts can range from CHF 60-150 depending on the artist and seating options.
- **Location**: Piazza Grande, Locarno
- **Dates**: Held in mid-July.
- **Website**: www.moonandstars.ch

Lugano Estival Jazz: A Free Music Festival

One of the highlights of Lugano's summer calendar is the **Lugano Estival Jazz**. This free outdoor festival brings together world-renowned jazz musicians for performances in **Piazza della Riforma**. The festival attracts both jazz enthusiasts and casual listeners, thanks to its relaxed atmosphere and diverse lineup, which often includes everything from classic jazz to Afro-Cuban sounds.

What to Expect:

- **Free Concerts**: The best part of **Estival Jazz** is that all the performances are free, making it a great event for both locals and tourists.
- **Outdoor Venue**: The concerts take place in **Piazza della Riforma**, allowing festival-goers to enjoy the music in Lugano's central square.

- **Ticket Information**: Free entry to all performances.
- **Location**: Piazza della Riforma, Lugano
- **Dates**: Usually held over two weekends in late June and early July.
- **Website**: www.estivaljazz.ch

Castle On Air: Concerts in Bellinzona's Castles

For a truly unique concert experience, check out the **Castle On Air** series, which takes place in **Bellinzona's** historic castles. These concerts feature a mix of rock, pop, and classical performances, all set against the stunning backdrop of **Castelgrande** or **Montebello Castle**. The combination of live music and medieval architecture creates an unforgettable atmosphere.

What to Expect:

- **Live Music in the Castles**: Concerts are held in the courtyards of the castles, providing a one-of-a-kind setting for the performances.
- **Eclectic Lineup**: Past performers have included everything from classical ensembles to rock bands, offering something for all tastes.
- **Ticket Information**: Tickets range from CHF 50-100 depending on the artist and seating options.
- **Location**: Castelgrande or Montebello Castle, Bellinzona
- **Dates**: Held in late summer, typically in August.
- **Website**: www.castleonair.ch

Cultural Events: Theater, Opera, and More

Ticino's cultural scene is deeply rooted in its Italian and Swiss heritage, and nowhere is this more apparent than in its theaters and opera houses. Visitors can experience world-class performances of opera, ballet, and theater, often set against the backdrop of historic venues and breathtaking scenery. If you're a fan of the arts, Ticino offers a rich cultural calendar that is sure to impress.

Lugano Arte e Cultura (LAC): The Heart of Ticino's Performing Arts Scene

At the heart of Ticino's cultural offerings is **Lugano Arte e Cultura (LAC)**, a state-of-the-art performance center located in **Lugano**. LAC hosts a wide range of events, including opera, theater, classical music concerts, ballet, and contemporary dance performances. The venue is known for bringing international productions to **Lugano**, while also supporting local talent through its collaborations with Ticino's cultural institutions.

What to Expect:

- **Opera and Ballet**: LAC is home to the **Orchestra della Svizzera Italiana (OSI)**, which performs regularly at the venue. You can also catch productions from renowned opera companies, including **Teatro alla Scala** in Milan, which frequently collaborates with **LAC** for special performances.
- **Theater**: The venue also hosts plays, ranging from classic works by **Shakespeare** to contemporary pieces by Swiss and Italian playwrights.
- **Exhibitions**: In addition to performances, **LAC** houses an art gallery, the **Museo d'Arte della Svizzera Italiana (MASI)**, which showcases modern and contemporary art.
- **How to Get Tickets**: Tickets for performances at **LAC** can be purchased online via the venue's website or in person at the box office. Prices vary depending on the event, with opera tickets typically ranging from CHF 50-150, and theater tickets from CHF 20-80.

Practical Information:

- **Location**: Piazza Bernardino Luini 6, 6900 Lugano
- **Website**: www.luganolac.ch
- **How to Get There**: The venue is centrally located in **Lugano**, just a

10-minute walk from the main train station. Public transport options are available, and parking is also available nearby.
- **Dress Code**: For opera and ballet performances, smart casual attire is recommended, though more formal attire is typical for evening performances.

Teatro Sociale Bellinzona: Historic Theater in the Heart of Ticino

Located in **Bellinzona**, the **Teatro Sociale** is one of Ticino's most historic and beloved venues for live theater. Built in 1847, the theater has been beautifully restored and today offers a mix of classical and contemporary performances, from Italian comedies to Swiss dramas. The venue's intimate setting, with seating for just over 500 people, makes for a unique cultural experience.

What to Expect:

- **Plays and Performances**: The **Teatro Sociale** offers a variety of performances, with a focus on Italian-language theater. Productions range from well-known plays by **Pirandello** to modern pieces by Swiss playwrights.
- **Concerts**: The theater also hosts classical concerts, with performances by local and international musicians.
- **How to Get Tickets**: Tickets can be purchased online via the **Teatro Sociale** website or at the box office. Prices for theater performances typically range from CHF 20-60.

Practical Information:

- **Location**: Via Teatro 2, 6500 Bellinzona
- **Website**: www.teatrosociale.ch
- **How to Get There**: The theater is located in the center of **Bellinzona**, within walking distance of the train station.
- **Dress Code**: Casual to smart casual attire is appropriate for most

performances.

Festival del Film Locarno: A Cinema Lover's Dream

For those who love cinema, the **Festival del Film Locarno** is one of the most prestigious film festivals in Europe, held each August in the stunning lakeside town of **Locarno**. The festival is renowned for showcasing a diverse range of films, from international blockbusters to independent films, all screened in **Piazza Grande**, one of the most beautiful open-air cinemas in the world.

What to Expect:

- **Film Screenings**: The heart of the festival is in **Piazza Grande**, where films are shown on a massive screen under the stars. With seating for over 8,000 people, it's an unforgettable cinematic experience. Films are shown in their original language with subtitles in Italian, French, and English.
- **Celebrity Appearances**: The festival often attracts big names from the film industry, including actors, directors, and producers from around the world.
- **How to Get Tickets**: Tickets can be purchased online through the festival's website, with prices ranging from CHF 20-40 for regular screenings in **Piazza Grande**. Festival passes are also available for those looking to attend multiple screenings.

Practical Information:

- **Location**: Piazza Grande, 6600 Locarno
- **Website**: www.locarnofestival.ch
- **How to Get There**: **Locarno** is easily accessible by train from **Lugano** and other major cities in Ticino. The venue is a short walk from **Locarno's train station**.
- **Tips for Attending**: Bring a light jacket or blanket, as it can get chilly

in the evening. Arrive early to secure a good seat, especially for popular screenings.

Family-Friendly Evening Activities

Ticino offers plenty of evening entertainment options for families looking to enjoy a fun and relaxing night out together. From outdoor movie screenings to nighttime zoo visits, there are a variety of activities that are both enjoyable and appropriate for children.

Outdoor Movie Nights: Films Under the Stars

One of the best family-friendly activities in Ticino during the summer months is attending an outdoor movie screening. Many towns and villages in the region host **open-air cinemas**, where families can gather to watch films under the stars. These events are often free or low-cost, making them a great way to enjoy a relaxed evening with the whole family.

What to Expect:

- **Films for All Ages**: The outdoor screenings usually feature family-friendly films, including recent animated movies, classic comedies, and adventure films.
- **Casual Atmosphere**: Families are encouraged to bring blankets or lawn chairs, and many venues offer food and drink stalls selling popcorn, ice cream, and soft drinks.

Best Locations for Outdoor Movies:

- **Lugano**: **Cine Lido Lugano** often hosts outdoor movie nights in **Parco Ciani**, located right by **Lake Lugano**. It's a scenic and relaxed setting, perfect for families.
- **Locarno**: In addition to the **Locarno Film Festival**, the town also holds regular outdoor movie nights at various venues during the summer

months.

Practical Information:

- **Cost**: Many outdoor movie screenings are free, though some may charge a small fee (usually CHF 5-10).
- **Timing**: Movies typically start around 9:00 PM during the summer months, when the sun sets.
- **How to Find Events**: Check local event listings or tourist information centers for the latest schedules.

Zoo al Maglio: Nighttime Visits for Families

Located near **Lugano**, **Zoo al Maglio** offers a unique experience for families: nighttime zoo visits. These special events allow children and parents to see the zoo's animals in a completely different light—quite literally! During the summer months, the zoo stays open late, giving visitors the chance to observe the animals' nocturnal behaviors.

What to Expect:

- **Animal Encounters**: Kids will love seeing animals such as **lions**, **tigers**, and **lemurs** in the evening when they are more active. Guided tours are available, providing interesting facts about the animals' nighttime habits.
- **Torchlight Walks**: Families can join torchlight walks through the zoo, adding an element of adventure to the visit.

Practical Information:

- **Location**: Via ai Magli, 6983 Maglio
- **Cost**: CHF 15 for adults, CHF 10 for children. Special pricing may apply for evening events.
- **How to Get There**: The zoo is a short drive from **Lugano** and is

accessible by local bus.
- **Website**: www.zooalmaglio.ch
- **Tips**: Bring a flashlight or torch if you're attending a nighttime event. It's also a good idea to wear comfortable shoes, as the zoo grounds can be uneven.

Lugano's Light Show: A Magical Evening for Families

For an enchanting evening activity, **Lugano's Light Show** is a must-see event for families visiting the region. Held in the evenings during the summer and winter months, the light show transforms **Lugano's main squares and buildings** into illuminated works of art. Children and adults alike will be mesmerized by the colorful displays and interactive light installations.

What to Expect:

- **Dazzling Displays**: The light show features a series of projected images and animations, synchronized to music, that bring **Lugano's historic buildings** to life. Some installations are interactive, allowing children to engage with the lights and sounds.
- **Festive Atmosphere**: The show is usually accompanied by street food vendors and market stalls, making it a fun and lively event for families.

Practical Information:

- **Location**: Piazza della Riforma, 6900 Lugano
- **Cost**: Free.
- **Timing**: The show typically begins around 8:00 PM during the summer and winter months.
- **How to Get There**: Easily accessible by foot from anywhere in **Lugano's city center**.
- **Tips**: Arrive early to get a good viewing spot, especially if you're attending on a weekend when it can get crowded.

Cultural Experiences in Ticino

Art Galleries and Museums to Explore

Ticino's artistic scene is diverse, featuring everything from cutting-edge contemporary art to exhibits showcasing the region's rich history. Whether you're wandering through a modern gallery in **Lugano** or stepping back in time at a historical museum in **Bellinzona**, there's plenty to see for art and history lovers alike.

Museo d'Arte della Svizzera Italiana (MASI) – Lugano

Located in the heart of **Lugano**, the **Museo d'Arte della Svizzera Italiana (MASI)** is one of Ticino's most important art institutions. MASI showcases a wide range of works from Swiss and international artists, with a particular focus on contemporary art and pieces that reflect the cultural heritage of the Italian-speaking part of Switzerland. The museum's collection spans from the Renaissance to the present day, and it regularly hosts temporary exhibitions that bring in works from renowned artists across the globe.

Must-See Exhibits:

- The museum's permanent collection includes works by artists such as **Giovanni Segantini**, **Félix Vallotton**, and **Paul Klee**.
- Temporary exhibitions often feature modern and contemporary art,

with past exhibitions showcasing works by **Pablo Picasso** and **Andy Warhol**.
- **Family-Friendly Programs**: MASI offers special family programs, including guided tours and interactive workshops that make art accessible and fun for children.
- **Admission Fees**: CHF 15 for adults, CHF 10 for students and seniors. Children under 16 enter free.

Practical Information:

- **Location**: Piazza Bernardino Luini 6, 6900 Lugano
- **Opening Hours**: Tuesday to Sunday, 10:00 AM – 6:00 PM. Closed on Mondays.
- **Website**: www.masilugano.ch
- **How to Get There**: Centrally located in **Lugano**, it's a short walk from the train station or easily reachable by local bus.

Museo Villa dei Cedri – Bellinzona

For a more intimate museum experience, visit the **Museo Villa dei Cedri** in **Bellinzona**. This charming museum is housed in a 19th-century villa surrounded by beautiful gardens and specializes in Swiss and Italian art from the 19th and 20th centuries. It's a peaceful place to explore art in a historical setting, offering a unique contrast to the larger and more modern galleries in **Lugano**.

Must-See Exhibits:

- The museum's collection includes works by artists such as **Carlo Carrà** and **Giovanni Giacometti**, as well as pieces by local Ticinese artists.
- The villa's architecture and garden are also highlights, making it a lovely spot for a quiet afternoon.
- **Family-Friendly Programs**: The museum offers art workshops for children and guided tours tailored to families.

- **Admission Fees**: CHF 10 for adults, CHF 5 for students and seniors. Free for children under 16.

Practical Information:

- **Location**: Piazza San Biagio 9, 6500 Bellinzona
- **Opening Hours**: Wednesday to Sunday, 10:00 AM – 6:00 PM. Closed on Mondays and Tuesdays.
- **Website**: www.villacedri.ch
- **How to Get There**: A 15-minute walk from **Bellinzona's train station**, or easily reachable by local bus.

Galleria Gottardo – Lugano

The **Galleria Gottardo** is a contemporary art gallery in **Lugano** that hosts rotating exhibitions featuring international artists. While smaller than **MASI**, **Galleria Gottardo** is known for its focus on innovative art forms, including photography, sculpture, and mixed media. It's a must-visit for travelers interested in modern art and cutting-edge exhibitions.

- **Must-See Exhibits**: The gallery's exhibits change frequently, but past shows have included works by notable artists such as **Mario Giacomelli** and **Josef Albers**.
- **Admission Fees**: Free.

Practical Information:

- **Location**: Via Besso 42, 6900 Lugano
- **Opening Hours**: Monday to Friday, 9:00 AM – 6:00 PM. Closed on weekends.
- **Website**: www.galleriagottardo.ch
- **How to Get There**: A short walk from **Lugano's main train station**.

Museo Nazionale del San Gottardo – Airolo

For those interested in the history of the **Gotthard Pass**, the **Museo Nazionale del San Gottardo** in **Airolo** is a fascinating stop. The museum explores the history of one of Switzerland's most important Alpine passes, showcasing everything from early engineering feats to the cultural impact of the **Gotthard railway**.

Must-See Exhibits:

- A detailed exhibit on the construction of the **Gotthard Tunnel**, one of the longest railway tunnels in the world.
- Artifacts and historical documents related to the region's transportation history and its significance as a cultural crossroads.
- **Family-Friendly Programs**: The museum offers interactive exhibits and guided tours that are particularly engaging for children interested in trains and engineering.
- **Admission Fees**: CHF 8 for adults, CHF 4 for students and seniors. Free for children under 12.

Practical Information:

- **Location**: Via San Gottardo 1, 6780 Airolo
- **Opening Hours**: Tuesday to Sunday, 10:00 AM – 5:00 PM. Closed on Mondays.
- **Website**: www.museodelsangottardo.ch
- **How to Get There**: **Airolo** is accessible by train, and the museum is a short walk from the station.

Ticino's Traditional Festivals

Ticino's festivals are an essential part of the region's cultural life, blending Swiss and Italian traditions in vibrant celebrations throughout the year. From religious processions to food festivals, these events offer visitors the chance to experience Ticino's rich heritage and lively community spirit. Here are some of the most notable traditional festivals in Ticino, along with tips on how to make the most of your visit.

Rabadan Carnival – Bellinzona

One of the most anticipated events in Ticino is the **Rabadan Carnival**, held annually in **Bellinzona**. Known as the region's largest and most colorful carnival, **Rabadan** transforms the city into a festive playground filled with parades, costumes, and live music. The carnival dates back over 150 years and is a major event in Ticino's cultural calendar.

What to Expect:

- **Parades**: The highlight of **Rabadan** is the grand parade, where locals dress up in elaborate costumes and parade through the streets of **Bellinzona**. Expect vibrant colors, floats, and plenty of music.
- **Music and Dancing**: After the parade, the streets come alive with music and dancing, as local bands perform and food stalls serve traditional carnival fare, including **polenta, grilled sausages**, and sweets.
- **Key Dates**: **Rabadan** takes place in February, coinciding with **Mardi Gras** celebrations. The festival lasts for five days, with the main parade typically occurring on the last Sunday of the event.

Practical Information:

- **Location**: Central Bellinzona
- **Cost**: Entry to the carnival area requires a festival pass, which typically

costs CHF 30-40 for the entire event.
- **Tips**: Dress warmly, as the carnival takes place in winter, and be prepared for large crowds, especially during the main parade.

Festa d'Autunno – Lugano

The **Festa d'Autunno** is **Lugano's** annual autumn festival, celebrating the region's harvest and local culinary traditions. Held in early October, the festival is a favorite among food lovers, with stalls offering everything from roasted chestnuts to Ticino's famous **Merlot** wines. The event also includes music, dancing, and family-friendly activities, making it a great cultural experience for visitors of all ages.

What to Expect:

- **Food and Drink**: The main attraction is the food, with stalls offering seasonal dishes like **polenta, grilled meats**, and **cheeses**. Local wineries also set up booths, offering tastings of **Ticinese Merlot**.
- **Live Entertainment**: Traditional folk music and dance performances take place throughout the festival, adding to the festive atmosphere.
- **Key Dates**: The festival usually takes place over the first weekend in October.

Practical Information:

- **Location**: Piazza della Riforma, 6900 Lugano
- **Cost**: Free entry, though food and drink prices vary by vendor.
- **Tips**: Arrive early to avoid the crowds, especially if you plan to visit the food stalls.

Processione della Settimana Santa – Mendrisio

For a more spiritual cultural experience, visit **Mendrisio** during Holy Week to witness the **Processione della Settimana Santa**. This religious procession is a deeply significant event in Ticino, featuring a dramatic reenactment of the Passion of Christ. Locals dress in traditional costumes, and the streets of **Mendrisio** are illuminated with lanterns, creating a solemn and moving atmosphere.

What to Expect:

- **Procession**: The main event is the Good Friday procession, which involves hundreds of participants dressed as biblical characters, reenacting scenes from the Passion of Christ.
- **Lantern Displays**: **Mendrisio** is known for its beautiful lanterns, which are lit during the procession, adding a special glow to the event.
- **Key Dates**: The procession takes place during **Holy Week**, with the most important events occurring on Good Friday.

Practical Information:

- **Location**: Mendrisio town center
- **Cost**: Free, though donations are welcome.
- **Tips**: Arrive early to secure a good viewing spot, as the streets can get crowded, especially on Good Friday.

Sagra del Borgo – Morcote

For a taste of traditional village life, head to **Morcote** for the **Sagra del Borgo**, a village festival celebrating local food, wine, and music. Held in the summer, the festival offers visitors a chance to experience Ticino's rural traditions, with open-air markets, wine tastings, and performances by folk bands.

What to Expect:

- **Food and Wine**: The festival features stalls selling local delicacies, including **cured meats**, **cheeses**, and **wine** from nearby vineyards. It's a great opportunity to sample regional specialties in a relaxed, festive

atmosphere.
- **Live Music**: Traditional folk bands perform throughout the festival, with some areas set up for dancing.
- **Key Dates**: The festival usually takes place in late July or early August.

Practical Information:

- **Location**: Morcote town center
- **Cost**: Free entry, though food and wine prices vary by vendor.
- **Tips**: **Morcote** is a small village, so it's best to park outside the center and walk to the festival.

Architectural Wonders of Ticino

Ticino's architectural landscape is a fascinating mix of traditional and contemporary design, with influences from its Italian neighbors as well as its Swiss heritage. From sleek modern buildings by **Mario Botta** to rustic stone houses, the architecture tells the story of a region that has always been at the crossroads of cultures.

Modern Masterpieces by Mario Botta

Ticino is home to several architectural works by **Mario Botta**, one of Switzerland's most famous architects. His style, characterized by geometric shapes and the use of natural materials like stone and brick, can be seen throughout the region, particularly in the city of **Lugano**.

San Giovanni Battista Church – Mogno

Perhaps the most iconic work by **Botta** is the **San Giovanni Battista Church** in **Mogno**, a tiny mountain village. This striking church, built in 1996, replaces a 17th-century chapel that was destroyed by an avalanche. The building's cylindrical shape, alternating layers of gray **Riveo granite** and white **Peccia marble**, and the open glass roof make it one of the most unique churches in Europe.

- **What to Expect**: The interior of the church is minimalistic, with no religious icons, allowing the natural light streaming through the roof to be the focal point. It's a peaceful place to visit, even for those not drawn to religious sites.

Practical Information:

- **Location**: Mogno, Valle Maggia
- **How to Get There**: Mogno is about a 1-hour drive from **Lugano**. Public buses also run from **Locarno** to the village.
- **Entry Fee**: Free
- **Opening Hours**: Open daily.
- **Tips**: The church can be visited year-round, but spring and summer are the best times to enjoy the surrounding nature.

The Banca del Gottardo – Lugano

Another notable **Botta** creation is the **Banca del Gottardo** building in **Lugano**. This office building, completed in 1988, is a prime example of **Botta's** use of symmetry and geometric precision. The building's exterior is dominated by horizontal bands of brick and windows, while the interior is equally striking with its clean lines and light-filled spaces.

- **What to Expect**: While the **Banca del Gottardo** is not open to the public, you can admire the exterior of this masterpiece. The building stands as a symbol of modern architecture in **Lugano** and is a must-see for architecture enthusiasts.

Practical Information:

- **Location**: Via della Posta 8, 6900 Lugano

- **How to Get There**: A short walk from **Lugano's main train station** or accessible by local bus.
- **Tips**: Since it's not open to visitors, combine your stop here with a visit to nearby **Piazza della Riforma** or the **LAC Lugano** for a cultural day out.

Other Notable Botta Buildings in Ticino

- **Centro San Francesco** (Fribourg)
- **The Church of the Sacred Heart** (Bellinzona)

Traditional Ticinese Houses: Stone Masterpieces of the Past

The rustic **Ticinese houses**, with their stone walls and slate roofs, are another architectural highlight in the region. These traditional homes are particularly common in the **Verzasca Valley** and the **Maggia Valley**, where they have been preserved for centuries, offering a glimpse into Ticino's rural past.

Valle Verzasca: The Quintessential Ticinese Village

A visit to the **Valle Verzasca** will take you through several charming villages where traditional **Ticinese** stone houses still stand. These homes are built from local materials—mainly **granite**—and are characterized by their thick walls and steep roofs, designed to withstand harsh mountain weather.

- **Best Villages to Visit**: **Corippo**, a tiny village with only a few residents, is the best place to see well-preserved **Ticinese** architecture. The entire village has been declared a heritage site, and the houses have been carefully restored to maintain their historical integrity.
- **Practical Information**:
- **How to Get There**: **Corippo** is accessible by car or bus from **Locarno**, a drive that takes about 30 minutes.

- **Tips**: Bring comfortable shoes as the village's narrow, cobblestone streets are best explored on foot.

Maggia Valley: Living in Harmony with Nature

In the **Maggia Valley**, the traditional stone houses blend seamlessly into the surrounding landscape. These homes, many of which are still in use today, have stood the test of time and continue to serve as symbols of Ticino's rural heritage.

Practical Information:

- **How to Get There**: The **Maggia Valley** is a short drive from **Locarno** or reachable by bus.
- **Tips**: If you're an architecture enthusiast, consider taking a guided tour of the valley, which often includes visits to private homes and historical buildings.

Churches, Chapels, and Sacred Sites to Visit

Religion has played an important role in shaping Ticino's cultural identity, and the region is home to many churches, chapels, and sacred sites, each offering a unique glimpse into its spiritual heritage. From grand basilicas to hidden countryside chapels, these sites are not only places of worship but also architectural marvels.

Madonna del Sasso – Orselina

The **Sanctuary of Madonna del Sasso** in **Orselina**, just above **Locarno**, is one of the most important religious sites in Ticino. Perched on a hill, the sanctuary offers panoramic views of **Locarno** and **Lake Maggiore**, making it a popular pilgrimage site for both religious visitors and tourists seeking breathtaking scenery.

What to Expect:

- The sanctuary is famous for its **16th-century frescoes** and intricate altarpieces. The interior is a blend of Renaissance and Baroque styles, and the quiet atmosphere makes it a perfect spot for reflection.
- The sanctuary is also known for its **funicular railway**, which connects **Locarno** with **Orselina**, offering visitors a scenic ride up the mountain.

Practical Information:

- **Location**: Via del Sasso, 6644 Orselina
- **How to Get There**: Take the funicular from **Locarno** to **Orselina**. The funicular runs every 15 minutes and costs CHF 6 for a one-way trip.
- **Entry Fee**: Free to visit, though donations are welcome.
- **Opening Hours**: Open daily, with extended hours during the summer months.
- **Tips**: For the best experience, visit in the late afternoon when the setting sun casts a golden light over the lake and mountains.

Chiesa di San Lorenzo – Lugano

The **Chiesa di San Lorenzo**, located in the heart of **Lugano**, is the city's main cathedral and a must-visit for anyone interested in religious architecture. Originally built in the 9th century, the church has undergone several renovations over the centuries, resulting in a mix of Romanesque, Gothic, and Baroque styles.

What to Expect:

- Inside, you'll find beautiful frescoes dating back to the 15th century, as well as ornate Baroque altars. The church's bell tower is also worth admiring, with its stunning views of **Lugano** and **Lake Lugano**.

Practical Information:

- **Location**: Via Cattedrale 5, 6900 Lugano
- **How to Get There**: A short walk from **Lugano's main train station**.
- **Entry Fee**: Free
- **Opening Hours**: Open daily.
- **Tips**: Try to visit on a weekday morning when the church is quieter, allowing you to fully appreciate its architectural details.

Santa Maria degli Angioli – Lugano

Another significant church in **Lugano** is the **Santa Maria degli Angioli**, best known for its impressive fresco of the **Crucifixion** by **Bernardino Luini**, a disciple of **Leonardo da Vinci**. This Renaissance masterpiece is one of the largest frescoes in Switzerland, covering an entire wall of the church.

What to Expect:

- The **Crucifixion fresco** is the main attraction, but the church also houses other Renaissance-era artworks that are worth admiring. The simplicity of the church's exterior contrasts with the richness of its interior art.

Practical Information:

- **Location**: Piazza Bernardino Luini, 6900 Lugano
- **How to Get There**: Centrally located in **Lugano**, it's easily accessible on foot from most hotels and attractions.
- **Entry Fee**: Free
- **Opening Hours**: Open daily.
- **Tips**: Visit in the early afternoon when the light best illuminates the fresco.

Hidden Chapels in the Ticino Countryside

Ticino is also home to many small chapels scattered throughout its valleys and mountains. These chapels, often found along hiking trails or in remote villages, are beautifully simple and provide a peaceful retreat for those seeking solitude.

Chapel of Santa Maria di Loreto – Ascona

One of the most charming chapels is the **Santa Maria di Loreto** in **Ascona**, a small, whitewashed chapel perched on a hill overlooking **Lake Maggiore**. The chapel dates back to the 15th century and offers stunning views of the surrounding countryside.

Practical Information:

- **Location**: Ascona, 6612
- **How to Get There**: A short walk from the center of **Ascona**.
- **Tips**: Pack a picnic and enjoy the peaceful atmosphere while taking in the views of the lake.

Day Trips from Ticino

A Day in Milan: Italian Culture and Shopping

Milan is just a short train ride or drive from Ticino, making it a perfect destination for a day of sightseeing, shopping, and indulging in Italian cuisine. Known for its stunning architecture, high-fashion boutiques, and world-class museums, Milan offers plenty to fill a day. Here's an itinerary that will help you see the best of Milan while making the most of your time.

Morning: Discover Milan's Cultural Landmarks

Start your day early by catching a train or driving from Ticino to Milan. If you're traveling by train, the journey from **Lugano** to **Milan Centrale** takes about 1 hour and 15 minutes. Trains run frequently, and tickets can be booked in advance on the **SBB** or **Trenitalia** websites, with prices typically ranging from CHF 20-40 depending on the class and time of day. If you prefer to drive, Milan is about 1.5 hours from **Lugano**, and parking is available at various lots in the city center.

Once you arrive in Milan, head straight to the iconic **Duomo di Milano**, the city's most famous landmark. This breathtaking Gothic cathedral is one of the largest churches in the world and is known for its intricate façade and spires that seem to reach the sky. Take the time to explore the interior and, if you're feeling adventurous, climb to the rooftop for panoramic views of Milan.

Duomo di Milano:

- **Opening Hours**: 8:00 AM – 7:00 PM (rooftop access until 6:30 PM)
- **Admission Fees**: €5 for cathedral entry, €13 for rooftop access by stairs, €17 for rooftop access by elevator
- **How to Get There**: From **Milano Centrale**, take the metro to **Duomo** station (Line 1). The Duomo is located right in the heart of the city.

After visiting the Duomo, walk over to the **Galleria Vittorio Emanuele II**, one of the world's oldest and most beautiful shopping galleries. This stunning 19th-century arcade, with its glass domed roof and intricate mosaics, is home to luxury boutiques, including **Prada**, **Gucci**, and **Louis Vuitton**. Even if high-end shopping isn't on your agenda, it's worth a visit just to admire the architecture.

Galleria Vittorio Emanuele II:

- **Opening Hours**: Open 24 hours
- **Cost**: Free to enter
- **How to Get There**: It's located next to the Duomo, just a short walk away.

Lunch: Savor Milanese Cuisine

For lunch, head to a local trattoria or café to try some authentic Milanese dishes. **Risotto alla Milanese**, made with saffron, and **cotoletta alla Milanese**, a breaded veal cutlet, are two regional specialties you won't want to miss. A great option for lunch is **Trattoria Milanese**, a traditional restaurant offering classic dishes in a cozy setting.

Trattoria Milanese:

- **Location**: Via Santa Marta 11, 20123 Milan
- **Price**: €25-40 per person

- **How to Get There**: About a 15-minute walk from the Duomo or reachable by tram.

Afternoon: Explore Art and Shopping Districts

In the afternoon, take some time to explore Milan's rich art scene. If you're an art lover, a visit to **Pinacoteca di Brera** is a must. This prestigious art gallery houses an impressive collection of Italian Renaissance masterpieces, including works by **Caravaggio**, **Raphael**, and **Titian**.

Pinacoteca di Brera:

- **Opening Hours**: 9:00 AM – 6:30 PM (closed on Mondays)
- **Admission Fees**: €15
- **How to Get There**: Take the metro to **Lanza** station (Line 2), or it's a 20-minute walk from the Duomo.

For those more interested in shopping, spend the afternoon wandering through Milan's **Quadrilatero della Moda** (Fashion Quadrilateral), the city's high-end shopping district. Located between **Via Montenapoleone**, **Via della Spiga**, **Corso Venezia**, and **Via Manzoni**, this area is home to designer boutiques and flagship stores from the biggest names in fashion, including **Armani**, **Dolce & Gabbana**, and **Versace**.

- **How to Get There**: It's a 10-minute walk from the Duomo.

Evening: Aperitivo and Departure

Before heading back to Ticino, make sure to experience Milan's aperitivo culture. This Italian tradition involves enjoying a pre-dinner drink (usually **Aperol Spritz** or **Negroni**) accompanied by small bites like **bruschetta**, olives, and cheese. **Navigli**, Milan's canal district, is the best place to enjoy aperitivo in a lively atmosphere. Many bars offer a buffet of appetizers that are included with the price of a drink.

- **Recommended Bar**: **Mag Café** (Ripa di Porta Ticinese 43)
- **Price**: Drinks from €8-12
- **How to Get There**: Take the metro to **Porta Genova** station (Line 2).

After enjoying the aperitivo, head back to **Milano Centrale** for your train or car journey back to Ticino. Trains run until late, and driving back in the evening typically takes about 1.5 hours.

Lake Como: An Enchanting Escape

A day trip to **Lake Como** is a great way to escape the hustle and bustle of city life and immerse yourself in Italy's natural beauty. Famous for its dramatic scenery, charming lakeside villages, and luxurious villas, Lake Como is a serene and picturesque destination just a short drive or train ride from Ticino. Here's how to spend a perfect day exploring this enchanting region.

Morning: Arrival and Exploring Como Town

To make the most of your day, start by taking an early train or driving from **Lugano** to **Como**. The train journey takes about 30 minutes, and tickets can be booked in advance on **Trenord** or **SBB** for around CHF 10-20. If you're driving, Como is about 45 minutes from Lugano, and parking is available near the town center.

Begin your day in **Como Town**, the largest town on the lake and a great starting point for exploring the area. Spend the morning strolling along the **Lungolago**, the lakeside promenade, where you can enjoy beautiful views of the lake and the surrounding mountains. Be sure to visit **Piazza del Duomo** and the **Como Cathedral**, an impressive Gothic-Renaissance cathedral that dominates the square.

Como Cathedral:

- **Opening Hours**: 8:00 AM – 7:00 PM
- **Admission**: Free
- **How to Get There**: A short walk from **Como San Giovanni** train station.

Late Morning: Ferry Ride to Bellagio

One of the best ways to experience Lake Como is by taking a ferry ride across the lake. From **Como**, hop on a ferry to **Bellagio**, known as the "Pearl of Lake Como." Ferries run regularly, and the journey takes about 1 hour. Tickets can be purchased at the ferry terminal, with prices ranging from €10-20 depending on the route and class.

The ferry ride offers stunning views of the lake's villas, mountains, and picturesque towns. Once you arrive in **Bellagio**, spend time exploring the town's narrow, cobblestone streets lined with boutiques, cafes, and restaurants.

Practical Information:

- **Ferry Schedule**: Ferries run every 30 minutes from **Como** to **Bellagio** during peak season.
- **Ferry Prices**: €10-20 one way, depending on the route.

Lunch in Bellagio: Lakeside Dining

For lunch, dine at one of **Bellagio's** lakeside restaurants, where you can enjoy fresh seafood and Italian specialties with breathtaking views. **Ristorante La Punta** is a popular spot offering a great selection of local dishes, including lake fish and pasta, along with a beautiful terrace overlooking the water.

Ristorante La Punta:

- **Location**: Via E. Vitali 19, 22021 Bellagio
- **Price**: €25-50 per person

- **How to Get There**: A short walk from **Bellagio's ferry terminal**.

Afternoon: Exploring Bellagio and Villa Visits

After lunch, spend the afternoon exploring **Bellagio** and visiting some of the area's famous villas. **Villa Melzi** and its stunning gardens are a must-see. The villa's English-style gardens are filled with rare plants, statues, and breathtaking views of the lake.

Villa Melzi:

- **Opening Hours**: 10:00 AM – 6:00 PM (April to October)
- **Admission Fees**: €8 for adults
- **How to Get There**: A 10-minute walk from **Bellagio's ferry terminal**.

If you have more time, consider taking a short ferry ride to **Varenna**, a peaceful village known for its pastel-colored houses and romantic atmosphere. A visit to **Villa Monastero**, with its terraced gardens and panoramic views, is highly recommended.

Villa Monastero:

- **Opening Hours**: 9:00 AM – 7:00 PM (March to October)
- **Admission Fees**: €9 for adults
- **How to Get There**: A 15-minute ferry ride from **Bellagio**.

Evening: Return to Ticino

As the afternoon winds down, head back to **Como** by ferry. Depending on your schedule, you can enjoy a casual aperitivo at one of the lakeside bars in **Como Town** before returning to Ticino by train or car.

- **Recommended Bar**: **Caffè Mazzini** (Via Mazzini 9, 22100 Como)
- **Price**: Drinks from €5-10
- **How to Get There**: A short walk from the ferry terminal.

The Swiss Alps: Adventure Beyond Ticino

For nature lovers and adventure seekers, a day trip into the Swiss Alps offers the ultimate escape. Whether you're interested in hiking along mountain trails, skiing down pristine slopes, or simply enjoying the stunning alpine scenery from a scenic train ride, the Alps are a must-see. The nearby towns of **Andermatt** and **Zermatt** provide access to some of Switzerland's most famous alpine landscapes, and each offers a unique experience for visitors.

Hiking and Scenic Train Rides in Andermatt

Andermatt, located about 1.5 hours from Ticino by car or train, is a charming alpine town that serves as a gateway to the Swiss Alps. Surrounded by dramatic peaks, **Andermatt** is a great base for outdoor activities, including hiking and skiing in the winter. For those looking for a less physically demanding adventure, the town is also known for its scenic train routes, which offer unparalleled views of the surrounding mountains.

Hiking in Andermatt

Andermatt is a hiker's paradise, with trails that cater to all levels of experience. One of the most popular hikes is the **Gemsstock Trail**, a moderate route that takes you to the summit of **Gemsstock Mountain**, offering breathtaking panoramic views of the Swiss Alps. For a more relaxed hike, the **Schöllenen Gorge Trail** leads you along a beautiful path through the **Schöllenen Gorge**, with the **Devil's Bridge** being a highlight of the route.

- **How to Get There**: Take the train from **Lugano** to **Andermatt** (about 2 hours). Trains run frequently, and tickets can be purchased through the **SBB** website for CHF 30-40.
- **Costs**: Hiking is free, but if you choose to take the cable car to the top of **Gemsstock Mountain**, tickets are CHF 30 for adults.
- **Best Time to Visit**: Summer and early autumn are ideal for hiking, with clear skies and pleasant temperatures.

Scenic Train Ride: The Glacier Express

If you prefer to take in the views without breaking a sweat, hop on the **Glacier Express**, one of Switzerland's most famous scenic train routes. Running between **Zermatt** and **St. Moritz**, the train passes through **Andermatt**, making it an easy day trip from Ticino. The train takes you through breathtaking mountain passes, deep valleys, and along rivers, offering spectacular views of the Swiss Alps along the way.

- **How to Get There**: Board the **Glacier Express** in **Andermatt**. Train tickets can be purchased online or at the **Andermatt** station. One-way tickets cost approximately CHF 50-70, depending on your class of travel.
- **Tips**: Be sure to reserve your seat in advance, especially during the summer and ski seasons, as the train can get fully booked.

Skiing and Mountain Adventures in Zermatt

For those seeking a more adrenaline-pumping adventure, **Zermatt** is one of Switzerland's top ski resorts, known for its access to the iconic **Matterhorn**. While **Zermatt** is best known for its skiing, the town offers activities year-round, making it a fantastic destination for both winter and summer adventures.

Winter Skiing in Zermatt

If you're visiting in the winter, **Zermatt** offers some of the best skiing in the world, with hundreds of kilometers of ski slopes and excellent snow conditions. The ski area is suitable for all levels, from beginners to experts, and offers stunning views of the **Matterhorn** from every angle. For non-skiers, **Zermatt** also offers other winter activities, including snowshoeing and sledding.

- **How to Get There**: Take the train from **Lugano** to **Zermatt** (about 3.5 hours). Tickets can be purchased on the **SBB** website for CHF 60-80.
- **Costs**: Ski passes range from CHF 70-100 per day, depending on the

season and access to different ski areas. Equipment rentals are available in **Zermatt** for CHF 40-50 per day.
- **Tips**: Make sure to book your ski pass and rentals in advance, especially during peak winter season.

Summer Adventures in Zermatt

In the summer, **Zermatt** transforms into a haven for hikers and mountain bikers. One of the most popular hikes is the **Five Lakes Walk**, which takes you through some of the most scenic spots in the area, including five crystal-clear alpine lakes that reflect the Matterhorn. For those looking for a less strenuous way to enjoy the mountains, the **Gornergrat Railway** offers a scenic train ride to the summit of **Gornergrat**, where you'll be treated to spectacular views of the **Matterhorn** and surrounding peaks.

- **How to Get There**: The **Gornergrat Railway** departs from **Zermatt**. Tickets cost CHF 60-80 for a round trip.
- **Best Time to Visit**: Late spring through early autumn is ideal for hiking and outdoor activities.

Hidden Gems for Day Trips and Excursions

While the Swiss Alps and popular towns like **Andermatt** and **Zermatt** are well-known, Ticino also offers access to lesser-known day trip destinations that are just as rewarding. These hidden gems are perfect for travelers looking to escape the crowds and explore off-the-beaten-path villages, hikes, and lakeside spots.

Morcote: Ticino's Most Beautiful Village

Just a 30-minute drive or bus ride from **Lugano**, **Morcote** is often referred to as the most beautiful village in Ticino. Perched on the shores of **Lake Lugano**, this charming village offers a peaceful escape from the larger towns and cities. **Morcote** is known for its narrow, cobblestone streets, traditional **Ticinese** architecture, and stunning views of the lake.

What to Do in Morcote

While in **Morcote**, take a stroll along the lakeside promenade, which offers some of the best views of **Lake Lugano**. Be sure to visit **Parco Scherrer**, a beautiful botanical garden filled with Mediterranean plants, sculptures, and fountains. For those interested in history, the **Santa Maria del Sasso** church is a must-see. The church is perched on a hill above the village and offers panoramic views of the lake and surrounding mountains.

- **How to Get There**: Take bus 431 from **Lugano** to **Morcote** (30 minutes). Tickets cost CHF 5-10.
- **Costs**: Entry to **Parco Scherrer** is CHF 5 for adults. Visiting the **Santa Maria del Sasso** church is free.
- **Tips**: Visit in the spring or autumn for the best weather and fewer crowds.

Valle di Muggio: A Hidden Valley for Nature Lovers

If you're looking for a secluded spot away from the main tourist routes, the **Valle di Muggio** is one of Ticino's best-kept secrets. Located about an hour's drive from **Lugano**, this unspoiled valley is home to traditional **Ticinese** villages, rolling green hills, and scenic hiking trails. It's the perfect destination for nature lovers and those seeking a peaceful retreat.

Exploring Valle di Muggio

Start your visit with a hike through the valley's meadows and forests, where you'll pass by stone houses, watermills, and vineyards. The **Sentiero delle Meraviglie** (Trail of Wonders) is a popular route that takes you through the valley's most scenic spots, including ancient bridges and waterfalls. Along the way, you can stop in the village of **Muggio**, where you'll find a small museum dedicated to the valley's history and culture.

- **How to Get There**: Drive from **Lugano** (1 hour) or take bus 519 from **Chiasso** to **Muggio**.
- **Costs**: Hiking is free, but entry to the **Museo Etnografico della Valle**

di Muggio is CHF 8 for adults.
- **Tips**: Bring a picnic and enjoy lunch by one of the valley's scenic rivers or waterfalls.

Monte Brè: A Panoramic Escape Above Lugano

For those who don't want to travel far from **Lugano**, **Monte Brè** offers a perfect day trip with stunning panoramic views of **Lake Lugano** and the surrounding mountains. At 933 meters above sea level, **Monte Brè** is one of the highest points around **Lugano** and is easily accessible by funicular.

Hiking and Scenic Views on Monte Brè

Once at the top of **Monte Brè**, you'll be treated to spectacular views of **Lake Lugano**, the **Alps**, and even **Italy** on a clear day. There are several hiking trails that lead from the summit, including a scenic route down to the village of **Brè**, where you can explore traditional **Ticinese** houses and enjoy a meal at a local restaurant.

- **How to Get There**: Take the funicular from **Cassarate** to the top of **Monte Brè**. Tickets cost CHF 25 for a round trip.
- **Costs**: Hiking is free, but funicular tickets cost CHF 25 for adults.
- **Best Time to Visit**: Late spring through early autumn is the best time to visit, with clear skies and warm temperatures.

Ticino for Families

Family-Friendly Attractions and Activities

Ticino is home to a wide range of attractions that cater specifically to families. From historical landmarks like the **Bellinzona Castles** to interactive parks such as **Swissminiatur**, these spots offer a mix of education and entertainment, ensuring that kids have fun while learning about Ticino's culture and history.

Swissminiatur: A Fun-Filled Journey Through Switzerland

One of the most popular family attractions in Ticino is **Swissminiatur**, an open-air park featuring miniature replicas of Switzerland's most famous landmarks. Kids and adults alike will enjoy wandering through this unique park, which covers more than 14,000 square meters and includes over 120 meticulously crafted models of Swiss buildings, castles, and monuments. The park also features a miniature railway with more than 3 kilometers of track, allowing kids to watch small trains wind through tunnels and cross bridges as they navigate the entire park.

- **What to Expect**: Kids can explore the tiny versions of landmarks like the **Château de Chillon**, the **Matterhorn**, and the **Zurich Hauptbahnhof**. The interactive nature of the park makes it particularly appealing for young visitors, as they can watch the trains and boats move across the landscape.

- **Facilities**: The park has a playground and picnic areas where families can relax and enjoy a meal. There is also a café that serves snacks, drinks, and meals.

Practical Information:

- **Location**: Swissminiatur is located in **Melide**, just a 10-minute train ride from **Lugano**.
- **Opening Hours**: Open daily from 9:00 AM – 6:00 PM (March to November).
- **Admission Fees**: CHF 19 for adults, CHF 12 for children (aged 6-15), and free for children under 6.
- **How to Get There**: Take the train from **Lugano** to **Melide** (10 minutes), then it's a short walk to the park. By car, there is parking available near the park.

Bellinzona's Castles: A Journey Through History

For a more historical experience, families can explore the **Bellinzona Castles**, a UNESCO World Heritage Site that consists of three medieval fortresses: **Castelgrande, Montebello,** and **Sasso Corbaro**. These castles, with their towering walls and ancient towers, offer a glimpse into the past and provide a great opportunity for kids to learn about Ticino's rich history while exploring the grounds.

- **What to Expect**: Kids will love running through the castles' courtyards, climbing up the towers, and imagining life in medieval times. Each castle has exhibits showcasing artifacts and historical information, making it a fun and educational experience for the whole family. **Montebello** has a museum with medieval weapons and armor, while **Sasso Corbaro** offers stunning panoramic views of the surrounding landscape.
- **Facilities**: The castles have picnic areas, and there are several nearby restaurants where families can stop for a meal. Bathrooms are available

at each castle, making it convenient for families with young children.

Practical Information:

- **Location**: Bellinzona, about 30 minutes by train from **Lugano**.
- **Opening Hours**: Open daily, 10:00 AM – 6:00 PM (April to October), 10:00 AM – 5:00 PM (November to March).
- **Admission Fees**: CHF 10 for adults, CHF 5 for children (aged 6-15), and free for children under 6. Family tickets are available for CHF 22.
- **How to Get There**: Take the train to **Bellinzona** from **Lugano** (30 minutes), and then walk or take a short bus ride to the castles. If driving, there is parking available near **Castelgrande**.

Falconeria Locarno: A Wildlife Experience

Another fantastic family attraction is the **Falconeria Locarno**, where children can see birds of prey up close and watch daily falconry shows. The park is home to eagles, hawks, owls, and falcons, and the shows are both thrilling and educational, providing insight into the ancient art of falconry.

- **What to Expect**: Kids will be fascinated by the majestic birds as they swoop through the air during the live demonstrations. The park also has an area where families can learn more about the different species of birds and their importance in history.
- **Facilities**: The park has a café and picnic areas, as well as restrooms and a gift shop where families can buy souvenirs.

Practical Information:

- **Location**: Falconeria Locarno is located in **Locarno**, about 45 minutes by train from **Lugano**.
- **Opening Hours**: Open daily from 10:00 AM – 5:00 PM. Shows are held at 11:00 AM and 3:00 PM.
- **Admission Fees**: CHF 18 for adults, CHF 10 for children (aged 6-15),

and free for children under 6.
- **How to Get There**: Take the train to **Locarno** from **Lugano** (45 minutes), then it's a short bus ride or 20-minute walk to the park.

Tamagno Funicular: A Scenic Ride for the Whole Family

Families looking for a more relaxed activity will enjoy taking a scenic ride on the **Tamagno Funicular**, which travels from **Locarno** to the hilltop town of **Orselina**. The ride offers stunning views of **Lake Maggiore** and the surrounding mountains, and once at the top, families can explore the **Madonna del Sasso Sanctuary** or take a stroll through the beautiful hillside gardens.

- **What to Expect**: The funicular ride is a fun experience for kids and adults alike, offering spectacular views of the landscape below. At the top, there's plenty of space for kids to run around, and the **Madonna del Sasso** offers a peaceful place to take in the scenery.
- **Facilities**: There are several cafes and restaurants at the top of the funicular where families can stop for a drink or meal, as well as picnic areas.

Practical Information:

- **Location**: The funicular departs from **Locarno**, near the train station.
- **Opening Hours**: Daily from 9:00 AM – 6:00 PM.
- **Cost**: CHF 8 for adults, CHF 4 for children (aged 6-15), and free for children under 6.
- **How to Get There**: Take the train from **Lugano** to **Locarno** (45 minutes), and then walk to the funicular station near the **Locarno** train station.

Best Playgrounds and Parks for Kids

Ticino is filled with beautiful parks and well-equipped playgrounds that provide perfect spots for families with young children to relax and play. Whether you're looking for a place to have a picnic, take a scenic walk, or let the kids burn off some energy, these parks and playgrounds are ideal for family outings.

Parco Ciani – Lugano

Parco Ciani is Lugano's largest and most beautiful park, located right on the shores of **Lake Lugano**. With sprawling lawns, tree-lined paths, and breathtaking views of the lake and surrounding mountains, it's a perfect spot for a family day out. The park features a large playground with swings, slides, and climbing frames, as well as plenty of space for kids to run and play.

- **What to Expect**: In addition to the playground, families can enjoy a leisurely stroll through the park's manicured gardens, which are filled with colorful flowers and sculptures. There are also several picnic areas where families can enjoy a meal with a view of the lake.
- **Facilities**: The park has public restrooms, picnic tables, and benches, making it a convenient spot for families. There are also several nearby cafes where you can grab a snack or coffee.

Practical Information:

- **Location**: The park is located in the center of **Lugano**, near the lakefront.
- **Opening Hours**: Open daily from dawn to dusk.
- **Cost**: Free to enter.
- **How to Get There**: A short walk from the **Lugano** train station or bus stops.

Parco San Grato – Carona

If you're looking for a more nature-focused park, **Parco San Grato** in **Carona** is a great choice. This botanical park, located in the hills above **Lugano**, is known for its beautiful collection of azaleas, rhododendrons, and conifers. It also has a large playground and several hiking trails that are suitable for families.

- **What to Expect**: The park's playground is set in a scenic location, with swings, slides, and climbing frames surrounded by trees and flowers. The park also offers plenty of open space for picnics and games, and the hiking trails provide an easy way to explore the surrounding nature.
- **Facilities**: There are public restrooms, picnic areas, and a restaurant where families can enjoy a meal with a view of the mountains.

Practical Information:

- **Location**: The park is located in **Carona**, about 20 minutes by car from **Lugano**.
- **Opening Hours**: Open daily from dawn to dusk.
- **Cost**: Free to enter.
- **How to Get There**: Drive from **Lugano** (20 minutes) or take a bus from **Lugano** to **Carona**.

Lido di Lugano: Beach Fun and Playground

For families who love the water, the **Lido di Lugano** offers a beach experience right in the heart of the city. This lakeside beach features soft sand, shallow waters that are perfect for young children, and a large playground where kids can play after a swim. The lido also has a pool area with water slides and a splash park, making it a great spot for a full day of fun.

- **What to Expect**: The beach area is ideal for families with young kids, offering plenty of space to play in the sand or swim in the lake. The

playground includes swings, slides, and climbing structures, and the pool area provides additional water fun.
- **Facilities**: The lido has changing rooms, showers, restrooms, and picnic areas. There's also a restaurant and café that serves food and drinks throughout the day.

Practical Information:

- **Location**: Viale Castagnola, 6900 Lugano.
- **Opening Hours**: Daily from 9:00 AM – 7:00 PM (seasonal).
- **Admission Fees**: CHF 6 for adults, CHF 3 for children (aged 6-15), and free for children under 6.
- **How to Get There**: A short walk from **Lugano** city center or accessible by local bus.

Educational Spots: Kid-Friendly Museums in Ticino

Ticino is home to several museums that are perfect for curious young minds. With hands-on exhibits and educational programs, these museums offer an engaging way for children to learn while having fun. Whether your child is fascinated by science, nature, or art, Ticino's museums provide an enriching experience for the whole family.

Museo in Erba: Art and Creativity for Kids

If your children love art, **Museo in Erba** in **Lugano** is the perfect place to nurture their creativity. This museum is specially designed for children and offers interactive, hands-on exhibits that introduce kids to the world of art in a fun and educational way. The museum features rotating exhibitions inspired by famous artists, with workshops and activities that encourage kids to explore different artistic techniques.

- **What to Expect**: **Museo in Erba** hosts art workshops where kids can create their own masterpieces, using inspiration from well-known artists like **Picasso** and **Kandinsky**. The workshops are designed to be interactive, allowing children to engage with art on a deeper level while developing their creative skills.
- **Educational Programs**: The museum offers educational programs tailored to different age groups, from toddlers to teenagers. These programs focus on hands-on learning and often incorporate elements of storytelling and music to make the experience more immersive for younger visitors.

Practical Information:

- **Location**: Via Cattedrale 12, 6900 Lugano.
- **Opening Hours**: Tuesday to Sunday, 2:00 PM – 6:00 PM.
- **Admission Fees**: CHF 10 for adults, CHF 6 for children (aged 4-15), and free for children under 4.
- **How to Get There**: The museum is located in **Lugano** city center, a short walk from the **Lugano** train station or bus stops.

Museo Cantonale di Storia Naturale: Nature and Science Exploration

For families interested in science and nature, the **Museo Cantonale di Storia Naturale** in **Lugano** offers a fascinating journey through the natural world. This natural history museum is packed with exhibits showcasing the geology, flora, and fauna of Ticino, making it a great place for kids to learn about the region's biodiversity.

- **What to Expect**: The museum features a range of exhibits, including fossils, minerals, and life-size models of animals native to Ticino. There are interactive displays that allow children to touch and explore different specimens, making it an engaging experience for young learners.
- **Educational Programs**: The museum regularly hosts workshops and

educational activities designed for school-age children. These programs cover topics like geology, zoology, and ecology, providing kids with hands-on learning opportunities.

Practical Information:

- **Location**: Viale Carlo Cattaneo 4, 6900 Lugano.
- **Opening Hours**: Tuesday to Sunday, 10:00 AM – 5:00 PM.
- **Admission Fees**: Free entry for all visitors.
- **How to Get There**: The museum is located in the **Lugano** city center, easily accessible by foot or public transportation.

LAC Lugano Arte e Cultura: Music, Theater, and Art

The **LAC Lugano Arte e Cultura** is a cultural hub in **Lugano** that offers a variety of family-friendly events, including concerts, theater performances, and art exhibitions. While not exclusively a museum, **LAC** hosts interactive programs and workshops designed for children, making it an ideal spot for families to explore the arts together.

- **What to Expect**: Families can attend live performances such as children's theater, musical concerts, or dance performances. The center also offers workshops where kids can engage in activities like painting, acting, or playing musical instruments.
- **Educational Programs**: **LAC** regularly organizes creative workshops for children, focusing on music, theater, and visual arts. These programs encourage kids to express themselves through different art forms, while also teaching them about Ticino's rich cultural heritage.

Practical Information:

- **Location**: Piazza Bernardino Luini 6, 6900 Lugano.
- **Opening Hours**: Varies by event.
- **Admission Fees**: Prices vary depending on the event or workshop.

- **How to Get There**: Located near the **Lugano** city center, **LAC** is a short walk from the train station or easily accessible by bus.

Museo Nazionale del San Gottardo: Discover the History of the Swiss Alps

Located near the famous **Gotthard Pass**, the **Museo Nazionale del San Gottardo** offers families the chance to learn about the history of one of Switzerland's most important alpine routes. The museum showcases the engineering feats behind the construction of the **Gotthard Tunnel**, as well as the natural history and cultural significance of the region.

- **What to Expect**: Kids will enjoy the interactive displays, which include models of the tunnel and historical artifacts from the construction of the pass. There's also a section of the museum dedicated to the flora and fauna of the Swiss Alps, with exhibits that allow children to learn about the unique wildlife found in the region.
- **Educational Programs**: The museum offers guided tours and educational programs that focus on both the human and natural history of the **Gotthard Pass**. These programs are ideal for older children interested in engineering, history, and ecology.

Practical Information:

- **Location**: Passo del San Gottardo, 6780 Airolo.
- **Opening Hours**: Open daily during the summer months, 9:00 AM – 5:00 PM.
- **Admission Fees**: CHF 8 for adults, CHF 4 for children (aged 6-15), and free for children under 6.
- **How to Get There**: The museum is located at the top of the **Gotthard Pass**, accessible by car or bus from **Airolo**.

Traveling with Babies and Toddlers: What You Need to Know

Baby-Friendly Accommodations

When traveling with babies or toddlers, choosing the right accommodation is key to ensuring a comfortable stay. Many hotels and vacation rentals in Ticino are well-equipped for families with young children, offering amenities like cribs, high chairs, and baby-friendly services.

What to Look for in Family Accommodations

- **Cribs and High Chairs**: Most family-friendly hotels in Ticino provide cribs (cots) and high chairs upon request. Be sure to mention that you're traveling with a baby when booking your room, so the hotel can prepare these items in advance.
- **Play Areas**: Some hotels, especially resorts, offer dedicated play areas for young children, complete with toys, games, and soft play equipment. This can be a great way for your little ones to burn off some energy.
- **Babysitting Services**: If you're looking for a break, certain high-end hotels in Ticino offer babysitting services, allowing parents to enjoy some time to themselves while ensuring their children are well cared for.

Recommended Family-Friendly Hotels in Ticino

- **Hotel Splendide Royal** (Lugano): This luxury hotel offers family suites, cribs, and high chairs. The staff is experienced in accommodating families, and the hotel's location near **Parco Ciani** makes it ideal for families with young children.
- **Hotel Serpiano** (Serpiano): A great option for families looking for a relaxing stay in the Ticino countryside. The hotel offers family rooms, cribs, and an indoor play area for children.

- **Villa Sassa Hotel** (Lugano): This hotel has a range of family-friendly amenities, including large suites, an outdoor pool, and babysitting services.

Restaurants with High Chairs and Kid-Friendly Menus

When dining out with babies or toddlers, finding a restaurant that offers high chairs and kid-friendly menus is important. Many restaurants in Ticino cater to families, providing high chairs, changing facilities, and child-sized portions of local favorites like **risotto** and **pasta**.

Recommended Family-Friendly Restaurants

- **Ristorante La Terrazza** (Lugano): This lakeside restaurant offers high chairs, a kids' menu, and plenty of space for strollers. The relaxed atmosphere and beautiful views of **Lake Lugano** make it a great choice for families.
- **Ristorante Al Faro** (Ascona): A family-friendly restaurant in **Ascona** with a kid's menu and high chairs available. The restaurant is located near the lakeside promenade, making it convenient for a post-meal stroll.
- **Grotto Morchino** (Lugano): This traditional **grotto** is popular with families, offering simple yet delicious **Ticinese** dishes and outdoor seating where children can play.

Stroller Accessibility

Ticino is a stroller-friendly destination, with most towns offering smooth, flat surfaces that are easy to navigate with a stroller. Attractions like **Parco Ciani** in **Lugano** and the **Lido di Lugano** beach are also fully accessible, with wide paths and ramps. However, if you plan to visit more mountainous areas or take part in hiking, you may want to bring a baby carrier, as some trails and villages (like **Monte Brè**) have steep inclines and cobblestone streets that can be difficult to navigate with a stroller.

Where to Find Baby Supplies

While Ticino is well-equipped for families, it's always good to know where you can find essential baby supplies like diapers, formula, and baby food. Most large supermarkets, such as **Coop** and **Migros**, carry a wide range of baby products. Pharmacies (**Farmacia**) are also well-stocked with baby essentials, including sunscreen, baby medicine, and wipes.

- **Coop Supermarket**: Located in **Lugano** city center and other towns across Ticino, **Coop** offers a full range of baby supplies, including diapers, baby food, and formula.
- **Migros**: Another large supermarket chain with locations throughout Ticino, **Migros** is a convenient stop for baby essentials and family groceries.

Practical Information

Emergency Numbers and Healthcare in Ticino

In the event of an emergency, knowing the right number to call can make all the difference. Ticino follows Switzerland's national emergency protocols, and help is always a phone call away. Whether you require police assistance, medical help, or the fire department, the emergency numbers are the same throughout Switzerland.

Essential Emergency Numbers in Ticino
   Police: 117

- The police handle all matters of public safety and law enforcement. Whether you need to report a crime or require immediate police assistance, calling 117 will connect you to the nearest police station.

Ambulance/Medical Emergency: 144

- For any medical emergencies, dial 144 to reach an ambulance service. Ambulances in Ticino are well-equipped and can reach most areas quickly.

Fire Services: 118

- In case of fire or hazardous situations involving fire or gas, dial 118. The fire department in Ticino is highly responsive and will dispatch help as quickly as possible.

European Emergency Number: 112

- The number 112 can be dialed for all types of emergencies across Europe, including in Switzerland. It's a universal number that can be used for any kind of help and is especially useful for non-Swiss residents.

Hospitals and Healthcare in Ticino

Ticino's healthcare system is highly developed, with modern hospitals, clinics, and pharmacies throughout the region. In case of a medical issue, there are several hospitals and urgent care centers ready to help.

Hospitals in Ticino

  1. **Ospedale Regionale di Lugano** (Regional Hospital of Lugano)

- **Location**: Via Tesserete 46, 6900 Lugano
- **Contact**: +41 91 811 60 11
- **Services**: The main hospital in Lugano offers full medical services, including emergency care, surgery, and specialized departments for pediatric and adult care. It is one of the largest hospitals in Ticino.
- **How to Get There**: Located in **Lugano**, the hospital is accessible by public transport (bus or train) and is close to the city center.

2. **Ospedale Regionale di Bellinzona e Valli** (Regional Hospital of Bellinzona and Valleys)

- **Location**: Viale G. Motta 30, 6500 Bellinzona
- **Contact**: +41 91 811 81 11

- **Services**: This hospital serves **Bellinzona** and the surrounding valleys, offering general emergency services, surgery, and a range of outpatient treatments.
- **How to Get There**: Located near the city center of **Bellinzona**, it's easily accessible by public transport or car.

Clinica Luganese Moncucco

- **Location**: Via Moncucco 10, 6900 Lugano
- **Contact**: +41 91 960 81 11
- **Services**: A private clinic offering high-quality healthcare services, including specialized treatments in cardiology, oncology, and orthopedics. It also has an emergency department.
- **How to Get There**: A short drive from **Lugano** city center, accessible by bus or taxi.

Urgent Care and Clinics

For less critical health issues that do not require hospital admission, there are urgent care centers and clinics that can provide medical help quickly and efficiently.

Centro Medico Lugano

- **Location**: Via Nassa 26, 6900 Lugano
- **Contact**: +41 91 922 21 21
- **Services**: Offers general medical care, walk-in services, and minor emergency treatments.

Centro Medico Bellinzona

- **Location**: Via Mirasole 5, 6500 Bellinzona

- **Contact**: +41 91 835 35 35
- **Services**: Provides urgent care, routine checkups, and specialized medical consultations.

Pharmacies in Ticino

Pharmacies in Ticino are widespread and well-stocked with medications and health products. Many pharmacists can speak English and are trained to offer basic medical advice.

Farmacia Internazionale Lugano

- **Location**: Via Pioda 9, 6900 Lugano
- **Contact**: +41 91 923 45 67
- **Opening Hours**: Monday to Friday, 8:00 AM – 7:00 PM; Saturday, 9:00 AM – 6:00 PM.
- **Services**: A full-service pharmacy with prescription and over-the-counter medications, as well as health and beauty products.

Farmacia Centrale Bellinzona

- **Location**: Piazza Collegiata 3, 6500 Bellinzona
- **Contact**: +41 91 825 21 71
- **Opening Hours**: Monday to Friday, 8:00 AM – 6:30 PM; Saturday, 9:00 AM – 5:00 PM.
- **Services**: Offers prescription medications, health products, and some natural remedies.

Embassies and Consulates in Ticino

Though Ticino itself doesn't host embassies due to Switzerland's unique diplomatic setup, you can find consulates in nearby regions or major cities, such as **Zurich** and **Milan** (Italy), which handle consular matters for travelers. Here's a list of key embassies and consulates relevant to foreign travelers in Ticino.

U.S. Consulate in Ticino

While there is no full embassy in Ticino, the **U.S. Embassy** in **Bern** serves U.S. citizens across Switzerland, and there's a **U.S. Consulate** in **Zurich** that can assist with certain consular services.

U.S. Consulate General Zurich

- **Location**: Dufourstrasse 101, 8008 Zurich
- **Contact**: +41 43 499 29 60
- **Opening Hours**: Monday to Friday, 8:00 AM – 5:00 PM.
- **Services**: Passport renewals, emergency assistance, and notarial services for U.S. citizens.
- **How to Get There**: From **Lugano**, take the train to **Zurich** (about 2 hours). The consulate is a short taxi ride from the **Zurich Hauptbahnhof**.

British Consulate in Milan

Given Ticino's proximity to the Italian border, the **British Consulate** in **Milan** is often the nearest place for British travelers needing consular support.

British Consulate General Milan

- **Location**: Via San Paolo 7, 20121 Milan, Italy
- **Contact**: +39 02 72300 01

- **Opening Hours**: Monday to Friday, 9:00 AM – 5:00 PM.
- **Services**: Provides assistance with passport issues, lost documents, and emergency services.
- **How to Get There**: From **Lugano**, it's about an hour by train to **Milan**. The consulate is located in the central part of **Milan**, near **Piazza del Duomo**.

Canadian Consulate in Milan

For Canadian citizens in Ticino, the nearest consulate is located in **Milan**, which handles a range of consular services.

Canadian Consulate General Milan

- **Location**: Via Palestro 14, 20121 Milan, Italy
- **Contact**: +39 02 62694 3111
- **Opening Hours**: Monday to Friday, 9:00 AM – 1:00 PM.
- **Services**: Passport services, legal assistance, and advice for Canadian travelers.
- **How to Get There**: The train from **Lugano** to **Milan** takes about 1 hour, and the consulate is located in the central part of **Milan**.

German Consulate in Zurich

For German travelers, the **German Consulate** in **Zurich** provides consular services for citizens visiting or living in Ticino.

German Consulate General Zurich

- **Location**: Zollikerstrasse 141, 8008 Zurich
- **Contact**: +41 44 385 85 00
- **Opening Hours**: Monday to Friday, 8:00 AM – 4:00 PM.
- **Services**: Assistance with passport issues, lost documents, and notarial services for German citizens.
- **How to Get There**: From **Lugano**, it's about 2 hours by train to **Zurich**.

Embassy of France in Bern

For French travelers, consular services are provided by the **French Embassy** in **Bern**. Although there is no consulate in Ticino, **Bern** is only a few hours away, and the embassy offers full consular services.

Embassy of France in Switzerland

- **Location**: Schosshaldenstrasse 46, 3006 Bern
- **Contact**: +41 31 359 21 11
- **Opening Hours**: Monday to Friday, 9:00 AM – 12:00 PM.
- **Services**: Passport services, legal assistance, and emergency help for French citizens.
- **How to Get There**: The train from **Lugano** to **Bern** takes about 3 hours.

When to Contact Your Embassy or Consulate

You may need to contact your country's embassy or consulate if you experience any of the following issues during your trip:

- **Lost Passport**: If you lose your passport or it gets stolen, your embassy or consulate can help you obtain a temporary travel document.
- **Legal Trouble**: If you get into legal trouble, your embassy can provide assistance or recommend legal services.
- **Emergency Situations**: In the event of a serious emergency, such as a natural disaster or civil unrest, your embassy can offer guidance on safety and evacuation procedures.

Accessibility: Tips for Seniors and Travelers with Disabilities

Accessible Public Transportation in Ticino

Ticino's public transportation system is efficient and largely accessible to travelers with mobility challenges. **Trains, buses, and boats** all provide accessible options for seniors and those with disabilities.

Trains: The Swiss railway system (**SBB/CFF**) is known for its accessibility. Major stations like **Lugano, Bellinzona**, and **Locarno** are equipped with ramps, elevators, and accessible platforms. Many trains have designated spaces for wheelchairs, and assistance can be arranged in advance if necessary.

- **Practical Information**: You can request assistance by contacting the **SBB Call Center Handicap** (+41 51 225 78 44) at least one hour before departure. They will help ensure you can board and disembark the train easily.

Buses: Ticino's **PostBus** network also accommodates passengers with disabilities. Most buses are low-floor models, making it easier to get on and off without climbing steps. Drivers are trained to assist passengers who may need help boarding or securing a wheelchair.

- **How to Arrange Assistance**: Notify the bus driver if you need additional help. Buses often have a retractable ramp for wheelchair users.

Boats: If you plan to enjoy one of Ticino's scenic boat rides on **Lake Lugano** or **Lake Maggiore**, you'll be pleased to know that most boats are accessible to wheelchair users. Ferries are designed with ramps and accessible toilets, making the journey comfortable for all passengers.

- **Practical Information**: Check with the boat company in advance to ensure accessibility, as not all older boats may have the same level of facilities.

Accessible Hotels in Ticino

Ticino is home to many hotels that have been adapted to accommodate seniors and travelers with disabilities. These hotels offer rooms with wider doorways, roll-in showers, and grab bars in the bathrooms. When booking, it's a good idea to contact the hotel directly to confirm that they can meet your specific needs.

Recommended Accessible Hotels in Ticino:

Hotel Splendide Royal (Lugano): A luxury hotel with accessible rooms that include roll-in showers, grab bars, and wheelchair access to all facilities. The hotel is also centrally located, making it easy to explore **Lugano**.

- **Location**: Riva Antonio Caccia 7, 6900 Lugano.
- **Contact**: +41 91 985 77 11
- **Price Range**: CHF 400+ per night.

Hotel Belvedere Locarno (Locarno): This mid-range hotel offers accessible rooms with amenities like lowered sinks, roll-in showers, and accessible entrances. It's located near **Piazza Grande**, a central area in **Locarno**.

- **Location**: Via ai Monti della Trinita 44, 6600 Locarno.
- **Contact**: +41 91 751 03 63
- **Price Range**: CHF 250+ per night.

Villa Sassa Hotel, Residence & Spa (Lugano): A family-friendly hotel with accessible rooms and a spa area that has been adapted for wheelchair users. It's located just outside the city center, offering beautiful views of the surrounding hills.

- **Location**: Via Tesserete 10, 6900 Lugano.
- **Contact**: +41 91 911 41 11
- **Price Range**: CHF 300+ per night.

Accessible Attractions in Ticino

Many of Ticino's top attractions, including parks, museums, and historical sites, have been made accessible to travelers with disabilities.

Swissminiatur: This open-air park featuring miniature replicas of famous Swiss landmarks is accessible to wheelchair users. The park has smooth pathways, and assistance is available at the entrance.

- **Location**: Melide, just outside **Lugano**.
- **Cost**: CHF 19 for adults, CHF 12 for children.
- **Contact**: +41 91 640 10 60

Bellinzona Castles: The three castles in **Bellinzona—Castelgrande**, **Montebello**, and **Sasso Corbaro**—are partially accessible to wheelchair users. **Castelgrande** is the most accessible, with ramps and elevators installed to help visitors explore the grounds.

- **Location**: Bellinzona.
- **Cost**: CHF 10 for adults, CHF 5 for children.
- **Contact**: +41 91 825 21 31

Parco Ciani: One of the most scenic parks in **Lugano**, **Parco Ciani** is a great place for seniors and travelers with mobility issues. The park has flat, paved paths that wind through beautifully landscaped gardens along the lakefront.

- **Location**: Lungolago Ciani, Lugano.
- **Cost**: Free entry.

Medical Services for Seniors and Travelers with Disabilities

Ticino's healthcare system is well-equipped to handle the needs of seniors and those with disabilities. Hospitals like the **Ospedale Regionale di Lugano** and **Clinica Luganese Moncucco** offer comprehensive medical services, including emergency care and specialized treatments. Pharmacies in major towns also carry medical supplies such as mobility aids and prescription medications.

For travelers requiring dialysis or other specialized treatments, it's best to contact local hospitals ahead of time to arrange appointments and ensure availability of the necessary services.

Staying Connected: Wi-Fi, SIM Cards, and Internet Access

Wi-Fi Hotspots in Ticino

Free Wi-Fi is widely available in Ticino, particularly in public spaces like cafes, hotels, and tourist attractions. Many towns and cities also offer free Wi-Fi in central areas.

- **Public Wi-Fi in Lugano**: The city of **Lugano** provides free public Wi-Fi in several locations, including **Piazza della Riforma**, **Parco Ciani**, and **Lido di Lugano**. To connect, simply select **"Free Wi-Fi Lugano"** on your device and follow the instructions to log in.
- **How to Access**: Once you're connected, you may be prompted to enter your email address for registration.
- **Free Wi-Fi at Train Stations**: Many train stations across Ticino, including **Lugano**, **Bellinzona**, and **Locarno**, offer free Wi-Fi through the **SBB Free Wi-Fi** network. You can connect by selecting the network and entering your mobile phone number to receive a verification code.
- **Cafes and Restaurants**: Most cafes and restaurants in Ticino offer free Wi-Fi for customers. Simply ask the staff for the password if

it's not displayed prominently. Popular spots like **Caffè Federale** in **Bellinzona** and **Grand Café Al Porto** in **Lugano** are great places to enjoy a coffee while staying connected.

SIM Cards for Travelers

For travelers who need more consistent access to the internet or local calls, purchasing a Swiss SIM card is a good option. Most Swiss SIM cards offer data plans, and they can be purchased at major airports, mobile shops, or supermarkets.

Where to Buy SIM Cards in Ticino

1. Swisscom: One of the leading mobile network providers in Switzerland, **Swisscom** offers prepaid SIM cards with data plans tailored to travelers. You can purchase a SIM card at **Swisscom** stores in **Lugano**, **Bellinzona**, or **Locarno**, or at major supermarkets like **Coop** and **Migros**.

- **Price**: SIM cards start at CHF 19, with various data packages available.
- **Coverage**: **Swisscom** has excellent coverage throughout Ticino, including in rural areas and along the lakes.

2. Sunrise: Another popular option for mobile services, **Sunrise** provides affordable prepaid SIM cards with a variety of data and calling plans. **Sunrise** stores can be found in **Lugano** and **Bellinzona**.

- **Price**: SIM cards start at CHF 20, with flexible data and calling packages.
- **Coverage**: **Sunrise** offers good coverage in cities and towns, but rural areas may have slightly weaker signals compared to **Swisscom**.

3. Salt: **Salt** provides more budget-friendly SIM cards and offers decent coverage across Ticino. You can find **Salt** SIM cards at kiosks and mobile phone shops in major towns.

- **Price**: SIM cards start at CHF 15, with different data plans available.
- **Coverage**: Coverage is solid in urban areas, but in more remote parts of Ticino, **Salt** may have less reliable service.

Mobile Apps to Stay Connected

Several apps can help you stay connected, navigate the area, and find local services while in Ticino.

- **SBB Mobile**: This app allows you to check train and bus schedules, purchase tickets, and view platform information for public transport throughout Switzerland.
- **Citymapper**: Perfect for navigating cities like **Lugano** and **Bellinzona**, this app provides real-time transit information, walking routes, and cycling paths.
- **WhatsApp**: For staying in touch with family and friends, **WhatsApp** is one of the most popular messaging apps, and it's widely used in Switzerland. Once you have a local SIM card or access to Wi-Fi, you can use **WhatsApp** for free calls and messages.

Using Swiss Francs in Ticino

Switzerland's official currency is the **Swiss franc (CHF)**, and this is the only currency accepted in most places in Ticino. The Swiss franc comes in both coins and banknotes:

- **Coins**: CHF 0.05, 0.10, 0.20, 0.50, CHF 1, 2, and 5.
- **Banknotes**: CHF 10, 20, 50, 100, 200, and 1000.

While Ticino is close to Italy, euros are generally **not accepted** in most shops, restaurants, or hotels. Some tourist-heavy locations might take euros, but the exchange rate will not be favorable. It's best to stick with Swiss francs for all transactions to avoid overpaying or confusion.

Where to Get Swiss Francs

- **ATMs**: The easiest and most convenient way to get Swiss francs is from ATMs (known as **Bancomat** in Ticino). ATMs are widely available in cities and towns such as **Lugano, Bellinzona**, and **Locarno**. They are found at banks, train stations, airports, and large shopping centers.

Major Banks with ATMs:

- **UBS**: Has a strong presence in all major towns.
- **Credit Suisse**: Another major bank with ATMs throughout the region.
- **PostFinance**: Available at most post offices and large train stations.
- ATMs typically offer the best exchange rate compared to currency exchange desks. You can use your debit or credit card to withdraw money, but keep in mind that international fees may apply depending on your bank. It's advisable to check with your home bank before traveling to learn about international transaction fees.
- **Banks**: If you prefer to exchange currency in person, banks like **UBS**, **Credit Suisse**, and **Raiffeisen** offer currency exchange services. Banks generally have good exchange rates, though a small fee may apply. Banking hours in Ticino are typically **Monday to Friday, 8:30 AM – 4:30 PM**. Most banks are closed on weekends, so plan accordingly if you need to exchange money.
- **UBS Lugano**: Piazza della Riforma 1, 6900 Lugano.
- **Credit Suisse Bellinzona**: Viale Stazione 3, 6500 Bellinzona.

Money Exchange Desks and Services

If you prefer to exchange money directly, there are several places to do so in Ticino, including at airports, train stations, and specialized exchange offices.

- **Currency Exchange at Airports**: Both **Lugano Airport** and **Milan Malpensa Airport** (often used by travelers heading to Ticino) have currency exchange desks. However, it's worth noting that airports tend to have less favorable rates than ATMs or banks.
- **Currency Exchange at Train Stations**: Major train stations like **Lugano**, **Bellinzona**, and **Locarno** offer currency exchange services. Look for **Change Migros** or **SBB Change** offices inside the stations.
- **SBB Change Lugano**: Piazza Riforma, Lugano Railway Station.
- **Migros Change Bellinzona**: Inside the **Bellinzona** train station.
- **Private Exchange Services**: Specialized money exchange offices in the city centers often offer competitive rates and may charge lower fees than banks or airport exchange desks. However, always double-check the rates and fees to ensure you're getting a good deal.

Tips for Exchanging Money in Ticino

- **Compare Rates**: Exchange rates vary, so it's worth checking several places before deciding where to exchange your money.
- **Avoid Airport Exchange Desks**: While convenient, airports generally offer poor rates and high fees. Stick to banks or ATMs for better value.
- **Carry Small Bills**: When exchanging currency, ask for smaller denominations. CHF 100 bills can be difficult to break at smaller cafes or shops, so it's better to carry a mix of smaller bills (CHF 10, 20, and 50).

Using Credit Cards in Ticino

Credit cards are widely accepted in Ticino, especially in larger cities like **Lugano**, **Bellinzona**, and **Locarno**. Major hotels, restaurants, and shops generally accept **Visa**, **MasterCard**, and **American Express**. However, it's important to note that smaller, family-run businesses, markets, or cafes may only accept cash or charge a minimum for card payments.

Important Tips for Using Credit Cards in Ticino

- **Always Carry Cash**: Even though credit cards are widely accepted, it's a good idea to carry some cash, especially when visiting rural areas or small local shops.
- **Chip and PIN Cards**: Switzerland uses **chip and PIN** technology for credit card transactions, so ensure your card has a chip. Some places may not accept cards with magnetic stripes.
- **Notify Your Bank**: Before you travel, inform your bank or credit card company about your trip to avoid having your card blocked for suspicious activity.
- **Currency Conversion Fees**: Be aware that using a foreign credit card may incur currency conversion fees. Some credit cards offer no foreign transaction fees, so it's worth checking with your provider.

Where Credit Cards Are Not Commonly Accepted

- **Small Cafes and Shops**: Many smaller establishments may have a minimum charge for credit card transactions or may only accept cash.
- **Public Transport**: Buses and some small ticket offices may not accept credit cards, so it's best to have cash on hand for local transport tickets.
- **Markets and Local Vendors**: While credit cards are gaining acceptance, cash is still the preferred method of payment at markets and with street vendors.

Tipping Culture in Ticino

Tipping in Switzerland, including Ticino, is generally not obligatory but is appreciated for good service. **Service charges are typically included** in the bill at restaurants, cafes, and hotels, so there's no pressure to leave a large tip. However, rounding up the bill or leaving a small tip for exceptional service is a nice gesture.

How Much to Tip in Ticino

- **Restaurants and Cafes**: Tipping is not expected, but rounding up the bill is common. For example, if your bill is CHF 47, you can leave CHF 50. If service is particularly good, you can leave a tip of 5-10% of the total bill, but this is entirely at your discretion.
- **Hotels**: Tipping hotel staff, such as porters and housekeeping, is appreciated but not required. A tip of CHF 1-2 per bag for porters or CHF 5-10 for housekeeping at the end of your stay is a kind gesture.
- **Taxis**: Taxi drivers do not expect tips, but rounding up to the nearest franc is common practice. For example, if your fare is CHF 18.50, you can round it up to CHF 20.
- **Guided Tours**: If you're taking a guided tour and feel that the guide has provided exceptional service, a small tip (around CHF 5-10) is appreciated.

Tipping Do's and Don'ts

- **Do**: Tip in cash directly to the server, porter, or driver if you wish to leave a gratuity.
- **Don't**: Feel pressured to leave large tips, as service is already included in most bills.
- **Do**: Round up the bill as a simple way to tip in cafes, taxis, and casual dining establishments.

Final Tips for a Memorable Ticino Trip

How to Avoid Tourist Traps in Ticino

While Ticino offers many well-known attractions, some areas are swamped with tourists, often leading to overpriced goods, crowded spaces, and less authentic experiences. Below are tips on how to avoid common tourist traps and discover Ticino's true gems.

Avoiding Overly Crowded Attractions

Certain locations, such as **Piazza della Riforma** in **Lugano** or the **Bellinzona Castles**, are very popular and can feel overcrowded, especially during peak seasons. To avoid long lines and crowded spaces, consider these alternatives:

- **Explore Lugano's Other Squares**: While **Piazza della Riforma** is bustling with tourists, **Piazza Cioccaro** and **Piazza Indipendenza** offer more laid-back atmospheres with fewer crowds. These areas still offer lovely cafes and shops but with a more local vibe.
- **Discover Lesser-Known Castles**: While the **Bellinzona Castles** are magnificent, **Castello di Morcote** is a lesser-known, picturesque option. Located in **Morcote**, a small lakeside village, this castle is often quieter, and the surrounding gardens offer breathtaking views over **Lake Lugano**.
- **Opt for Alternative Hiking Trails**: Popular hiking spots like **Monte**

Brè and **Monte San Salvatore** can get busy. Instead, try **Monte Generoso** for equally stunning views without the heavy tourist traffic. The hike is more relaxed, and you can even take the scenic cogwheel train from **Capolago** to the summit.

Seek Authentic Local Experiences

Tourist traps often involve overpriced restaurants or experiences designed to cater more to visitors than to locals. For a more genuine Ticino experience, try these tips:

- **Dine Where the Locals Eat**: Many tourist-heavy areas have restaurants with high prices and average food. To avoid this, step off the main streets. For example, instead of dining in the touristy restaurants around **Piazza Grande** in **Locarno**, head to **Grotto Baldoria** for authentic Ticinese cuisine. It's a local favorite, offering simple, delicious meals like risotto and polenta at affordable prices.
- **Visit Local Markets**: Markets are excellent places to experience the true flavor of Ticino. The **Bellinzona Saturday Market** is one of the best for fresh produce, local cheese, and handmade crafts. Here, you can mingle with locals, enjoy authentic products, and avoid the overpriced souvenirs often found in tourist shops.
- **Stay in Family-Run Accommodations**: Instead of booking big chain hotels, choose locally-owned guesthouses or **Agriturismi** (farm stays). These options often provide a more personal touch, a glimpse into local life, and homemade meals using regional ingredients. **Agriturismo Dosso dell'Ora** near **Mendrisio** is a great example of a charming, family-run farm stay.

Money-Saving Hacks for Budget Travelers

Traveling in Ticino doesn't have to be expensive. With a few practical tips, you can experience the region's beauty and culture without breaking the bank. Here are some helpful hacks to save money during your trip.

Use Public Transportation

Ticino's public transport system is efficient, clean, and reasonably priced. Instead of relying on taxis or car rentals, use the extensive **SBB/CFF** train system and **PostBus** services to get around.

- **Swiss Travel Pass**: If you're staying for several days, consider purchasing a **Swiss Travel Pass**, which allows unlimited travel on trains, buses, and boats across Switzerland. The pass also gives free entry to many museums and discounts on certain mountain excursions.
- **Cost**: Prices start at CHF 232 for a 3-day pass.
- **Ticino Ticket**: If you're staying in registered accommodation (such as hotels, hostels, or campgrounds), you'll receive the **Ticino Ticket** for free. This ticket allows unlimited travel on public transportation within Ticino and offers discounts on attractions.
- **Cost**: Free with your stay in a registered accommodation.
- **Rent a Bike**: For a more active and affordable way to explore, rent a bike. Cities like **Lugano** and **Locarno** have bike rental services, and many areas have dedicated bike lanes. Plus, cycling along **Lake Maggiore** or through **Valle Maggia** offers beautiful scenery at no extra cost.

Find Budget Accommodations

While luxury hotels are abundant in Ticino, there are plenty of budget-friendly options that don't skimp on comfort.

Hostels: Hostels in Ticino are clean, safe, and ideal for budget travelers. **Youthhostel Lugano Savosa** is a great example, offering affordable private rooms and dormitories. It also has a garden, swimming pool, and kitchen facilities, making it a popular choice for backpackers.

- **Price Range**: CHF 30-50 per night.

Campgrounds: Camping is another excellent way to save money while enjoying the outdoors. **Camping Tamaro Resort**, located by **Lake Maggiore**, offers stunning views and great facilities. You can rent a tent pitch or stay in a cabin for a more comfortable experience.

- **Price Range**: CHF 20-40 per night for tent pitches.
- **Airbnb and Guesthouses**: For a more local experience, consider staying in an **Airbnb** or guesthouse. These options often provide more affordable rates compared to hotels and offer a homier atmosphere.

Eat at Local Markets and Grottos

Dining out every day can quickly add up, but there are ways to enjoy delicious food on a budget.

- **Markets**: As mentioned earlier, markets are an excellent place to pick up fresh, affordable food. You can buy local cheeses, bread, fruits, and pastries at markets like the **Bellinzona Saturday Market** or the **Lugano Farmers' Market**. Enjoy a picnic in a park or by the lake to save on restaurant costs.
- **Grottos**: These traditional Ticinese restaurants, often set in rustic, countryside locations, are known for simple but hearty meals at reasonable prices. **Grotto del Cavicc** near **Locarno** is one such place where you can enjoy local dishes like **polenta** and **risotto** without paying tourist prices.
- **Price Range**: CHF 15-30 per meal.
- **Coop and Migros Supermarkets**: If you're really looking to save, head to **Coop** or **Migros**, two major supermarket chains in Ticino. Both offer fresh produce, ready-made meals, and baked goods at affordable prices. You can grab a sandwich or salad for a fraction of what you'd pay in a restaurant.

Other Tips for Budget Travelers

- **Visit Free Attractions**: Ticino has many beautiful places that won't cost you a thing. **Parco Ciani** in **Lugano** is a lovely lakeside park perfect for an afternoon stroll. The **Brissago Islands** also have gardens you can explore for free, and many hiking trails in **Valle Verzasca** are accessible at no cost.
- **Use Museum Passes**: If you plan to visit museums, the **Swiss Travel Pass** includes free entry to many museums in Ticino. Alternatively, look for free museum days, which many institutions offer once a month.
- **Save on Mountain Excursions**: Cable cars and mountain trains can be expensive, but by using the **Ticino Ticket**, you'll get discounts on trips up mountains like **Monte Brè** and **Monte San Salvatore**. Plan ahead to make the most of these savings.

Additional Tips for an Authentic Experience

1. **Learn a Few Words of Italian**: Though many people in Ticino speak English, learning a few basic Italian phrases can go a long way. Simple greetings like **Buongiorno** (Good morning) and **Grazie** (Thank you) will help you connect with locals and show that you respect their culture.
2. **Travel Off-Season**: The best way to avoid crowds and high prices is to visit Ticino during the shoulder season (April-May or September-October). You'll find cheaper accommodations, less crowded attractions, and pleasant weather perfect for hiking and exploring.
3. **Ask Locals for Recommendations**: Locals always know the best hidden gems, whether it's a secluded swimming spot on **Lake Maggiore** or a family-owned restaurant serving up the best **pasta al pesto**. Don't hesitate to ask your hotel staff, hosts, or friendly shop owners for their suggestions.

Making the Most of Your Ticino Adventure

Ticino is a region where you can easily switch between thrilling outdoor adventures and tranquil moments by the lake. Whether you're hiking in the mountains or enjoying a leisurely boat ride on **Lake Lugano**, it's important to strike a balance between action-packed activities and peaceful downtime. Here are some must-do experiences and tips on how to fully enjoy your adventure in Ticino.

Blend Relaxation with Adventure

Ticino is famous for its stunning landscapes, and it's important to pace yourself when exploring them. Here's how to mix relaxation and adventure into your itinerary:

- **Start Your Day with Adventure**: Ticino offers many outdoor activities that are best experienced in the morning when the air is cooler and the trails are quieter. Start your day with an adventurous activity like hiking, mountain biking, or paddleboarding.
- **Hiking Monte Brè**: One of the most popular hikes near **Lugano** is **Monte Brè**, offering beautiful views of the lake and city. It's a moderate hike that takes around 2 hours. If you prefer something less strenuous, take the funicular up and enjoy a short walk at the top.
- **How to Get There**: Take the funicular from **Cassarate**, just outside of **Lugano**. Tickets cost CHF 25 for a return trip.
- **Afternoons by the Lake**: After an active morning, head to one of Ticino's lakes for some downtime. **Lake Lugano** and **Lake Maggiore** both offer plenty of opportunities for relaxing by the water. Whether you're sunbathing on the shores, swimming, or taking a gentle boat ride, the lakes provide a peaceful contrast to the morning's adventure.
- **Tip**: If you're visiting **Ascona** or **Locarno**, you can rent a paddleboat for around CHF 15 per hour and explore the lake at your own pace.
- **Wind Down with a Sunset View**: End your day at one of Ticino's many scenic lookout points. The views from **Monte San Salvatore** or

Parco Ciani in **Lugano** offer the perfect backdrop to watch the sun set over the water. These spots are popular but rarely overcrowded, making them ideal for a quiet evening.

Must-Do Experiences for First-Time Visitors

If you're visiting Ticino for the first time, there are several experiences that should be at the top of your list. These are the moments that will give you a true sense of the region's beauty and culture.

Boat Tour on Lake Lugano or Lake Maggiore: One of the best ways to appreciate Ticino's landscape is by boat. A guided boat tour on **Lake Lugano** or **Lake Maggiore** offers a different perspective of the region, with stops at charming villages and scenic islands. During summer, sunset boat cruises are also available, providing a magical way to end the day.

- **Cost**: Guided tours start at CHF 20 per person. Most boats depart from **Lugano** or **Ascona**.

Visit the Bellinzona Castles: A UNESCO World Heritage Site, the **Bellinzona Castles—Castelgrande**, **Montebello**, and **Sasso Corbaro**—are a must-see for history lovers. You can explore the castles' ancient walls, enjoy panoramic views, and even attend one of the medieval festivals held throughout the year.

- **Cost**: Entry fees are CHF 10 for adults and CHF 5 for children.

Explore Local Markets: For a taste of local life, visit one of Ticino's many outdoor markets. The **Bellinzona Saturday Market** is one of the largest, offering fresh produce, local cheeses, cured meats, and artisan crafts. It's the perfect place to pick up some souvenirs or enjoy a picnic by the river.

- **Opening Hours**: Saturdays from 8:00 AM to 12:30 PM.

- **Ride the Funicular to Madonna del Sasso**: The **Madonna del Sasso Sanctuary** in **Locarno** is one of Ticino's most sacred sites, offering not only religious significance but also incredible views over **Lake Maggiore**. The funicular ride up is an experience in itself, winding through lush green hills.
- **Cost**: CHF 12 for a round-trip on the funicular.
- **Taste Ticino's Wine and Cuisine**: Ticino is known for its **Merlot** wines and hearty mountain cuisine. Visit a local vineyard, such as **Vinoteca Ticinese** in **Lugano**, to sample some of the region's best wines, or dine at a traditional **grotto** for a meal of **polenta** and grilled meats.

Must-Know Tips for First-Time Visitors

Ticino is a unique region in Switzerland with its own cultural nuances and practical travel tips. Here's what every first-time visitor should know to make their trip as smooth and enjoyable as possible.

Cultural Nuances and Language Tips

Ticino is the only canton in Switzerland where **Italian** is the official language, but many locals also speak **German** and **English**, especially in tourist areas. Still, learning a few basic Italian phrases will go a long way in making a good impression:

- **Buongiorno** (Good morning)
- **Grazie** (Thank you)
- **Per favore** (Please)
- **Quanto costa?** (How much does it cost?)

While most people in the larger towns will speak some English, trying out a few Italian words will be appreciated and help you connect more with the locals.

Embrace the Laid-Back Italian Influence

Ticino has a slower, more relaxed pace compared to other parts of Switzerland, thanks to its Italian influence. Don't be surprised if service in restaurants is slower, as meals are meant to be savored. Take this as an opportunity to slow down and enjoy the moment, whether you're sipping coffee at a café or sharing a meal at a **grotto**.

What to Pack for Ticino

Packing for Ticino depends on the season, but here are some essentials for any trip:

- **Comfortable Walking Shoes**: Whether you're exploring the cobbled streets of **Ascona** or hiking in **Valle Verzasca**, comfortable shoes are a must.
- **Layered Clothing**: Even in the summer, temperatures can drop in the evenings or at higher altitudes. Pack layers to stay comfortable throughout the day.
- **Swimwear**: With so many lakes and rivers to swim in, you'll want to have a swimsuit ready for a spontaneous dip.
- **Sunscreen and Hat**: The sun can be strong, especially by the lakes. Bring sunscreen, sunglasses, and a hat to protect yourself during outdoor activities.
- **Light Rain Jacket**: Even if you're visiting in summer, sudden rain showers are not uncommon in the mountains. A light rain jacket will keep you dry without taking up much space.

Travel Essentials

Before departing for Ticino, make sure you have these essentials prepared:

- **Swiss Travel Pass** or **Ticino Ticket**: For easy access to public transportation and discounts on attractions.

- **Currency**: The official currency is the **Swiss franc (CHF)**, though some tourist spots may accept euros (at unfavorable exchange rates). ATMs are widely available, and most places accept credit cards.
- **Power Adapter**: Switzerland uses **Type J plugs**, so bring a power adapter if needed.
- **Download Offline Maps**: The mobile signal can be weak in more remote areas, so it's a good idea to download offline maps of Ticino in advance.

Checklist of Things to Do Before Departure

To ensure your trip goes off without a hitch, here's a handy checklist of things to do before you leave for Ticino:

1. **Check Passport Validity**: Ensure your passport is valid for at least 6 months beyond your planned stay.
2. **Confirm Visa Requirements**: Depending on your nationality, you may need a visa to enter Switzerland. Check the requirements in advance.
3. **Book Accommodations**: While you can sometimes find last-minute deals, it's a good idea to book your accommodations ahead of time, especially during peak seasons.
4. **Buy Travel Insurance**: Medical care in Switzerland can be expensive, so make sure you have comprehensive travel insurance that covers health, accidents, and cancellations.
5. **Research Local Festivals**: Ticino hosts several annual festivals, from the **Locarno Film Festival** to **JazzAscona**. Check the dates to see if your visit coincides with any exciting events.
6. **Plan for Sunday Closures**: Many shops, including supermarkets, are closed on Sundays in Ticino. If you arrive on a weekend, plan accordingly by buying any essentials beforehand.
7. **Check the Weather Forecast**: Ticino's weather can be unpredictable, especially in the mountains. Make sure to check the forecast and pack

accordingly.
8. **Learn Key Italian Phrases**: While English is widely spoken in tourist areas, knowing a few basic Italian phrases will enhance your experience.

Conclusion

As your journey through Ticino comes to an end, it's clear that this region is not just a destination—it's an experience that leaves a lasting impression. Whether you've immersed yourself in the culture of its charming lakeside towns, explored the heights of the Swiss Alps, or tasted the flavors of traditional Ticinese cuisine, there's something here for everyone.

Ticino's beauty lies in its contrasts—where Swiss efficiency blends seamlessly with Italian flair. The serene lakes of **Lugano** and **Maggiore**, the quiet elegance of **Ascona** and **Locarno**, and the rugged outdoor adventures in **Valle Verzasca** or on **Monte Brè** create a diverse yet harmonious landscape that invites exploration.

But beyond the must-see sights and experiences, what makes Ticino truly special are the small moments: sipping a **Merlot** at a local grotto, wandering through local markets, or taking in the sunset from a scenic mountain perch. These are the experiences that connect travelers to the heart of the region.

A Few Final Tips:

- **Take Your Time**: Ticino rewards those who move at a slower pace. Whether you're meandering through a local market or lingering over a lakeside meal, give yourself time to soak in the beauty and culture around you.
- **Engage with Locals**: Ticino's residents are proud of their region, and

CONCLUSION

   they love sharing it with visitors. A simple "**Buongiorno**" can open doors to richer, more authentic experiences.
- **Plan to Return**: Ticino's magic is hard to capture in a single trip. As you explore, you may find there's more to discover than your itinerary allows. That's the beauty of Ticino—it always leaves you wanting more.

As you close the pages of this guide and embark on your Ticino adventure, remember that the best travel experiences aren't just about checking places off a list. They're about immersing yourself in the moments, connecting with the culture, and leaving with stories that you'll carry long after you've left. Ticino offers all of that and more, and whether you're visiting for the first time or returning again, the region is sure to surprise and delight you at every turn.

***Safe travels, and may your time in Ticino be filled with unforgettable memories.**

Printed in Dunstable, United Kingdom